WHEN THE FIGHTING

IS ALL OVER

THE MEMOIR OF A

MARINE CORPS

GENERAL'S DAUGHTER

By Katie Letcher Lyle

LONGSTREET PRESS, INC.
Atlanta, Georgia

Published by
Longstreet Press, Inc.
A subsidiary of Cox Newspapers,
A subsidiary of Cox Enterprises, Inc.
2140 Newmarket Parkway
Suite 122
Marietta, GA 30067

Printed in the United States of America

Library of Congress Catalog Card Number: 97-71939
ISBN: 1-56352-426-0

Electronic film prep by OGI, Forest Park, GA
Cover photo: *The author and her father, 1941*

*For Royster, who has the amazing grace
to have put up with me
for more than a third of a century*

ALSO BY KATIE LETCHER LYLE

The Foraging Gourmet
(1997)

The Wild Berry Book
(1994)

The Man Who Wanted Seven Wives
(1986)

Scalded to Death by the Steam
(1985)

Finders Weepers
(1982)

Dark But Full of Diamonds
(1981)

The Golden Shores of Heaven
(1976)

Fair Day, And Another Step Begun
(1974)

I Will Go Barefoot All Summer for You
(1973)

Acknowledgments

A childhood memoir cannot be written in isolation with any hope of accuracy. I am in much debt and warmly grateful to the following friends and family members who have in various ways helped me bring this book to fruition: my dear sister Betsy, my aunt and godmother Polly Curry, and my brothers Johnny and Pete, for their thoughtful readings, wise suggestions, and occasional corrections.

I must express special thanks to my lifelong friend and mentor, Louis Rubin, who has had much to do with the completion of this book, as he has had in everything I have ever written.

Many old friends, people who knew my grandparents and my parents in ways that I, being a child, could not, have contributed information, opinions, and different perspectives, for which I am very grateful. They include Nell Paxton, Iris McNeil, Dr. David Brothers, Tina Mallory, and General Jimmy Morgan.

My immense gratitude goes to Sally Hill McMillan, my genial agent, who believed in this book and encouraged me to finish it.

I count myself truly lucky to have a heavenly host of wonderful writerly friends, and I want to thank heartily my perceptive and eagle-eyed readers and listeners Chip Barnett, Perry Epes, Mark Hazard, Sarah O'Connor, Dorene Home, Jeannie Lee, Fletcher and Margaret Collins, Hale Broce, LaWanda Shellan, and especially my beloved Royster for their reading, comments, and encouragement.

And finally, a special word of gratitude to all the Good Old Girls, who for ten years have listened to and helped shape the pieces of this work, good writers and critics all: Judy Ayyildiz, Mary Bishop, Rene Crackel, Janet Lembke, Monty Leitch, Anne McCaig, Charlotte Morgan, Patty Pullen, Miriam Rogin, Joan Schroeder, Jeri Watts, and Toni Williams.

Contents

WHEN THE FIGHTING IS ALL OVER, and He calls His children home,
And Tojo's hanging from the wall of Valhalla's golden dome,
God will wink at General Vandergrift as he eats his Spam and beans,
Saying, "God on High sees eye to eye with the United States
    Marines!"

— ROGUE STANZA FROM "THE MARINE CORPS HYMN"

WHEN THE FIGHTING

IS ALL OVER

Andaddy, Mama, me, Daddy, and Nainai.

Introduction

I am in the middle of telling some terrific story when Mama comes in and accuses me, in front of Andaddy, of exaggerating. Andaddy laughs easily and says, "Oh, but Betty, it makes life so much more interesting."

"Cap'n!" she protests. "You ought not to encourage it!"

He says, "Now, Miss Betty, the truth is generally boring. But everyone loves storytellers!" And he winks at me.

IT IS BELOW FREEZING, and why didn't we think of this last August when we were here for Daddy's funeral, how cold it would probably be? It is January 1995. How we decided on this date had to do with all the dates some one of us couldn't come. Scattered from Maine to the Midwest, from mountain farm to city house, we have returned for this moment, the four of us together to this house for the first time since we can remember, resentful loving strangers, exasperated siblings, stressed aunts and uncles, forced grown-ups, now that our last excuse for being children is gone.

We are wary and weary participants in this tearing apart of a house containing all our own parts and pasts, roughly a half century of the material all families accumulate. As if pulling out rats' nests, or tomb-robbing, we are

newly surrounded by the moldy detritus of our six lives. In addition, Daddy
was heir to the effects of six of the governor's, his grandfather's, children as
well, another vast collection of stuff that must be dealt with.

My sense of history wars with my sense of economy: what, for
instance, do we do with a broken tortoise-shell hair-comb with a spidery
note attached saying this was a gift from Mrs. Robert E. Lee from her
husband to his goddaughter, our great-aunt Lizzie, one of Governor
Letcher's daughters? With a small locket (initials indecipherable) carrying the picture of an unidentified child, found among Aunt Jennie's
effects? With a ghastly pair of Victorian andirons on marble bases sport-
ing stags, twined grapevines, and crystal pendants that we can't just
throw out, as they were once in the Governor's Mansion in Richmond?
("They'd look *great* in *your* house!" I tell my sister. "Oh, mercy, no!" she
counters. "You're the oldest. You *deserve* them!" We make faces at each
other, shove them toward the auction piles.)

We are bound by the strange (and, at first glance, generous-seeming)
directive of our father's will: any of us can purchase from the estate any
part of it, at eighty percent of the appraised value. But this means that
every item of value not already clearly someone's property, small or
large, must be appraised. Items whose ownership is in question go to the
highest bidder among us. Not conducive to loving resolution. Speaking
for myself, I never liked competitive games. I particularly dislike this
one, which seems devised to turn us mean-spirited.

So here we are. In order to sell the house, we have to clear it out, dis-
tribute books, china and crystal, bolts of silk from China wound on bamboo poles, the carved walnut furniture, the painted Shansi chests, the
double baby carriage, the wheat grinder, the red cider mill, the old 78
Vernon Dalhart records, the 33 rpm Stravinskys and Sousa marches, the
Chinese rugs, the fishing tackle, the little carved walnut cabinet with a
marble top that Daddy bought for Mama when she was dying.

The outside of the house Daddy built for Mama in the back yard of
Andaddy's is still bare of planting, for Daddy was convinced roots would

undermine the foundation. The poured concrete is exposed like ugly legs under a too-short dress.

The front-porch aluminum window frames, which never did work right, now have rigor mortis. Bamboo chairs and chaises are piled there like bones in an ossuary.

Off the back porch is the treacherous rock "terrace" Daddy laid with undulating river rocks hauled home one at a time from all over Rockbridge County.[1] There is one space left empty up under the bathroom windows. In this hole there are two exceptions to the no-planting rule: a fig tree and its progeny threaten to tear the house apart, for Daddy loved figs, and had cultivated them in California before the War. Afterward, he actually managed to grow them here in the mountains of Virginia where figs do not grow. Now the old tree annually offers up a lesson in resurrection as it sprouts bravely each spring, flirts its Rubensesque leaves throughout the summer, tries valiantly to make it through our harsh winters, dies down, and sends up more stolons to try again next year. Occasionally, figs still appear on it. The other exception is Mama's mint bed, gone wild and scraggly among the stones.

This white asbestos shingle house has its back set resolutely to the big house, our Andaddy's, which stands facing Letcher Avenue in front of it.

The inside of this postwar salt-box is plain and ugly with its two small bathrooms, peach and blue, in which we tangled each morning, all six of us (and finally seven), in each other's ways, in each other's smells. The other rooms are more or less square, five on the first floor, four on the second, and have low ceilings, small windows, odd thin squatty baseboards, cheap floorboards. Unimaginative paints (light green, pale blue, peach, boiled custard yellow) tint the walls.

[1] Rockbridge County, named for its famous Natural Bridge, was formed in 1778 out of vast Augusta County, Virginia, reaching from the Shenandoah Valley all the way to the Mississippi. George Washington, one-time surveyor of Natural Bridge, once said, during a dark period of the Revolution, "If I am defeated, I can retire to the wilds of west Augusta and hold out indefinitely."

In addition to the furniture, we have cleared out the junk long crammed under and into the unfinished eaves and attic (somebody recalls that at some point Daddy hid some of the silver under the fiberglass insulation on the attic floor, and sure enough, blacker than night, a tea set and a small fortune in flat silver come to light).

More stuff is piled in nightmarish profusion in the half-finished basement: picnic gear, cookpots, metal outside furniture, the old front-porch glider now paralyzed with rust. Jars of screws and nails. Tins, ammunition, tools. Years of canned tomatoes and blackberry jelly, honey, applesauce, and chutney.

Our piles of sad treasure block all but the most perilous passage through the rooms. My sister has claimed the marble-topped walnut night-stand. My own stash, things I can't use but also can't let go: the filthy and now-rotten tarp that enclosed the back porch where I slept throughout the fall of 1947, the brittle Blue Horse notebook with my first novel scrawled and illustrated on twenty-seven of its pages, a big glazed crock that once held baked beans, a brittle tiger-belly-fur laprobe from Peking, my little blue 78 Victrola from California, long defunct, but its smell still capable of recalling with one breath the whole feeling of my early years. I have claimed, too, my old blue-rimmed enamel potty with Chinese lettering on the bottom that stayed in whatever car we owned until I was past grown up, the red plaid suitcase that crossed and recrossed the continent with me nearly fifty years ago, Boppie's (our other grandfather's) old coffee grinder that Mama got when he died. It still retains the ghost of the A&P Bokar coffee ("Vigorous and Winey," said the label) that he ground each morning fresh.

I can conveniently keep more than the others, for I still live in the same town where we grew up. The others will have to ship home the rolled rugs, the boxes of books, the silver, whatever they keep, wrestle it all into a back seat, or a truck, or take extra luggage on the plane.

In this terrible cold I have broken out with the hives that I get every time I go down to the house for more talk, more work. Whatever parts of

me are exposed — face, hands, calves, throat — sport itching red conti-
nents and islands rising out of a sea of white skin, for as long as we are
about this stressful task.

Here is the tin tomato juice can with the wire handle that was our
cooking pot on the trip Daddy and Johnnie and I made across the continent; into the trash it goes, along with stained leg bandages from my
horseback riding days. Every item is a landmine, exploding memories from
somewhere deep in the past. There is a dried-up bottle of *L'heure Bleue*,
Mama's party scent, with only a brown tobacco-juice stain in the bottom. I
stash it until my pile grows unwieldy, then it too goes into the trash.

My hives, I know, have to do with another coldness: that of our family, gathered here to absorb, or make disappear, the leftovers of three
generations. Out in the yard are other piles of things: scrapbooks, boxes,
cookpots, a parachute, wardrobe trunks. Johnnie wants the six-foot brass
telescope Daddy got off a dead Jap, and we haul it into the yard in its
heavy case with rope handles. Peter wants the silver, guns, and tools.
Betsy would like the rare Czechoslovakian plates. Of the valuable items,
I want jewelry. I spot and grab the scratched tin plate my grandfather
used to feed the birds on every morning. A quizzical look from Betsy,
and I realize: nobody else cares or remembers what it was used for. And
what will I do with it?

The entire situation seems orchestrated by our dead father in order to
pit us against each other, though that was surely not his conscious intention. What we always did know was that Daddy was reluctant to give us
things, and that in his mindset, *money* corrupts. Both would make us soft,
he believed. I don't know why — apparently, things and money didn't
corrupt him, but he believed that if any of his kids ever got flush, we'd
instantly become bums, dope addicts, alcoholics, or gamblers.

In this January, we will sometimes pay our own money for things
from our childhood, Ming vases and lamps, fine Chinese plates. Betsy
and I run up the price bidding on a real gold matchbox someone once
gave our grandfather.

The rest of the household goods will be dispersed the following summer at an auction, with some bizarre results. Our walnut sideboard will sell at the auction for $200, and change hands again later the same day for $1600. Chairs, china, and cupboards will show up for months at local antique stores identified as "being from the Letcher estate," but which did not come from there at all. Local dealers are apparently trying to cash in on the faded past of a family that once gave Virginia a governor.

At a cocktail party a man will say, "I bought one of your family portraits at Henry's. I can't understand you all letting them go."

"But there *were* no family portraits," I say, truthfully. I can tell he doesn't believe me. Another man will call from Pennsylvania to say he has bought a Letcher piece and will I tell him what I know of its history? When a photograph of the piece arrives, it is a cabinet I've never laid eyes on, certainly not from the Letchers.

And the next summer my brothers can't believe until I show them the receipts and the cancelled checks, that we netted less than two thousand dollars apiece from the Ruritan Club auction, which we four children agreed was more palatable than a sale on the premises.

"2 deerhides, $1.00," the sales slips say. "Box of 19th c. lawbooks, 75 cents." "Bk of Know. Encyclopedia, $5." (My childhood dream-fount, the pictures of ruined Mayan cities rising out of jungle, of Roman temples and Greek colonnades.) "Chinese rug, 12 x 15, $45." "Wardrobe trunk, $6." "Box of Blue Willow china, $5." "Posthole digger and Misc. tools, $1." "Parachute, $1." We know they'll all be hauled off and possibly sold for many times what was paid for them, but what can we do? Or what say to the million people who ask, "How could you sell all those family things?"

THE BLACK WALNUT TREE halfway to the woodshed still drops its exhausted load of fruit onto the tin roof and into the sagging gutters, and sucks up the nourishment from the side yard, leaving only moss and brown grass as thin on the soil as an old man's hair. We cross back and forth from the house to the cold woodshed/office, trampling last year's harvest, trying to decide what to do: what to keep, what to toss, what to sell, what to give away.

The woodshed. When I first came to Lexington to live in 1943, it held wood and coal in bins. It had a stall for the horses Daddy and his brother Gee once owned. It was a wonderful filthy trove of abandoned tools and boxes. Now we pry open its ancient wooden door, breaking the lock, and find it full of garden tools. The woodshed was my playhouse. It was where Andaddy had taken Daddy to whip him for wrongdoings in the early years of the twentieth century, and where I was twice taken in the middle of the century for serious transgressions, lying I think it was, both times. Around 1960 after Andaddy died and Daddy sold the big house on Letcher Avenue to Virginia Military Institute, he renovated a part of the sagging old structure, adding a tiny coal stove and bookshelves, and jury-rigged himself an office. For years it's been crammed with file cabinets, old maps, artillery shells, med-packs from World War II, books, boots, uniforms, collapsed tents, luggage, unopened crates of low-quality silver compote dishes from China. There are a dozen snake and alligator skins from animals Daddy had flayed in the south Pacific or the Virginia mountains, the worst a rattlesnake skin six feet long, eight or nine inches wide. All are curled permanently into useless keratin-hard bundles. Tottering piles of framed degrees, citations, photographs, religious art, maps, grim-faced people peering out of cracked glass in whom I imagine I can see one of us, balance uneasily. Beneath greasy coal dust we discover more Chinese platters, a silver samovar, the beaver coat Daddy made for Mama (now brittle as cardboard) in a box tied with cord, the huge brass bullet casing we'd used as an umbrella and walking-stick stand. My wedding dress, carefully wrapped in blue tissue paper.

Six tall filing cabinets are packed with papers. Some can go: decades of annual reports from companies Daddy owned shares in. Others vote to throw out all the papers, letters, files of Andaddy's law cases. I cry *No*, and offer to haul them home. I agree to arrange them in file cabinets.

Things surface like fragments in dreams: Daddy's three white BVD nightshirts that I know he wore on their honeymoon. A box of Betsy's schoolbooks. An entire *barrel* of old lace, napkins, and linens, stained and rodent-chewed. Books that fall into crumbs when picked up. Over everything, black greasy soot, years and years of it. Precious goods, or worthless trash? Unclear.

THERE IS AN OLD HINDU FOLK SAYING that the prisoned monkey, given paper and colors, paints a picture of the bars of its cage. I take this to mean we can only portray things the way we see them. I doubt whether there is much use in *looking for the truth*, though that is why I began this book. My mother had a sad, if not terrible, life with my father during most of the forty-three years they lived together. My stepmother, who married and lived with my father for the last dozen years of his life, had a wonderful life with him. My own life with him was something in between wonderful and terrible, always contradictory. I wanted to know the truth of him, the truth of me, the truth of our relationship.

I was a girl; he wanted a boy. So I learned, more than the boys, to be daring and fearless (though it was already in my nature, for of his four children I was and am the most like him).

He was a good hater, and I wanted to be a good hater. It was something he got from his mother. I never thought to ask what that was, or what good it was, but it got defined and redefined all the time. I loved him maybe more than anyone else; I don't know if he loved me.

I often made him very mad. He often made me very mad. What I wanted was to make him love me back. What he wanted was not clear. One thing I knew he wanted was for me to be less trouble; but I could never help being lots of trouble.

He considered children lesser creatures than grown-ups, and approved of them solely on how well behaved they were. But I was not insubstantial, or subtle, or well behaved, and it made me mad as hell to be so disregarded, and so unfairly judged.

Once, before he went off to war, he'd loved me, I was sure, but the tall ungainly urchin my father kept bumping up against after the war was nobody he knew, and, quite evidently, nobody he wanted to know. He didn't like the hoyden I'd become, and, not at all given to sentiment, he didn't seem to recall the past and its idylls as I did. I was soon given to know that I was difficult, disobedient, and headed for jail, or perdition, probably both.

He wanted me to go into the Marine Corps; I went flouncing off instead with a "So there!" and got an M.A. in creative writing and philosophy and sang in a nightclub, more than partially just to show him I could, after getting a similarly useless B.A. in English. I wanted to excel at things he couldn't touch. But oh, how I wanted him to approve of them!

I hated a lot of things about my father: his narrow-mindedness, his suspicious nature, his erratic and uncontrolled temper, his tight-fistedness — while admiring extravagantly his energy, his ability to do absolutely anything he made up his mind to, his outrageousness and defiance of what anyone else thought of him, and most of all his downright charm.

Daddy could be the best company of anybody. He was a great storyteller. He chose his stories; he only told ones that confirmed his view of the world — and revealed only part of himself. For example, I learned only from other people that in his early days, my father was a rounder, a wild man. He never told us that.

With my mother I had a placid, pleasant, loving, and therefore not terribly interesting relationship. We were always good friends, and I knew she loved me and was proud of me. I heard and saw her side of things, and agreed with them, but I couldn't see then why she wouldn't fight back. She was a grown-up, not a little child. I now know that she was as physically afraid of Daddy as the children were. I carefully chose a life different from hers.

This book glosses over many aspects of my childhood; specifically, it fuzzes the fact that we children were four interactive and very different siblings, and it avoids the truth that as I grew up I was in many ways closer to my friends and certain other adults than to my family. It skirts the fact that I left home early and for good, though ten years later I did return to marry, and have been in Lexington since. So I've left out a lot, and I've changed the names of some minor characters, especially where naming them didn't add to the story. Once or twice, I had to make up a name because I couldn't remember it, such as the Flournoys' dog, or because there were two people with the same name.

I have attempted throughout to be mindful that, as Stephen Jay Gould so perfectly put it: "(The) propensity to tell stories grants us resolution, but also spells danger in avenues thereby opened for distortion and misreading." I believe a writer has the right, even the obligation, to interpret events and shape them into story, which automatically means you are fiddling with cold facts. This is my own etiological tale, though the tale of, say, my sister, eight years younger, a girl born of the same (but tireder, older) parents eight years later, with two older siblings and a twin, into a postwar family that was by then no longer affluent, would be a far different tale.

But this is not apology. None of this is made up. I have rearranged some material, but this is the way I remember things.

Something similar to this story must have happened to thousands of American families who somehow survived World War II. Writing this has instructed me in how difficult it must have been to hold together families sundered by years of separation and radically changed roles, and given me enormous respect for all those who managed to stay together with grace or near-grace.

Katie Letcher Lyle, February 1997

Me, Andaddy, and Johnnie, 1943.

Magic

*A*fter the war, I sometimes asked about it when Daddy and I were going somewhere in the car: of course I knew that Daddy was a Marine, a war hero, a good fighter, that he'd hated the Japs, and that he couldn't count the number he'd killed.

"Why, though?" I asked him, more than once. Okay, so the Japs were little and mean and sneaky and slant-eyed, but I still didn't see why he had to kill them. His explanations didn't make enough sense to me to remember them, so I'd bring it up again.

"They were the enemy," he'd say.

"But why did you have to kill them?"

"I had to kill them, or they'd have killed me."

"Why?"

I could see him growing irritated. "That was my job," he'd growl, and I knew I'd better not push him further.

I still couldn't understand why anyone had to kill anyone. But it wasn't something he could examine or explain, at least not to a seven-year-old. "You just do," was about it, or that old basic standby, "It takes a good hater to get ahead *in the world. You got to be a good hater."*

Once in 1933 while a tourist in Germany, he was mistaken for one of Hitler's close circle, the Brown Shirts. He awoke from a nap under a tree in a castle courtyard to find four soldiers marching in strict formation around him. As he stirred and woke, they came to smart attention, saluting him and saying in unison, Heil Hitler. He yawned, rubbed his eyes, and returned the foreign greeting. That kept happening during his trip; soldiers and sometimes even civilians, on seeing his Marine Corps drab t-shirts, would snap to attention and salute him. He later learned that his garb, an innocent American brown t-shirt, inadvertantly imitated that of Hitler's exclusive cabinet. He loved to tell that story.

"LITTLE SWEETHEART," Andaddy, my grandfather, used to say, "the world is full of mysteries." We went to Lexington to live with my father's parents during the war. He'd go on to ponder one of the mysteries, such as, "Did you know that ginseng plants walk at night?" He'd tamed a fox when he was a boy, got it as a cub and fed it warm milk. It stayed almost a year, and acted, he said, like a cross between a cat and a dog. He wondered if you could ever really tame a wild animal.

"Have you ever seen a ghost?" I asked him once.

And as usual he wrinkled up his old red face, thinking. "Well, one time I saw a ball of lightning, bigger than a basketball, roll across the parade ground at the end of a thunderstorm. Just about twilight. It was going the way someone would walk, about that rate, just moseying. Didn't know what it was.

"Finally I figured it just might be Hootie — my brother. Your father's Uncle Hootie. You see, he'd died several weeks before. So I don't reckon I'll ever know, but maybe. . . ."

THE PANCAKES ARE LACE-EDGED from the bacon fat they were fried in. The dining room smells hammy and the chairs and table feel slightly sticky. There is a whole lake of maple syrup over and around my pancakes. Nobody in the dining room but me. I can hear the cook, Nannie, banging in the kitchen, a pot hitting another pot, a spoon clattering to the floor. Outside it is dark. Everyone is still sleeping until Andaddy comes. He believes that if you sleep late, you will never amount to anything. My mother sleeps late on purpose, but I am ready when Andaddy comes, not wanting to be caught napping.

His odd smell, like distant onions just when you start to smell them, is the result of his belief that tub baths weaken a person. He says all those baths are what did in the Romans. Andaddy washes every morning in a china basin of cold water from the bathroom, which is probably what he's doing right now. There has been a tub hooked up to the water since 1929, hot as well as cold, but he isn't taking any chances.

Though it's summer, the year 1943, it's cold in the mornings, and I can feel the goosebumps rising on the backs of my arms. I have shorts on and a striped halter Mama made me. I am barefoot, which Andaddy likes because it reminds him of Daddy, my grandparents' only son, called Buzz. He loves to tell me or anyone who will listen how Daddy survived when his brother Gee died of measles and pneumonia — and how Buzz went barefoot from then on, for years. Absolutely barefoot. Day and night, because the doctor thought wet feet caused sickness. How I still love that reassuring story! So my father went to school barefoot. He went to Sunday school barefoot. He delivered newspapers barefoot. In the snow. Graduated from high school barefoot, in a cap and gown. He was the only cadet who ever started VMI barefoot, though at the beginning of his second year there, he began to wear shoes. His feet were so tough then, he once told me, that he could carve his initials on the bottoms. Barefoot Buzz Letcher! My daddy, tough and strong.

The stairs creak, then I hear the shuffle of carpet slippers outside the door, and sit up straight in the pale light. "Good morning, Little Sweetheart!" Andaddy sings out. "The early bird catches the worm!" As he lifts the silver covers and fills his plate from the sideboard with sausage and bacon and enormous pancakes, two, three, four of them in a great brown hump, he goes on to quote me Benjamin Franklin on going to bed and rising early and the triple benefits thereof, as he does every morning. At the table he continues, telling me that Henry David Thoreau believed that all art dated from a communion with the earliest part of the day!

He tends to tell me things over and over, but when I point that out, he says that way I will remember them. He talks to me as if I were a grown.

Though of course he does not say it, I know he feels that the rest of them, my grandmother Nainai, Mama and Johnnie, are sluggards, wastrels, no doubt of it, as we sit together, alert conspirators in the dark dining room. I dribble syrup off my fork onto the pile of pancakes that seems to have grown since I took them. Daddy, of course, is not a sluggard. He is away in the Pacific, fighting Japs, killing them, mowing them down. He's a hero. He's the cat's meow. He's like us.

Andaddy carves and eats loudly, slicing across his huge hotcakes until they are a pile of squares. (Mama says it is rude to cut up everything at once; you only cut what you are going to eat next.)

One hotcake is left on the tin plate on the sideboard. This is the part I wait for, what I rise early, cold, in blue pellucid shadow, to experience. When he is through eating his breakfast, Andaddy goes to the sideboard again, and cuts that last pancake up into a million little pieces, crossing his knife and fork again and again, metal screeching against metal.

Then he picks up the tin plate and nods, and we leave the dining room for the dark hall. Now the others will wake up if they haven't already, grumpy or silent, snuffling or whining, blowing noses, and the day will begin. Ordinarily I have to be quiet when the others are asleep, but this is Andaddy's house, and, taking my cue from him, I stomp up the stairs, my feet slapping on the sticky treads right behind the felt smacks of his slippers.

In his front bedroom is no screen, and the window stays wide open almost year-round. A huge heavy bookcase sits exactly in front of the window, a foot back from the radiator. Andaddy explains that mosquitoes can't go around corners, so with the bookcase, just a bit larger than the window, set as it is, he is never bothered by these pests.

Mama won't go in his room, not for anything. He told her there was a black snake in there for quite a while last summer, four feet long he estimated, though it wouldn't stay still long enough to measure accurately. Andaddy assured her it was harmless, and would go of its own accord when it was ready, and he didn't see any reason to do anything about it. Mama reckons it is still in there somewhere. She's heard of black snakes living for years in old houses and attics. I check around myself.

Outside, the branches of the black walnut tree reach almost exactly to Andaddy's window. Inside, Andaddy's bed is unmade, the sheets rumpled, and bird lime drips off the tarnished brass bedposts. The dark wood floor is patterned with splats of white and littered with walnut shells. We close the door to keep out Soot, the stray cat I've adopted.

I tense myself for this next moment, when Andaddy clangs the tin pan on the window sill, a deafening signal that will awaken not only everyone in the house but also everyone in the neighborhood — and magically, instantly, there is a ruffle of feathers, a scrabble of feet, birds and squirrels arriving out of nowhere, flapping, and grabbing hotcake bits out of the pan Andaddy holds. Next door, Cerberus (the ugliest, smelliest black dog I've ever seen, who barks day and night, confined in a flimsy wire pen behind the Flournoys' house) starts his day, barking with frustration because he can't get any of the feast.

Despite the profusion of walnut bits on the floor, the squirrels for now prefer pancake. They duck the greedy blue jays that swoop in and out, stopping to sit up brightly with their tails high in the air, darting around looking for another bite, colliding at the corners of furniture. One piece of pancake gets dropped on my head, is retrieved. Andaddy laughs to weeping, wipes the tears off his wrinkled face at a tug-of-war between a jay and a gray squirrel. Cardinals, jays, robins, and squirrels flap, hop, scoot, and scamper all over the place for a glorious five minutes, a mad peaceable kingdom.

We stand in the middle of it all, and I have to be still, as they don't know me as well as they know him. The jays land on his head, his shoulders. It tickles him to death. They swoop near me, but don't land. I feel proud and elated to be a part of this circus, this wild celebration.

When the plate is empty, not a scrap left, the commotion dies as suddenly as it began. Two squirrels still gnaw at walnuts on top of the desk which stands at the foot of his bed, but they glance nervously at me and dive out the window and down the gnarly arm toward the trunk. Cerberus has stopped.

The washstand still holds the dirty water where Andaddy washed earlier; he brought the china bowl, with water in it, back to his room, a ritual Mama cannot get used to — always there is slopped water along the hall where we all have to walk. She pointed out to him that the drain is in the bathroom, but this is the way he has always done it, since 1902 when he built the house, and it is Nannie's job to empty his wash water. And I know that the slop jar is still under his bed, still used from a lifetime of habit, though the bathroom is only twenty feet (count them! Mama tells her friends) down the hall.

MAMA COULD NOT STAND IT, despite her promise to Daddy that while he was defending his country, she'd take me and Johnnie east from California and go live in Virginia with his parents.

She liked Nainai and Andaddy all right, but felt she had nothing in common with them except her absent husband. She used to say they *weren't her kind of people,* and left it to me to figure out that that meant they weren't city people, as hers were, and they weren't sophisticated in ways she felt folks ought to be. And they certainly weren't clean enough to suit her.

Nainai derived much pleasure from others' comings and goings, and cheered Mama on as she did battle with Daddy long-distance on the subjects of permanent waves, lipstick, off-shoulder blouses, nail polish, rings. My mother liked all those things; Daddy objected to them all. Though Nainai herself did not indulge in any such frivolities, she couldn't wait to hear from Mama the latest skirmishes in what Nainai saw as a perfectly reasonable battle for independence.

So it wasn't that Mama didn't like Nainai, or didn't feel welcome. It was the *dirt* Mama couldn't bear. She believed, as my grandparents obviously did not, in germs. If she'd had her way, I'd have taken a bath every couple of days. She told her women friends in my hearing that Johnnie's knees would not come clean from crawling on the floors, that the windows had not been washed in years, and that she had seen mouse droppings on the kitchen *counter*!

We moved officially to a newly painted apartment about a mile uptown. But that was never home to me as much as Andaddy and Nainai's.

The war years were years of great peace for me. I roamed freely about the hilly town of Lexington, Virginia, safe, known, and basically happy. There was lots to do: the tiny library welcomed me to read in its dusty sunlight, just as soon as I learned how. The wonderfully intricate campuses of Washington and Lee and Virginia Military Institute invited exploration. The woods surrounding the town were safe then, with benign hoboes along the railroad tracks to jaw with, who more than once gave me coffee to drink in speckled blue tin cups with Carnation milk in it. And there were quaint museums commemorating Robert E. Lee and Stonewall Jackson. The books at Andaddy's I loved best were *Gray's Anatomy* (I was absolutely fascinated by innards) and *American Flora*, two volumes published in 1851 with gorgeously hand-tinted pictures of American flowers.

I remember how slowly time moved, how long it was from one Christmas to the next, from one summer to the next, then later, from one school term to the next. People sat out on their porches in nice weather, and I stopped by and visited with many of them, inhaling the sweet smell of privet or the tang of quince, the odor of wet cinders, with which all the driveways in Lexington seemed to be paved. In summer the air was heady with honeysuckle. I stored up local folklore without trying; the stories became a part of my mind.

I dressed my compliant baby brother Johnnie up like a girl and took him in my doll-baby carriage to visit our friends Bo and Dess, two ladies who lived next door to our apartment when we moved out of Andaddy's house. We had solemn tea parties, with good china, and slices of the rich pound cake that Bo made every week. They were sisters, the widowed Mrs. Bowman and the never-wed Miss Jessica, and they always had time for us. I learned that the one we called Dess had had a lobotomy years before for her nerves, which was probably why she giggled so, and loved tea parties with children, and gave me hankies and tins of scented bath powder to take home.

At Andaddy and Nainai's, I studied pictures of Daddy and his brother Gee, who had died at sixteen. Gee looked nothing like Daddy and me, but had black eyes and black, naturally curly hair, and a sweet mouth. Yet some of the old ladies I ran into opined I was more like Gee than Daddy, what with my singing and recitations and all. Gee had played the ukelele, and I wanted to play the ukelele.

After we moved from their house, I still went down almost every day to see Andaddy and Nainai. I had found my home in that old house where Nainai, nearly blind, drank coffee from a thermos all day, trying even at her advanced age to lose weight. She was always home, and always glad to see me, would give me a cup of coffee or tea and let me put as much sugar in it as I wanted. And not tell Mama.

Up the stairs at the very top of the house was the most wonderful attic, smelling of dust and brittle paper and leather, that pale warm odor of the blond folders which I thought for years were called *vanilla envelopes* (both because of their color and their smell). I managed to spend most of my nonschool days and quite a few nights downtown at the house on Letcher Avenue, where Daddy's concave old metal bed was kept made up and ready for me.

In the attic were trunks full of Nainai's old clothes, as well as clothes that had belonged to the Governor's many daughters; there were printed cotton dimity dresses with huge skirts, dance dresses, summer dresses, fur capes and velvet capes, a dirty pale-pink feather boa, all guarded by a benign seamstress's dummy whose headless form watched my play. The attic was littered with the remains of childhood toys that had belonged to Daddy and Gee: sleds, scooters, birds' eggs, chemistry sets, mineral collections, and books. Throughout the rest of that house were drawers that had ostensibly never been cleaned out or even straightened: every time I opened one I found treasure. Money was everywhere scattered among jewelry, sewing equipment, pens, old letters, unopened bottles of perfume, half-used boxes of sweet talcum, a dear little cabinet with forty tiny drawers, tins of chocolate gone white with age, and old, old bottles of ginger ale never opened but waiting, maturing, just, it seemed, for me! I might open a book, and out would flutter a dollar—or sometimes a Confederate bill.

They didn't care what I found, and they didn't care what I took. If I admired Nainai's tinkling collection of silver bangles, she removed one and gave it to me; it wasn't long before I had them all, to wear to this day. We cleaned them with her wintergreen tooth powder until they shone and gleamed with their own light in that dark house.

Everything in the house drew me, the dark staircases, the rooms behind rooms, and the anterooms before you got into the real rooms, the beveled glass panes. I loved the paintings, the china, the lavender-scented linens, the dull-looking cigarboxful of nuts and bolts and screws and packets of needles that might yield the surprise of a blackened bracelet I could polish up, or a couple of nickels, or even a gold hatpin with diamonds that gleamed untarnished in the dust-filled recesses. I adored jewelry.

Of course Mama thought it was awful of me to go rummaging, and forbade it absolutely. "Do *not* open drawers. That's *rude*. Those are *not* your things."

And I couldn't wait to get down there and go at it again. I loved treasure-hunting, loved my grandparents, and I loved Nannie's cooking, which was greasy, salty, rich, and buttery. Further, Nannie and my grandmother let me cook if I wanted to. Everyone agreed that my cheese sandwiches, cheddar on white bread fried in big lumps of yellow country butter thrown hissing into the frypan on the little electric one-eyed stove, zigzagging crazily across the tin surface and smoking, the cheese oozing out of the sides, were the eighth wonder. I was enchanted by the mice that skirted the edges of Nannie's shelves, that sometimes came out and sat still to watch me with their beady black eyes as I whipped up something.

Nannie, who had been born the child of slaves the year the Civil War ended, was happy to instruct me in how to make corn pudding or cherry cobbler: "You scrapes the co'n . . .'nen you takes some aigs, two or three, and you mixes um wiv some sugar, and some milk —"

Me: "How much sugar?"

Nannie: "Jes' a tad."

Me: "How much milk?" I'd have my pencil poised above the notebook page.

And Nannie, thoughtfully, "Ah doan know — 'bout a slosh, reckon." She had dark hands with pink palms, fingers gnarled from arthritis, and odd, splayed, round nails.

And they had dessert every day at lunch, an amazing luxury, the final enticement that pulled me there like a magnet. Trifles, puddings, deep-dish cherry or peach or apple pies with cream poured over them to the top of the dish, ice cream with hot chocolate sauce, bread pudding, rice pudding, something wonderful with liquor in it called Charlotte Russe. Was it any wonder that I finagled to be there for lunch as often as possible?

"SIT A SPELL," THEY USED TO SAY TO ME — MY GRANDPARENTS, THOSE OLD ladies along Letcher Avenue or Jefferson Street, where our apartment was. I had that invitation from the men in country stores, my friends' grandfathers, and my grandfather's friends. Part of it was that I made them nervous with my tireless energy, but part of it was they wanted to talk.

"Sit a spell" promised a discourse on the ways of the lightning blinking up a storm, and arguments about why thunderstorms occurred either in the late afternoon or at night, hardly ever in the morning, or what it meant when the cows on a hill all stood facing the same way: maybe rain was coming, maybe fish were biting.

Sometimes they'd bring the war into the discussion, usually concerning the picture in a local paper of one of the hometown boys in England or Germany or on one of those islands, sometimes even Daddy. Andaddy would occasionally philosophize about Hitler; it was his theory that all this wouldn't be happening if Hitler would just get married and settle down. Marriage, he maintained, was man's natural state; you didn't know what to expect from a bachelor.

To sit a spell was also to have woven about me a spell, of information and misinformation, of shocking fact or pale innuendo. "You take old man Hostetter," one would say, of someone they all knew. "Now he cured that ol' arthur-itis by Sadie putten six ole mean bees in a jar and shaken it up real good until them bees was ma-ad, then putten the mouth of that ol' jar right onto his chest. When them bees stung him, hit just took away that pain, and he could walk again, first time in ten year. . .. He's been doin' it ever since."

They had opinions about the way people *looked*, and said things like, "Did you ever notice Tardy Gerber's ears? No lobes." They'd nod sagely to each other. I soon came to understand that what that meant was, Tardy Gerber, say, was not one of them, of us — that the bigger your earlobes were, the more aristocratic you were. Same with eyes. Criminal elements had little eyes, and they tended to be close together. What you wanted was wide, big eyes in a person. Little feet on a man were suspect, too, they all agreed. Meant you couldn't trust him.

They speculated on whether they'd ever find gold, or any more tin, or iron, or cassiterite in the nearby mountains, or if it was all mined out. Someone had found the biggest diamond in the world near the West Virginia border, fifty-six pounds. Used it for a doorstop. How many carats you reckon that was, anyway? Didn't that mean there were bound to be others?

Or they'd tell one on a famous town drunk: "Passed him the other day, just sound asleep there in front of the courthouse, right on the grass. I said to him, 'Jack, you takin' a little nap?' and he opened one eye, 'bout like this, and said, 'Nope, just drunk.'"

And we'd all laugh until the old men had to wipe their eyes with their handkerchiefs. They didn't mind what I heard.

It was open season on anyone who was different. Harry Cheat had made what everyone called "an unfortunate marriage," and parted early from his wife to move in with Dancey Gibson. The old men liked to elbow each other in the ribs about those two fussy men who lived together and quarreled like fishwives, and one time, one of the men's wives had said tentatively, "Do you think they're queer?"

"Well, *of course* they're queer, Martha," her husband said testily.

Martha drew herself up huffily and said, "Well, how was I to know? They never made an advance to me!"

Then they'd all slap their knees and whoop and haw, laugh until they were all red-faced, and all take out their handkerchiefs again.

Daddy, the devoted fisherman.

Eel

*O*nce in California when I was two or three, I cut my foot badly on a piece of glass on the beach at Coronado Strand. Trip home, I stood up on the plush seat between them, holding Mama's hand in my right, Daddy's in my left, my foot on a shockingly bloodstained towel. Daddy spoke of iodine, which he pronounced, "Eye-deen," and I protested, from past experience. Mama wondered aloud about peroxide, but he didn't approve.

Daddy idled the car on a steep hill outside a drugstore, and Mama went in to consult with the pharmacist. She came out, and stuck her head in the window, saying across me, "They have two new things for cuts, Dovey, called Mercurochrome and Merthiolate. They both stain the skin red. One stings, and the other one doesn't."

And my father said, "Get the one that stings. It'll do more good."

IN THE PEACOAT BLUE FOG, I could smell everything more strongly than usual: Daddy's tea in the blue mug, the bacony smell from breakfast that clung to my clothes and skin, the car's interior, wet-woolly, smelling of tidal bays like the fog itself, the peppermint toothpaste I had just used to clean my teeth.

I turned anxiously as he swore, pushing and pushing the starter. I glanced back to the blurry square of the kitchen window to see if Mama was watching, but she was nowhere in sight, and I figured she must be on the other wall of the kitchen probably, already washing up the dishes, resigned and silent in her old pink chenille bathrobe, her face pale from all the throwing up she'd been doing lately, Johnnie lying quietly awake sucking his thumb or playing by himself making soft engine noises, and Ivy still asleep in her iron bed in the maid's room behind the kitchen.

This fishing trip was not anything I wanted to do, but I was doing it anyway. The thing Daddy seemed to love most since his return from the war was fishing; he did not mind reaching into the coffee can and feeling around as if it were cold spaghetti, to find a fat frantic worm that would reach wildly out and take hold of any nearby finger or wrist while he threaded it two or three times onto the hook. He did not mind holding the slimy jerking fish, whacking it so that it shuddered, stiffened, and died in his hand. He did not mind raking a finger down through a rip in the fish's stomach, to drag out all manner of evil bloody things. He made fun of my squeamishness, pushed near my face handsful of guts, or worms, laughed when I jerked away in fear.

I was tired of being bullied. My intent had been to stay as far as possible from my father's hobby, but there was something in me that wanted to make him approve of me. He had gone away to fight Japs when I was not yet four, and come back four years later, banging around the place like he owned it, thinking I had been spoiled in his absence.

So when he had challenged me to go fishing with him, I said yes, telling him that I would go only if I would not have to thread a hook or kill a fish. He had laughed, but he had agreed. I wanted to be companionable, but it was hard, as already I'd learned that he did not believe in bathroom stops on trips, instead running me into the woods to pee. He did not allow sweets or soft drinks in the country stores where we stopped to buy sardines and crackers and milk for lunch. I detested sardines, their fishy taste, slimy falling-off skin, mean little bones. But I ate them, and didn't let him know — afraid he'd use that against me. I'd already figured that out — he would tease me about any of the things I was nervous about. Bugs. Worms. Fish insides. The dark.

Right after we moved to the Norfolk Naval Base, around the time I turned eight, I planted a little patch of carrots and beans and radishes in my own corner of the garden, and grew what turned out to be the biggest radish anyone around Norfolk had ever seen, big enough to get a reporter out to the base to take a picture of the CO's daughter holding it up, big as a potato, big as a heart. When I brought it in the house, Daddy had stood beside me staring at the ugly thing, split and fading and hairy, with dirt in the cracks, saying over and over, "I'll be damned. Well, I'll be damned!"

Though I knew the radish was a fluke, and all the rest were just plain little radishes, still I wanted desperately to hear that tone of voice again, for it seemed a ghost from a dimly recalled past, some happier time and place.

The car was chilly, but I was warm in my navy blue pea jacket, and the scenery was ghostly and fairy-tale-like. "Daddy," I said, "see how the trees just appear? In England they believe in ghosts. I bet that's why. It's the fog, it must make things do that all the time."

For a moment he drove silently. Then he said, "I never thought about it. The only ghost I ever saw was a fireball in a field once, after a storm in the fall. Gee and I were deer hunting, walking along, and it was warm for fall, and we both saw it, rolling away from us across the field. I believe Pop saw one once, too."

"Yeah, he told me it was Uncle Hootie. You didn't follow it?"

"No —"

"I would have. Didn't you want to know what it was?"

"Reckon not," he said.

"Didn't Gee?"

The old ladies in Lexington during the war had sometimes told me how charming Gee had been, how sweet his voice was, how he flirted with the old ladies, how good-looking he was with his dark curly hair and black, black eyes. . . . Gee had the Paul coloring and eyes from Nainai's family. Daddy and I had the blue Letcher eyes, the florid skin, the pale thin hair.

Ahead, a tree loomed from beside the road that looked like a monster with its arms long-fingered, upheld in the act of reaching for us. When I asked Daddy if he'd noticed, he said no. Daddy, though seemingly interested in many of the natural phenomena I was, often appeared not to think about things that I pondered. For instance, he had gone into caves, but never looked for prehistoric wall-paintings like the ones in the Book of Knowledge. He'd been in the South Pacific jungles and seen exotic animals, but never thought of bringing one home to tame. "Too much trouble," he said shortly, when I asked. Yet in all his war letters, he'd written about animals, about how we'd have them after the war, on our farm. Now it was as if that was all just a dream, for here we were in Norfolk, and he never talked about the farm anymore.

He told me that there was a rumor that underneath the barracks at VMI where he had gone to college was a secret tunnel leading out to the river where Confederate soldiers had hidden from the Yankees. It was supposed to start at the luggage room, where the thousand or so cadets stored their trunks. Yet he had not gone there even once, at the end of the year, maybe, when the trunks were all or mostly gone, to see if it was true!

If I lived in Egypt, I'd find the secret tunnels in the Great Pyramid I'd read about. Daddy turned corners, swaying me one way, then the other.

Suddenly, the car stopped. I blinked and tried to see why. Before us the road disappeared and water began. I leaned forward to see what was happening, but the fog was thick, and the headlights barely cut into the solid bank of air. "What happened?"

"Ferry," he said. "You fell asleep."

"I did?" My mouth felt furry. Had he seen a fairy?

"Yep. It'll be here in a minute."

"The fairy?"

"Yes."

I waited, transfixed, alert, trying to force my eyes to see through the fog. I wondered what stopped people from driving on into the river.

"You got the doughnuts?" he asked.

They were cold, but still good. I decided I really liked sitting in the car in the fog with my father, eating doughnuts out of a bag together, the powdered sugar sifting like light snow onto our laps. Maybe this was going to be fun after all. He didn't usually let me have things like doughnuts. He was like Mama that way; everything had to be good for you.

Looming out of smoke, something like a bridge appeared, a boat, but square, with rails on both sides. In a moment, it docked with clanging and scraping of metal against concrete, and a garbling of heavy chains, and we drove on board, directed onto the humped deck by someone in the wolf-gray fog with a gray hooded coat. Chains were drawn across behind us, and motors started up fearsomely.

I felt abashed, realizing my mistake. The *ferry*, for of course that's what he meant, shuddered, and then we were powered strongly through water, the fog opening before us, swirling closed around us. "Want to get out and stand by the rail?" he asked. "Ought to be good fishing today," he said. "High tide in the bay at seven oh five."

The words sounded like a magic spell, promising and mysterious, and I was relieved that for once I had not made a fool of myself by mentioning a fairy, for he'd have teased me about my mistake. The fog wrapped us in pungent salty dampness. Presently stone abutments appeared, mono-colored in the mist and ancient-looking. As we drew near the bank, where the black water lapped and sucked, he made me get back in the car.

He drove carefully off the ferry, as if over chains. "It's just a mile or so down this way," he said.

"What is?"

"The boat we're going on. It takes six people. There'll be others. We'll go out a mile or two, into the current."

The fog hadn't let up, but it was a lighter gray, so morning was coming. We walked out on a long dock that smelled fishy, down wooden stairs that seemed to bounce up and down in the water.

The fishing boat had a little cabin in the middle. Someone gave me some cocoa that was watery and dark, in a tin cup like a can with a handle. For what seemed a long time, I stood at the rail looking down at the dark water moving swiftly by, while Daddy talked to the soft-voiced woman behind me. He told the woman where all he'd been, those places like Guam and Iwo Jima and Corregidor. He told the woman how he had just bought in to the Menhaden Fertilizer Company.

We were all holding fishing rods and the sinkers dragged through the water. Now the sun was a thin silver coin floating higher in the fog. The seaweed smell was in my nose, and when I licked my lips I could taste the brine, as salty as my own sweat.

You're an owner? the woman asked behind me.

Yes. One of the best investments I ever made, came Daddy's voice.

This your kid?

Yes, Daddy said, at my back. I listened eagerly, but that was all, nothing about that radish, my good standing at school, my bravery in coming here.

The ocean looked pearly now, and green and raggedy seaweed occasionally whipped out into the foamy wake from underneath the boat, caught on the line. I liked the way the string of the poles cut through the water like knives, leaving little winglike trails that disappeared as the string pulled on.

All at once Daddy, standing beside me, jerked his body, and his elbow jabbed into my shoulder. "Got a big one," he said tensely. "Come here and help me reel this thing in."

Wary, I hesitated, then moved reluctantly closer. I could smell his acrid breath, almost like Mama's nail polish remover, as he turned the handle on the green spool. The cold drops of water splashed my face as the line spun by. I was stung by salt water until the fish appeared, flung upward from churning spray, a huge black letter S in the air.

Immediately I revised that to an enormous iridescent spotted black snake, a sea monster! In that awful spray, it landed, a giant eel I shortly recognized from one of the fish books, and before I could move, it wove strange loops around my feet. In nightmare, I stared, frozen, at its blotched black slick body. For an instant I knew it would be possible to fly askew and never return to the self I was at that moment. The serpent writhed on the gray boards of the deck, smacking against my legs.

I didn't mean to, but heard myself screaming, felt his hard hand as it slapped me on my face. Angrily he yelled, "Stop it! Hold this. You hold it!"

"You promised!" I wept, though I doubt if anyone could have understood my words.

"You hold this!" he repeated, yelling in my ear and forcing my hand down toward it.

He would not make me. I would decide. I would not, I would not, ever be what Mama was, tired in a dirty pink bathrobe, shoulders sloping off hopelessly as she bent to wash clothes, or dishes, or the floor. There was another choice.

I would do it. With my cheek burning, I gathered strength, willed my hand, quickly before I could change my mind, to reach out, to grasp the monster, to put my hand firmly upon the cold slimy muscular length of that enormous snakefish that thrashed its fury beneath my grasp, to see at close range the flaking gelatinous skin, layer upon layer of cloudy-clear, to grit my teeth and hang on fiercely to the bad dream.

I tried not to see and hear while he cut off its head, sawing through flesh and bone and cartilage, those button fish eyes zombie-like upon me, the immense jaws evil and senseless opening and closing their needle teeth horribly on nothing but air, then the thick length still whipping even without a head, its red blood flying everywhere, adding a coppery smell to the fishy air, a sickening pink wash to the gray deck.

I held on and on and on, hearing voices around me but not listening, and did not let go until my father unclamped my hand from the slime and the razor fin.

He laughed then, and turned and told the woman how hard I'd held on, and showed off the great eel. He stretched it along the rail to show how it was four feet even without the disgusting head, and still, beheaded, it spelled its horrible message cursively on the air like one of his fishing worms that a bad dream had swollen huge.

Now I stared at my palm, cut across as if by a knife, the blood gathering in a thick line, and dripping down onto my dungarees. I had not failed myself. As for him, I felt hardened forever.

Clearly I saw that there was no promise implicit or explicit, so hard it could not be broken. He'd broken the promise by making me help kill the eel. Then I made an odd distinction in my head: he had not made me, I had chosen.

I began to cry, and I cried until two men came back from the other side of the boat and stood above me, concerned, talking to Daddy in low urgent tones. I luxuriated in the crying. The woman pushed me into the cabin and tried to wipe the slime and blood from my hand, and so I screamed then, great heaving gulps, while Daddy stood leaning in the door and trembling in fury because now they were turning around, heading back to shore. I had the final say.

My palm felt sticky with a taint that would not go away, though the woman rubbed and rubbed at it with some water, then wrapped a handkerchief around it. I glanced up at his red face, then hid mine again in the handkerchief the woman had given. I felt the interrupted movement of the boat, smelled a heady perfume, saw the shadows change.

When I was sure I had won, because the sun was now visible through the opposite murky side window, that we were returning to shore, I stopped crying and allowed the woman to rock me in her arms.

Daddy and Mama in Peking, 1938.

Genesis

Over elegant dinners with lots of Sauterne or sparkling burgundy at restaurants like Normandy Farms and L'Escargot, they wove a fantasy in which they became the exiled royalty of a European principality whose name changed every time it was written: Groftonburg-Hosenbach, Zutenhof-Grosendorfer, Zaffingen-Hofstadan. Stripped of their wealth and titles, they were presently forced to live ignominiously in exile until they could muster an army and return to reclaim their thrones and treasure.

DADDY WOULD SAY ONLY that he'd gone to Quantico and been dazzled by Mama, and that was that. He wasn't high on psychologizing. When they weren't mad, they called each other Doveychick or Dovey. When they were, it was Buzz and Betty — or worse, no names at all. Just *You*. Later my nickname would be Chickie, to be used when all was well. When I was called Katie, I knew something was not right.

As Mama told it, she met Daddy at Quantico, where her father was the Commanding Officer. Betty Marston had gone to secretarial school and worked at a dreary job. She wanted to be married, but felt overshadowed by her charismatic and popular sister Polly, who attracted midshipmen by the fleetful.

My future mother felt tall, awkward, and shy. It was a complicated blow when her sister Polly, two years younger than she, and not nearly as pretty, got engaged and married first.

Betty was supposed, of course, to be happy for her sister, but she felt only jealousy; she was supposed to feel love and compassion, but all she could feel was humiliation and resentment. And then of course she felt guilty about *that*.

So you could say she was primed, when, shortly thereafter, in 1935, she met Daddy. My father, when he appeared on the scene as one of the young Marine lieutenants her father commanded, looked perfect to her. He was the grandson of the Civil War governor of Virginia, big and blond, handsome and florid, even a bit wicked. Right out of the hills, not always refined. But that was fixable. A strong point in his favor was that he outranked her younger sister Polly's new husband.

Although Buzz was small-town and unsophisticated — perhaps if she were to be honest, even something of a hillbilly, with his earthy language, his crude table manners, his affinity for tramping around in the Virginia mountains — she could overlook that because now he was comfortably a part of the service she'd grown up in, and he had a fresh honesty, an unjaded charm, about him. As they were committed to staying in the service, she'd never have to have much to do with his people, small-town southerners, people who'd once, not all that far back, *owned slaves*.

And he was just back from a glamorous tour of chasing down dangerous *banditos* in the Nicaraguan jungles, where she too had lived as a child, so they had that in common. Though she had loved living there, making pets of jungle animals and birds, he told her stories that shocked and fascinated her: once he had come into a jungle clearing to discover a clutch of half-naked women and children cooking a large pot of beans.

"And where are your men?" Lieutenant Letcher asked in Spanish. The women claimed not to know. The Marines in my father's band observed that there were too many beans being cooked to feed just the women and children present.

Oh, no, said the women, no men anywhere around. No, indeed, they were certainly *not* cooking those beans for any Nicaraguan soldiers.

My father, even then, barely over twenty, deeply cynical about human nature, concluded that the Nicaraguan women were lying, and to make sure that the beans would not feed the enemy, or the women and children, he ordered his men to spit and urinate, and to perform any other physical acts they could manage, into the pot of beans, before they rode off. The story shocked Mama, but she pushed it aside.

Another time, to discipline a soldier, Lieutenant Letcher had him tied to a post atop an anthill overnight. The Central American ants are known for their aggressive stinging.

He lived up to his own ideal; in the Marine Corps, he was known as a Good Soldier. There is no doubt in my mind that he'd have died bravely. In Nicaragua, way before he was twenty-five, he'd already won the Navy Cross and the *Medallo de Merito* for exceptional bravery and leadership.

Despite some reservations, Mama made up her mind that she wanted Daddy. She felt too old for school, and was not much good at it anyway. He, like her family, loved good food and wine, tennis, and riding. Apparently he found her good company.

A closet writer of delicate feminine poetry, a devotee of Sara Teasdale and Amy Lowell, Betty Marston let her enchantment grow, decisively ignoring anything she didn't want to deal with. He was Prince Buffito, she The Countess. If his language was indelicate on occasion, his table manners less than elegant, his temper quick, she closed her ears, her eyes, her attention.

And then, as is the way in the service, Buzz Letcher was transferred — in this case, to Fort Sill Field Artillery School. On the 26th of August, 1935, Daddy wrote what may have been his first letter to Mama. It begins, "My dear Countess, Your missive, if I may use an old country term, arrived here today forwarded from the ancestral castle, and it was indeed a cheering thing in this Oklahoman desert so far, so very far from my beloved Virginia. And really I needed just the cheerfulness that it brought because ever since I arrived here I have been wondering whether I was intoxicated or out of my senses or just having a spell of mental aberration when I told your exalted father that I was so desirous of coming out here. The five days' drive was tiring, but the look of this place would make me welcome thrice the five days driving if only I were going away from here."

Through the winter of their epistolary courtship, 1935 and 1936, Daddy wrote Mama often, and amusingly. He explained that he expected to spend Christmas drinking 3.2 beer "because, as you perhaps know among the many things that are wrong with Oklahoma not the least is that they still have prohibition, and never have I seen a place where a drink or two was more needed." Upon her request of a photo of himself, he wrote that he had no snapshot, but would try to have one taken, although "I take a terrible picture . . . we had to be photographed for the official records and I saw mine a few days ago. Really if Dillinger wasn't known to be dead I'm sure someone would shoot me for him." When he finally got around to sending the picture, he apologized ruefully for being "already stricken with premature balditude."

Of Oklahoma society, he commented, "The Army juniors . . . try to appear blase and sophisticated as they sit around sucking their cigarettes and looking bored. They affect the bored look, but I don't need to affect it."

In November of 1935 Betty got a position as a secretary in the Persian embassy in Washington, and soon she was being pursued by an amorous clerk a foot shorter than she, whom she described to "Prince Buffito" as "foreign, little, dark and greasy."

Prince Buffito congratulated her on getting the job as secretary to the Persian ambassador, and gallantly remarked that he knew they could, given her beauty and grace, choose no other. Two months later, he warned that if the Eastern Europeans didn't stop molesting her he would have to come back and shoot them for her, and then he would be guilty of homicide and it would be all her fault. Betty in fact detested being a secretary — which circumstance no doubt made the concept of rescue more alluring.

They wrote letters for a year. Clearly, Daddy was in his element. He wrote funny, inventive letters. Hers were not of the same quality, and had throughout an oddly querulous tone. Over and over she begged him to reiterate that he loved her, complained at length about the boring people around her, and groused about her awful job. After seeing Marc Connolly's hit show, "Green Pastures," she remarked, "It was good but it dragged a bit in parts." The critique of a play about southern Negroes and their religious beliefs — certainly not commonplace in her world — seems shallow and obligatory. She wasn't a deep thinker, but her responses to everything were serious: she wanted to discuss religion, and conscience. She urged Buzz to read *Anthony Adverse*, an adventurous historical novel with a very noble hero which she believed was "the best book ever written."

Of course she wrote many nice things: "You are so funny about your car. I'd rather ride in that car with you than a Packard roadster with anybody else, and that includes the King of England and Clark Gable." She asked him in a letter *to teach her how to fish*, and wrote that she'd gladly live in a "tent or whatever sort of place we have to live in." When a snapshot she had taken of him on a picnic turned out to look "rather like three-quarters of a pound of cheese," in her mother, Laolo's, view, she wrote him indignantly that she didn't appreciate her mother laughing at him. (Laolo was my name for her; I think it was a Chinese word for "ancestor" or some such.)

Before he'd left for Fort Sill, at the end of the summer, Betty had for the first time visited Buzz and his parents, Captain and Mrs. Letcher (whom I later would call Andaddy and Nainai) in the dark old house in Lexington. Upon returning to Annapolis, she wrote, "I even liked Teddy, which is the supreme test."

Indeed it was. She must have been deeply in love by then to say that about the family dog. Her entire family despised dogs deeply.

By Christmastime Buzz was writing to her from the train on his way to spend a few days in Mexico, "Don't worry about me having anything to do with any senoritas, Countess. If I can claim any virtues at all it is that I'm a 'one-man dog.' Well I have attached myself to none other than you, Countess, and you are my sole star in the feminine firmament so the senoritas will get none of my time."

Promises and intentions were exchanged, but then something went awry. There are letters leading up to it, cooling a bit, his inquiring repeatedly if *she* is quite sure. . . . There was, too, in his past, a girl named Bunny whom he'd been engaged to, and whom he couldn't get out of his mind, even though Bunny had broken off with him.

When he returned to Quantico a year later to own up, in person, that he didn't think he loved her, Mama felt she would die, and told him so. She told him no one else could ever love him as much as she did. She told him she'd already made her wedding dress. She told him her father had already booked them honeymoon passage on the SS *Pastores*, a Columbian steamship.

So he did the manly thing; he abandoned his plan to try to retrieve the thing with Bunny, and he married Betty, in a big ceremony at St. Alban's Church in Washington. Captain Letcher came by himself from Lexington. Mrs. Letcher, he explained, was too ill to travel.

Mama's wedding pictures are pensive. She had already tasted the ashes of getting what she wanted when she knew *she* was not what *he* wanted.

In the Marine Corps, everyone knew everyone else, and it may be true that Boppie, the family name for Betty's father and Daddy's CO, had sent Buzz Letcher to Fort Sill knowing that the young lieutenant he wanted for a son-in-law had been engaged to another girl, one from Norfolk, and at Fort Sill there were no quarters for married men. Aunt Polly thinks Boppie's ploy may have been to keep Buzz and Bunny apart, to give his daughter Betty time to work her spell via epistolation.

It is to my father's credit that he looked only forward, never back. Although he kept a picture of Bunny hidden at the bottom of a trunk from then on, which I discovered after Mama died and Daddy got over his mourning and married Sallie, and my sister Betsy and I were cleaning out three generations of accumulated possessions, he never held it against Mother that she held him to a promise he didn't want to be held to.

And once married, he did not nourish himself on regret. They were stationed in China, and left on a ship only five weeks after they returned from their honeymoon.

In Peking, Mama and Daddy lived like the royalty they had fantasized about. They played tennis and bridge, drank martinis and wine, enjoyed picnics at the Emperor's Summer Palace and sumptuous dinners at exotic restaurants and officers' clubs, and rode thoroughbred horses. (Later they swore off hard liquor entirely, hardly ever had dinner parties, and rarely went out at all. Daddy's odd explanation of why he quit drinking at forty was that everyone was born with a certain capacity for drinking, and some just used it up sooner than others. He also said he'd decided time drunk was time wasted.)

They lived in the Legation, a section of Peking where all the foreign dignitaries lived. There were Germans, Italians, Russians, Belgians, to socialize with, as well as Americans. My father headed up a detachment of Marines at the American Embassy, while my mother shopped for bolts of gorgeous Chinese silks and brocades in colors unavailable at that time anywhere else in the world, then settled in to make slipcovers and curtains, bedspreads and pajamas, daydresses, elegant bathrobes, and evening gowns. Daddy, not overtaxed in his work, which was a peace-keeping mission left over from the Boxer Rebellion, combed Peking's back streets every afternoon bargain-hunting for ancestor portraits painted or embroidered on silk, tapestries, ivories, statuary, royal robes, ancient books, vases. Together and separately, they shopped. Neither could turn down a bargain in those heady days.

Once on a visit to the Ming tombs outside the city, Daddy saw one of the carved gargoyle downspouts that had fallen from the roof lying on a trash heap, and asked a guard if he could buy it. They settled on one dollar American, and he shipped home the ninety-pound white-jade Ming dragon head carved in the fourteenth century. It stayed packed in excelsior and crated in beautiful (and well-seasoned) walnut boards until Betsy and I came across it in 1985.

In the afternoons, and again in the evenings, they partied, hard. They played bridge. Lieutenant and Mrs. Letcher joined an international gourmet group that sought out Peking's exotic cuisine. My mother went only once, but Daddy kept going, and ate, among other things, shark's fins and monkey's brains, soup with whole mice in it, and artistic gelatin creations that looked like miniature fishponds, and turned out to have live goldfish trapped in the jelled "water." Mama took to bed following the miscarriage of twin boys. While she was sick, Daddy shopped by himself.

They fired one houseboy for stealing salt, one for toasting their breakfast bread between his filthy bare toes over the space heater in the kitchen. My mother relieved a ricksha driver of his duties because he chewed garlic all the time, and she, riding at close range behind him, could not bear the perfume. Perhaps her squeamishness was because I was on the way. They bought rugs, coats lined with snow leopard pelts, Ming vases, a white lapine (rabbit) evening coat for Mama, fur lap rugs, china, and silver.

If indeed our coming from spirit into flesh is by choice and by contract, then I was seduced by their youth, humor, vibrant health, glamour, and privilege, and came eagerly to blend with those two in flesh, exhilarated by the bright promise of their lives. If our coming here is mere accident, then I was luckier than most other creatures born to this planet.

But all was not well, even then.

My mother is walking in Peking along a canal one evening after it has been raining. Playfully, my father shakes a water-laden branch off onto her new perfectly lacquered hairdo.

She protests the meanness of the trick! He laughs. They walk on.

A few minutes later, my father reaches up, and shakes another water-laden branch of plum blossom down on her. She turns, furious, realizing that she is not surprised. She feels something inside her grow cold, seeing that the teasing means more to him than her feelings do.

She tells him again, this time coldly and firmly, how she feels.

So, when he responds by laughing at her and shaking down a third wet branch to wreck the perfection of her set, it creates a turning point in their relationship. Daddy laughs it off, forgets in seconds, but Mama never forgets. At this moment she hardens her heart against him.

SHE TOLD THAT STORY OFTEN; all of us knew it.

I was born in May of 1938, the only pink-and-white baby, my mother liked to say, in a Chinese hospital among hundreds of yellow-and-black babies. Mama told it that she was comforted that there was no way they could have gotten me mixed up. In fact, I look so much like both my parents that I never even wondered if I had been adopted. Later, of course, I sometimes wished I had, by richer, or kinder, or more sympathetic, people. And I often, as I grew up, wished I was an only child, for I ended up with a lot of responsibility for the littler ones. But for better or worse, I knew I belonged to them.

I am told that I understood and responded to Mandarin before English because I spent so much time with my Chinese *amah*. My mother feared Amah would spoil me, and so decreed that for one hour of each afternoon I must be left alone in my crib. A typical Taurean from Day One, abounding with appetite and stubbornness, I cried every single day for the entire hour, separated from my doting nurse, while she sat on a chair in the corridor with her head against my closed door, weeping in tandem. The other servants hovered about nervously; they had no control over this wrongdoing by the American Missie. In China, if a baby cries, it reflects badly on the nurse, and so Amah *lost face* each afternoon during this ordeal, which was to a Chinese person a terrible humiliation.

Because Amah, in her great fear of dirt, carried me everywhere, I never learned to walk until I was nearly two, on shipboard coming back from China to California. Because Amah anticipated every whim, I never tried to talk either until then.

From letters he wrote home to his parents, in which he described me as "feisty," "an engaging little wretch," "an entertaining little frump," and "her imperious highness," I am sure Daddy adored me then.

It is too bad in my case that we don't remember the first couple of years of life, because mine were spent as a pampered exotic little princess in that household with eleven doting servants. And beginning life as an only child to unusually privileged parents would probably be a good start for anyone. No matter what happened later, I am grateful for being allowed to burst upon the scene like a single beautiful firecracker in the night.

I RECALL NOTHING OF THOSE FIRST TWO YEARS. But I remember a great joyous lot about San Diego, where we lived for nearly three after that, though in memory the time there seems endless, as long as the rest of childhood.

The very earliest memory I am sure of: an aunt from the east sent me a stuffed animal, and immediately I named it Wabboo. Mama told someone in my presence that I had named my *bear* Wabboo. But it wasn't a *bear*; it was a rabbit, and I had called it correctly Rabbit, Wabboo. I could *not* make them understand, and it just made me furious.

Daddy was stationed at Camp Elliott, and we lived on steep Goldfinch Street, which dead-ended at our house, a sweet Spanish stucco one-story with a glass porch running down the side of it. Just across the driveway was a precipitous fall-away into a deep canyon where I was not allowed to go, and being the child I was, went continually. Ten yards or so down its rim was a greenhouse that had previously tilted and slid there during one of the earth tremors that we felt nearly every day. I went hunting the tiny red cherry tomatoes that volunteered in the precarious structure. Mama fussed and fussed, but that was all. I gauged her early; she could be worn down easily, and she hardly ever spanked. I knew she hated spanking me. Even when she did, it was just pretend. All I had to do was holler real loud at the beginning, and she'd quit.

I loved watching Mama put on lipstick, carefully on her top lip only. Then she'd compress her lips together to get some on the bottom, then run her little finger, its pad permanently red from doing this, over first the top, then the bottom lip. Though she loved makeup, she had a horror of appearing over-painted. I liked and imitated her style when I took to wearing lipstick, in my third year.

We had an avocado tree with a swing for me in it, and a huge fig tree, and we ate those fruits even richer than God had made them. The sun-yellow avocadoes we ate halved, with mayonnaise mounded in the centers, and the figs, already honey-sweet, we cut up into bowls with honey and thick cream.

Poinsettias grew in huge bushes around the house, surprising the rainy winter gray of San Diego. We had olive trees out back, several different kinds, green and brown and black, and in the cellar, two barrels of olives. In one, the olives cuddled in brine, shiny, salty, crisp; and in the other dry-processed olives aged slowly, wrinkled, leathery. Daddy puffed smoke at them to give them a pungent, smoky taste.

We had a hillside of beehives. My brave daddy, when he got home from work, put on a hat draped with mosquito netting, and big heavy gloves, and Mama tied cords around the bottoms of his pants and his cuffs, and he marched off to battle with a contraption like a coffee pot or the tin woodman's oiling can, and drove away the bees by puffing clouds of smoke at them, and brought us back honey, and never got stung. I chewed dripping square chunks of beeswax until my jaws hurt, working out every iota of sweetness.

The memories are as golden as Goldfinch Street's name. Sunlight falls on a table top, and Daddy swiftly, neatly, decaps soft-boiled eggs in Blue Willow china cups. The yolks run yellow as the sun, yellow as Mama's bath towel that smells of her lavender soap when she hugs me, reunited after the separation of her bath, which she insists on taking all by herself.

Not so with Daddy; he cheerfully invites me into the bathroom to talk with him as he wets down, then soaps all over, every single inch, with orange Lifebuoy soap, white with suds and lather, his hair like clouds aflame, his eyes squeezed shut in his red face, his loins blurred with drippy foam. Together we sing, "I'm dreaming of a white Christmas . . ." or "Don't fence me in," at the top of our lungs. He finishes by turning on the water again, getting suds all over the shiny chrome faucets, and washing away all that white, rinsing down the faucets, stepping out onto the yellow bathmat, yellow towel in a sarong around his hips.

In a yellow bowl the scooped-out eggs are stirred with crumbled bacon, crisp toast, yellow butter, in the glassed-in breakfast porch looking out across the canyon in San Diego.

DADDY, ARRIVING HOME AT MY BATHTIME, brings a fish still alive, bursts into the bathroom, arcs a golden rainbow of urine into the toilet, and slides the live fish into the tub with me. Trying to catch it, we swamp the bathroom, our laughter echoing off the walls, spraying the mirror, soaking the towels. Daddy's face is shiny and red, though Mama, her elbows jutting out in the same shape as the diamond windowpanes in her room, doesn't think it's so funny. She's trying to get me to bed, keep the bathroom nice for the company due to arrive. But Daddy and I don't care about company. We love it that Mama is scandalized.

Mama in her shell-pink chenille bathrobe, Daddy dressed fit to kill in his uniform with ironed creases, smelling of Lifebuoy, and I in my pink nightgown, all drive to the train station in Old Town where Daddy takes his train to Camp Elliott. Mama drives; I sit in the middle; Daddy eats his breakfast in the car. He leaves the empty dish in the glove compartment, and I can smell bacon on his breath when he kisses me goodbye, and says, *Don't fight nobody, don't call nobody Fool*, an incantation that his mother used to say to him. Occasionally after the train has gone I can wear down Mama's protests and am allowed to scramble barefoot onto the platform, put a penny into the gum machine, and get two Chiclets neatly wrapped in cellophane. Green is spearmint, blue is peppermint; it is a small agony to decide which I will have.

Back home, it is my job to retrieve Daddy's blue dish and spoon from the glove compartment and take them past the round fishpond, up the back stairs, to the kitchen.

All day we do things, Mama and I: we sew, we make up beds, we cook. We go to the Piggly-Wiggly. We feed the goldfish, and run errands. Sometimes we meet Laolo at the zoo and wander around among the monkeys and peacocks. My grandfather had years earlier (when Mama and Polly and Jack were kids and they were stationed in Nicaragua) shipped a lot of animals to the zoo, and so my grandmother is given the red-carpet treatment, and I am given free candy.

And at night we drive back in the car, to pick up Daddy from the train. Then, he smells unlike us, sweaty and officey. And we all go home together and have supper and read, until it is time to sleep. Daddy reads me my favorite book, about Jackie Rabbit and the Last Carrot, over and over, and pretty soon I recite it with him. Before the end, when poor Jackie and his sister Susie have to wear newspapers to school, they are so poor, Daddy makes out like he's crying loudly, and lets me comfort him. "It's just pwetend!" I urge, night after night.

No child ever had a happier babyhood; I made my parents laugh, and I knew I was their singular most favorite thing. In my baby pictures I held out flowers to the parent pointing the camera. Grinning, I toddled barefooted toward the anchors of my life with my hands stretched out as tar-scented California breezes lifted my wispy hair from my face. Sometimes in photos I was solemn, staring levelly at the camera, huge-eyed.

"Chickie!" they called, and I ran to their good big warm smells. "Katie Paul Letcher!" they cried.

Daddy, over the Lifebuoy's odor, smelled the way milk used to when it sat for a few minutes in the sun, and Mama smelled yeasty and toasty. The smell I hated most was *L'heure Bleue*, because Mama put it on her wrists and behind her ears when they were going out, going to leave me with someone else for whole *hours* of time!

We have been to the beach, Daddy and I, and are homeward bound when we cross Mission Bay at low tide and Daddy spots three lobsters, trapped in a pool when the tide went out! All we have to collect them in is my potty, which we keep in the car for emergencies, so we wade in and scoop up lobsters out of the sand. Three of them, and the pot is bulging.

Car won't start, goes Harnh! Harnh! when Daddy turns the key. We walk to the nearest streetcar line where we take the trolley, still holding the potty containing three indignant lobsters bent on freedom; we ride home juggling the potty to keep its gesticulating denizens corralled, to the delight of the other commuters.

At home, Mama shows by her outrage how awful we are to make such a scene, to be so near nude in public, still in our bathing suits! Daddy winks at me, shrugs, says, "What could we do? The car wouldn't start, so we had to leave it on the bridge." His face glows with pleasure, and I savor the delight of being regarded as a maverick, and feel triumphant along with Daddy. I love the attention our exhibitionism attracts; in fact, it is most certainly preferable to the dourness of my mother who stands fully dressed, hands on hips, frowning disapprovingly at her two happy bad kids. This early, I learn what fun it is to shock Mama. To Mama, the worst sin is to make a spectacle. But at the same time she admires us, and that's a part of it. She just shakes her head.

But Daddy is not ashamed of anything he does. He tells me he never wore shoes as a child, never, and I find that appealing and nervy. "Not in wain?" I ask, and he shakes his head. "Not in snow?" "Not in school?" It is a game we play night after night.

"Not ever," he has to say. Hooray for his wondrous lack of inhibition!

ONCE DADDY CAME CRASHING THROUGH the back door barely in time for a dinner party, flung a fish he'd caught into the icebox, and sprinted for the shower. Later, I was eating my supper with Amela, the Mexican maid — a poached egg on rice. Mama came breathlessly into the kitchen to fetch the shimmering red tomato aspic already turned out and waiting on a bed of lettuce, decorated with piped mayonnaise. She opened the door of the refrigerator to discover that it had been wrecked by the still-live flopping fish that had made its way down several shelves to where the lovely salad was, overturning the cream pitcher on the way. Daddy soon had Amela and me screaming with laughter as he tried gamely and vainly to reshape the now disgusting aspic. We infuriated Mama by thinking it was so funny. Daddy even got the dinner guests in on the joke, but it was days before Mama forgave him. She clung to her grudges.

What's your name, little girl? Kaypawleckie.

Who do you love? Mamandaddy.

There are just we three. "Mamahand, Daddyhand," I demand, standing between them on the plush seat of the new 1939 Ford sedan. And there the hands are: his, big and rough and red, with hairs like gold wires on the back, and hers cool and smooth and white, blue veins like tiny rubber tubes beneath the skin, white spots on her nails.

My parents in the pictures are young, and their body language does not reveal any unhappiness. My mother, dark-haired, tall, and slender, in nearly every snapshot of her tilts her head coyly, with a small smile she must have thought made her look prettier than usual. My husky Nordic-looking father squints like all us blonds do in bright light, and grins engagingly, over and over, smack into the camera. Page after page of pictures against black blotter paper: beach, lawn, fishpond, tricycle, sunlight, wind, with me the center of each. There is no doubt in my mind that they were happy then, no matter what Mama told me later.

In the afternoons, I nap on a tiger-belly lap robe that we got in China, as soft as the stomach of any cat. On my bed is a turquoise silk quilt Mama has made to snuggle under when the nights are cold. Mama rubs

yellow-green-smelling citronella on the windowsills and dots it on my pil-
low, to keep the mosquitoes away. At naptime, I learn that I can roller-
skate instead of rest, if I put the silk quilt on the floor and skate on top of
it, in muffled triumph.

In arguments, I win a reasonable percentage of the time: I win a sip of
Mama's iced coffee or iced tea, I get another helping of Spanish cream, I
get *Jackie Rabbit and the Last Carrot* read again, though it is past my bedtime.

BUT I DO BADLY AWAY FROM HOME. They sign me up for a nursery school
where we sing and eat graham crackers and draw, and there are some children I like. But I cannot stand it after snack when we have to lie down on
mats orange or gold or turquoise blue and take a nap. In order to avoid
going at all, I throw up every morning in the car on the way to school.
Mama becomes less and less sympathetic.

At some party I have been brought to, I sit in a small chair just my
size, and eat gumdrops (purple and peppery) out of a little ruffled basket,
vari-colored. But I am miserable here, a galaxy or more away from my
house, and I want to go home. Other children, across the room, seem
happy. The Woman comes again, says, "If you cry you'll ruin your pretty
dress." She means to be kind, but I can't stand this. My nose and eyes are
wet and blubbery, and the soft chewy candies she's given me are for some
reason covered with sand, but I am getting used to the taste. "Your daddy
will be here soon!" The Woman hovers and worries, invites me to join the
others, but I stay alone, crying. There is a cake, but I'm not interested, I
just want to go home — and poppers, See!, she exclaims, showing me the
two in her hand, but I want only Daddy. At last he arrives, filling the
doorway with his wonderful shininess, swoops me up onto his shoulders
laughing, and rescues me!

Twice, Daddy really saved my life. We were on a dock in San Diego
to take possession of some of the furniture sent from China. I apparently
walked to the end of the long dock and simply did not stop: I disappeared

into deep water, and sank like a stone. After me dove my daddy, and found my pale baby hair in the blackness floating out above my head, and grabbed it, and dragged me to the surface, and yelled for a life preserver.

And there was the Dalmatian, right out of a nightmare, vicious, huge, spotted. It was a scary neighborhood dog, and my fright was reinforced by my mother who detested dogs, found them unbelievably disgusting, and let the world know it. I grew up with her opinion deeply embedded.

On moving day I got left accidentally for a moment on the sidewalk, and the Dalmation apparently simply attacked me, was standing over me when they heard me scream, with half my face in its teeth. I have no memory of the attack, of the more than one hundred tiny stitches in the side of my scalp, along my hairline, in my nose, no memory at all except for one thing: that when I looked up into that pinkish-white mouth as it descended, there were spots inside it, on the arched roof of the dog's mouth, just like the spots that covered its outside. I heard later how Daddy snatched the vicious dog off me, and flung it yipping into the street, but I don't remember that.

My potty, white enamel with a thin blue edge, brought from China, rolled around reassuringly on the floor of our new car. I understood that once I got the hang of telling them in time, they would take me out with them at night: I learned quick, and my favorite place was a San Diego restaurant called Bernadini's, where I sat in a green leather booster chair and ate wonderful spaghetti. Movie stars patronized the restaurant, and once Mickey Rooney came over to speak to us, remembering Mama from a party in Washington that Jimmy Roosevelt took her to once when she was a secretary.

In December of 1941, two things occurred that, as it turned out, took my father from me forever. The first, of course, was the Japanese attack on Pearl Harbor, which didn't register in my three-year-old consciousness, but which would take Daddy to the south Pacific and a glorious war record. In the next four years he would rise to the rank of colonel, the youngest in the Marine Corps.

The second event, of which I was most indignantly conscious, was the birth of my brother Johnnie two days after Pearl Harbor, in San Diego, in a blackout.

As soon as I heard the news, I went around the neighborhood, knocking on doors, telling people when they answered that I had a new baby brother and that his name was Mary Sue. I felt sure that if I could get to them before Mother did, that by the power of naming I could turn him into the girl playmate I wanted. A boy? Who needed a boy?

They grinned. They laughed. "A baby brother? What did you say his name — ?" I had no idea why they thought that funny, no idea why my plan did not work out.

My salvation at the time of Johnnie's birth arrived in the form of Harriet, a cheerful plump girl who came to live with us, as Daddy had to leave almost at once. The chewing gum she slipped to me the first day she was on board was all it took to win my shallow affection.

In the confusion that followed America's entry into World War II, Johnnie and Mama came home from the hospital, Daddy was shipped overseas, and my babyhood ended. I blamed the baby. It drove me crazy for Mama to nurse him, which she did with disgusting frequency, while I rollerskated in the hall loudly, broke things, crashed about making noise any way that I could, pushing Mama to the point where she would yell at me, and I could collapse, weeping at her treachery. I turned to Harriet for consolation.

At home, Johnnie did little but sleep. I wasn't allowed to dress him up in doll clothes. I wasn't even allowed to pick him up. They wouldn't call him Mary Sue for all my pleas. My daddy was gone, and with him his jokes and laughter, his lobsters posturing absurdly on the kitchen floor, his fish swimming in my bath, his good smell and his smoking beehives, and great rides high in the swing, Mama standing on the front porch cautioning us both to be careful, hold on tight, while I grew dizzy with bliss and went higher.

Mama, never possessing the electric energy Daddy had, now stayed in bed a lot, her eyes puffy. The house, once so bright and sunny, was a place shaded and shushed. The damn baby had to sleep. Mama had to rest. Harriet had to cut up potatoes, or mop the floor. I was terrified to leave for a second, for what else might happen while I was gone?

Harriet took my side in every argument, even the ones about chewing gum, and sometimes managed to make me a little kinder about Johnnie.

Mama, sad and frightened without Daddy, had been left alone in the world with two children in a place where the Japs might attack any moment, killing us all. To me it seemed only that her eyes were far, not near, her hands jerky, not smooth, her face not attending when I asked her something. It was clear to me that she preferred Johnnie. I had no choice but to expand my world to include Shirley, a raggedy girl with naturally curly hair on the next street whose mother never made her bathe, and a girl named Sally Swarbrick who lived across the street. She was older, and took pleasure in tormenting me. She told me mockingly when we were in a room alone, "Jesus can see through walls. He can see what you do at night."

Before he left, Daddy extracted from Mama a promise she couldn't refuse, for he well might have been going off to his death: he made her promise she'd go to Lexington, Virginia, and live with his parents while he was off at war. Her own father was still active in the Marines. She couldn't say no. It was her worst nightmare coming true. She waited a year before complying.

So when we left for Virginia in the car with Harriet, Mama must have felt dreadfully sad and alone, driving toward a life in a small rural community, in the South, with people she didn't know or care for, moving even farther away from Daddy, who was at least in the same ocean we'd been living on.

Me, Johnnie, and Mama at Andaddy's during the war.

Women

he men living in Lexington during the war were all strange: though I change their names here, Lee Jackson was nearly blind, with thick glasses, Tote Bradley had something called Angina that made his chest hurt, Dave Grossinger was flat-footed, and Nutty Jenkins was shell-shocked from World War I, which was why he drank all day long. The professors we knew at the colleges seemed all right, though of course their not being in the war damned them so that people wondered about their secret handicaps. From Mama and Andaddy and Nainai I knew that all real men were at the war.

AS I REMEMBER IT NOW, I danced through the war years to the light music of gossiping women who seemed, in retrospect, more at ease together then than they did later, after the war, when there were men again. All summer long we were surrounded by the perfumes of fruits being put up, simmered into sweet clear jellies, mashed into sauce, blended with spices for pickles. When we weren't spending afternoons corralled in sullen isolation from the dreaded polio, we might be found running with pails along the railroad tracks for the wild strawberries we knew we'd find; we

gathered watercress, and grapes, and blackberries for pies, swapping stories about the enormity of the rattlesnakes that were reputed to hang out
in the blackberry thickets.

Back home in anyone's kitchen there was the music of kettles of
water bubbling in tropical humidity for the skinning of peaches or
tomatoes. Or there were mountains of blackberries to be picked over
with purple fingers. Mama, with her obsession for cleanliness, was fond
of saying that I had enough dirt on me, or under my nails, to grow a
victory garden.

She was good at what was required: economy and ingenuity. She
made me for Christmas one year during the war a most wonderful doll-
house, without a single commercial item in it. The house itself was con-
structed of orange crates from the grocery, four of them, to make eight
rooms. The wallpaper was made out of anything she could find, from
butcher paper and laundry paper and saved gift wrapping paper, and the
wallpaper paste she mixed up out of flour and water, with salt and something else, maybe powdered alum, added to discourage silverfish and
other insects.

The family of dolls were padded bendable pipe-cleaners, every limb
lovingly shaped and covered with pink cotton fabric, hair made of
sewing thread, little faces painted on.

Boxes turned into intricate furniture, padded with the cotton from
old medicine bottles. Four wooden thread spools and a Christmas card
box bottom made a fine bed, and Mama sewed a tufted mattress for it.
Leftover bits of material, mostly Chinese silk, were transformed into curtains and bedspreads, and the sheets she monogrammed with flowery L's.
A bandage-tape spool was transformed into a round table. Band-Aid
boxes made dressing tables and sideboards when covered or painted. She
made tables and chairs out of cardboard, wood scraps, anything she
could find in that war-scoured world. The bath tub was modeling clay.
She built the fireplace out of wood scraps, and carefully cut a scrap of fur
from an old collar into a bearskin rug to go in front of it.

Buttons served for plates, a bottle cap with modeling clay in it became a tiny pie; she framed tiny bits of magazine pictures and "hung" them on the walls. She hand-carved tiny soap bars from real soap, tiny sponges from real sponge. She molded oranges and loaves of bread and bananas from flour dough, dried them in the oven, and painted them. It was a wonder. Furthermore, she did the entire thing after I went to sleep every night, for it was an utter surprise to me on Christmas morning.

The women discussed the war, their absent husbands, the few men left in town, their victory gardens, the scarcity of cotton fabric, a Negro child who died of polio, a new bolt of material at Adair's, recipes for eggless cakes, child psychology, a certain farmer who was selling black-market beef. They were quick to condemn other women in town who bought black-market meat when their own families were doing without, and they were proud of their honest patriotism. Everyone, even strangers, knew my father, and seemed anxious to relate some event of his childhood: Buzz putting pepper in a fellow camper's nose, Buzz skinning a snake, picking a fight and getting thrashed by the principal, and of course always Buzz going barefoot to school in the snow.

I recall the women and children pooling gas ration stamps for a blackberrying trip to the mountains one August day, returning with pails and cans and cooking vessels brimming, and everyone with stained scratches that stayed purple a long time. My mild mother killed a copperhead with a big stick, and the other women closed around to praise her and thank her, and advise her how to get the spatters of snake blood out of her peach-colored shirt. That incident still stands out as an idyll, an instant in history of women cooperating gracefully, of children for once helpful and attentive. We were holding the world together. After the fathers came home from war, the women never killed snakes.

Buzz Letcher on Guadalcanal, 1944.

Naming the Enemy

When I was a kid, nobody (with the affectionate exception of my first-grade teacher, Miss Edmonia Smith) ever told me anything but good things about Daddy. Of course that's how the world was, and is; nobody tells a kid mean things about her father. The idea I got was that he was perfect, that he won every battle he ever fought, that he did everything right, and that everyone loved him. In comparing myself with him, I fell short in every respect. Miss Edmonia did tell me how often Buzz had to stand in the corner, and she did imply that he was not full of scholarly alacrity.

I did not know that after the horrendous drawn-out battle of Iwo Jima, 2,600 Marines went insane, most of them permanently.

With grim humor, some wag put a sign on a buoy marking the course for landing craft that read BUY WAR BONDS. Off Iwo, Daddy decided he needed salt tablets to stand the heat of the crowded transport. Seeing a stack of white tablets on a wardroom table, he took one, couldn't chew it for the life of him, and finally got it down his gullet with several quarts of water. Soon after, someone began counting the stack of tablets. "Why are you counting salt tablets?" Daddy demanded. Whereupon, he was told they were poker chips. His response: "Well, it's *just as well; I didn't think I was going to be able to take any more salt tablets."*

My father was one of the ones who were able to regard the Japanese hidden in the lava caves among the hot springs of that Stygian island as mere vermin — and to set about exterminating them in much the same way he'd later mount attacks against roaches or mice or Japanese beetles. It wasn't nice, but it kept him sane. It was something he kept hidden in his heart. Did he nearly wet his pants with terror, or was he fueled by righteous fury alone? I never knew; he never said. How might our lives together have been different if he'd been the kind of man who could talk to his children about his real feelings?

Peter, the youngest of us, remembers a story Daddy told him. I never heard it, but here it is. Daddy returned in August of 1945, which means he must have left the South Pacific before the war was over. The Japs slowed the fighting after we dropped the bomb on Hiroshima on August 2, then stopped entirely on August 15, but the peace agreement was not signed until September 2. Daddy, making his way home at a leisurely rate, stopped on the West Coast to visit some friends for a week.

He arrived at Andaddy and Nainai's house one day, apparently unexpected, because he was confronted by his father, who instead of greeting his only son, demanded angrily, "Buzz? What are you doing here? The war isn't over. You go back and finish it!"

JOHNNIE CLAIMS THE FIRST MEMORY of Daddy's arrival home from war: he was swinging one day on our grandfather's alley gate when he saw a tall stranger in uniform approach from the end of the long driveway. Johnnie, who never got disciplined because he never did anything naughty, swung and swung, enjoying the sun and the breeze, and the stranger strode closer, then frowned and said, "Little Boy, if you don't stop swinging on that gate, I'm gonna *bong* you." The words scared Johnnie, who didn't like the sound of bong, which he would soon learn indeed approximated the Chinese word for spanking.

By bad luck, I had a terrible case of more or less infected chicken pox when Daddy arrived home, made worse by a vaccination I'd gotten not long before. With my propensity to scratch, I'd revaccinated myself all over my body, wherever there was a chicken pock. To finish off the portrait, I had recently had a disastrous permanent — so as to be gorgeous for Daddy's return. All that on top of the fact that even pretty girls, which I was not especially, go through an ugly year somewhere around seven or eight.

And all three-and-a-half-year-olds are beautiful. Johnnie was now almost exactly the age I had been when Daddy left. To Daddy's longing eyes, weary and hungry after the war, I think it must have seemed that the red-cheeked cherubic child he had loved so, and had to leave on the West Coast, had miraculously turned into the boy he had always in his deepest soul wished I'd been.

From the first day home, Daddy would take Johnnie on his lap and say, "What we going to do when you get bigger?"

Daddy coached Johnnie to reply, "Huntn, fissin, campin, fwimmin," and his face would redden with pleasure listening to the little boy's recitation.

I watched, irritation and jealousy bubbling up inside me. "I can say 'The Cremation of Sam McGee,' the whole thing," I'd say, but Daddy wanted to play with Johnnie.

I danced a hoochy-koochy dance for his favor, accompanied by my rendition of a song called "Wait Till You See Bessie and Her Bustle"; he only told me to stop showing off.

I sang the songs I'd learned; I tried to recite the poems, but I could see his eyes turn to Johnnie or blur with boredom when I got to maybe the third verse.

I tried harder; he grew more irritated. I grated on him, I could tell.

He took Johnnie on walks, but Johnnie always came home crying. He had cut his hand, fallen and banged up a knee, gotten too cold, was hungry. I watched for my chance, and offered to go on a walk. I was the one, I explained, who liked those kinds of activities, not Johnnie. But by then Daddy would be discouraged and irritated, and wouldn't be interested in another walk. Mama, annoyed at Daddy for making her perfectly agreeable little boy cry, would take Johnnie on her lap and comfort him; Daddy would tell her to leave him alone and not turn him into a sissy; supper would be a silent affair, the hot air heavy and prickly on the back of my neck.

Within days of his homecoming, he said to me, "You can't tell time? You're *seven years old* and can't tell time?"

"I can read," I said, deeply offended.

"Well, Hell's pecker, I certainly hope so," he said. "You go get a clock and come in here."

"I can't," I said. "I told Mary Ann I'd be out to —"

"Get a clock," he said rudely, "You're not going anywhere until you can tell time."

"Oh, yes I am," I said, smooth and confident, used to having my own way. "I'm going to play out in the side lot, with Mary Ann," I said. I was not used to being contradicted.

That was the first time he hit me. Mama had always used a hairbrush on the few occasions when she spanked me, but he used his big hairy hand and then made me sit there until I could tell time. It was in my room afterwards, shaking with fury, that I began to write my first book. And to be the good hater he and my grandmother, Miss Katie, Nainai, had said I should be. Good haters in her opinion (and in his) were tough and resilient.

I still believe that, instructed with reason, I'd have been a more reasonable child. But Daddy believed a child ought to do whatever a parent said, without question, and it was the "without question" that was not in my nature any more than it was in his. His example, as usual, was a particularly terrifying one, and one I couldn't answer: *What if you were standing in the middle of a track, and a train was coming, and I told you to move, and you asked why? What then?*

Before they were married, that winter he spent at Fort Sill, Buzz Letcher wrote to Betty Marston of his last day in Lexington with his parents before leaving for Oklahoma: "Pop [whom I would later call Andaddy] and I went around the county to look over the various properties and because Pop is so good hearted and easy-going the tenants just act terribly. At one place they had torn down the house and carted it away in the three years that Pop hadn't visited, but it never seems to ruffle him at all. I wish I had his complacency in the face of all and every kind of irritating circumstance."

This letter was an important clue to his nature, but my mother was looking for different things, and probably skimmed over that part.

DADDY GOT ORDERS SENDING HIM to the Norfolk Naval Base. We packed up everything, and drove to Norfolk, the old '39 Ford creaky and loaded to the limit.

We hadn't been living there long when I noticed the round of metal pipe sitting there in a nest of crumpled-up newspaper. As I did not like the father who had brought it home from the barracks and laid it on a shelf and apparently forgotten about it, I saw no reason to feign an interest in it. There was nothing about it to arouse my curiosity, but still one day I looked more closely at the burnished cylinder, and saw that it was a fine coil of flat wire about three inches across and the same height. When I touched it, it wobbled.

Sighing, I turned away. I wanted diamond bracelets, candy — perhaps a whole Whitman's Sampler all to myself. I wanted us back the way we'd been during the war in Lexington with Andaddy and Nainai. I wanted Daddy to leave again. I wanted it to be like it had been in California. I didn't know what I wanted.

It was summer, the air heavy with the scent of the spirea hedge that grew all along the front of the CO's quarters; the war was over but I was in a war of my own.

Daddy had arrived home heavily decorated just a few months before, and now he was in charge of a barracks full of Marines stationed at the

Norfolk Naval Base. I might have to live with him, but I didn't have to like him. I figured that the metal coil was for Johnnie anyway, whose room was full of boring stuff like that.

Our house, with our name plate in the yard, was right next door to the bowling alley, where the Marines and sailors came to hurl the heavy balls down shiny lanes to knock over the wooden bottles. Choosing to stay away when Daddy was in the house, I spent a lot of time behind the bowling alley where it was private and shady, hunkered down with my backbone to the wall, a sailor hat on my straight yellow hair, hiding out for three reasons I could have named. The first one was that Daddy did not allow us to have candy, and I had a sucker working, big, green, and bumpy on the front, smooth on the back. The clear lime candy was foggy from the humidity because I'd been saving it and savoring it a long time, in one of my secret places, which I had several of since he had come back from the war and I had been driven underground.

The second reason for being behind the bowling alley was not as clear, but demanded some hard thinking. I had that day at school been given a Conduct Card, and told that I could not return until both of my parents had signed it. I was caught breaking one of the school rules, the one that forbade gum chewing.

The third reason I was behind the bowling alley was that I was going to be a writer, already completing my first book, in a Blue Horse notebook, and I needed a place to be alone. It was called THE MYSTERY OF THE DIAMOND BRACELET, by Katie Paul Letcher, its heroine a teenaged girl named Linda Lou Larkspur. It was already twenty-some pages long, and I was so in love with the story, with the writing and illustrating of it, that even school, which I loved, seemed so tedious that I could hardly bear to go and attend to the work there. Everything paled beside this adventure mystery I was composing.

I had three sailor hats I had found: one in the gutter by the bus stop, one left at the swimming pool, and one in a trash can at the shopping center. I wrote names and funny sayings on them, turned down the brims, and wore them as I'd seen the high school girls on the bus doing. Girls who had boyfriends wrote their boyfriends' names on them. I wrote "Billy Craig," on one of mine, remembering a blue-eyed boy with a cowlick, safely two or three hundred miles away in Lexington, who'd been in first grade with me.

A hitch-hiking Marine whom Mama and I picked up one day had given me a wonderful new type of pen and showed me a trick I could do with it. It had a kind of ink that wouldn't spill and run, and a tiny little ball in the end of the pen, and this thick ink ran onto the ball, and when you wrote, it made the ball turn and deposit ink on the paper.

The Marine drew a seagull in the middle of the palm of his hand, and showed me how it was dry, no running ink. Then he huffed a gust of hot breath on it, smacked his hand down on a piece of paper, and the gull came off onto that paper. He did it five times before the gull grew so pale you couldn't tell what it was.

Then he gave me the pen, since Mama had driven him all the way into Norfolk. I couldn't wait to do the trick for Johnnie, for all the kids at school. A girl in the compound offered me a dollar for the pen, but I vowed never to part with it. It was perfect for writing on sailor caps with; the writing didn't run even when it rained. Mama found it amazing, but Daddy thought it was a flash in the pan. "It'll never replace the fountain pen," he said.

I could hear the bowling balls coming right at me inside the building, the long ominous roll before the explosion of the pins against the wall. I heard when the balls went in the gutters, a softer growling sound. I liked tensing up as they approached, and the little shocks of release as they crashed.

It was the perfect place to write.

So for the moment I was happy, listening to the bowling games behind me, sometimes with my eyes closed, sucking the lollipop as I read or let echo my own words, or gazed proudly at my own illustrations: Linda Lou walking home from school, Linda Lou's mother fainting onto a couch, fancy ribbony letters with flowers at the beginning of each chapter.

At first the sucker had been lint-covered from being in my pocket, but my tongue had worn it smooth again and slick-sweet. I read, aloud, "All around them was deathly darkness. In the dolefulness, Linda Lou's father whimpered pathetically."

In the first chapter of my book Linda Lou Larkspur had come home from school, and her mother had said, "Where is your three thousand dollar diamond bracelet you wore to school today?"

"I guess the assembly speaker must have stolen it. He was from India," replied Linda Lou. I had drawn her mother fainting at that point. Linda Lou had naturally curly hair and loafers with bobby socks, and she appeared in all of the drawings, even in one with her sweater buttoned up the back, just the way high school girls wore them. When Linda Lou's father came home from the office, in chapter 2, he was interested and understanding, and agreed at once that they must go to India and get the bracelet back.

Unfortunately, my father was not a bit like Linda Lou's, and I couldn't begin to think what to do about him. He stomped around, and I held my breath at the strange mildewy odor of the uniforms he'd worn that hung now in the understairs closet. He had been home for ages, and it was beginning to look as if he would *never* go away again.

Mama and Johnnie and I had been getting along fine for years without him. For all I cared, he could have stayed out there with the dead Japs.

He bossed us all around. He snatched us up away from Nainai and Andaddy, then moved us to this flat hot place where the air always smelled fishy, before I could win the double-dip ice-cream cone at Wayland's for the best record in second grade.

I was lonesome for my old friends from Lexington, my pals Tut (short for Ann Carrington Tutwiler) and Jeanne Tracy and Susan Coe. Patty Pullen and Carol Adams and Mary Ann Miller. I hated this new school, a long bus ride from home, full of taunting mean boys.

I had been ahead of Susan and Patty and Carol, and way ahead of all the boys, and I would have won it, but Daddy was interested only in himself. All he said, when I'd brought it to his attention for the third or fourth time, was, "I'll buy you a damn ice cream cone." But he hadn't, and I was still waiting.

I noticed he ate a lot of ice cream; in fact, he loved it. He had a poem he'd recite, "I scream, you scream, we all scream for ice cream!" as he headed for the refrigerator. If there wasn't any, he'd go right out and get some, often inviting me along, and those trips were fun, for he was always happy in anticipation of the ice cream we were getting.

But he wouldn't let me have iced tea anymore. He said, "You're supposed to drink milk." He had some idea that tea would stunt my growth. I knew it wouldn't, for I'd been drinking it ever since we moved to Lexington. It never once occurred to me to stop drinking it: I just sneaked it. I loved imagining that the iced tea was the sea, with an inch or so of sugar sand in the bottom, and mint for seaweed, and a lemon slice for a fish. I could imagine treasure chests buried in the sand at the bottom of the sea. In my spare time I drew ruined underwater castles of Atlantis, and spilling chest of pearls, rubies, and gold coins. Now I could have iced tea only when he was at his office.

I could tell that Mother was worried, her hair curled on her neck from perspiration. She'd acted nothing like her old self when she came home from the commissary earlier than I'd expected and caught me hard at work on my book at the kitchen table with a glass of iced tea. She sat down heavily, then took it away from me and poured it down the sink. She refused to discuss it, but said I had to do what Daddy said.

"But why?" I said. "Why?"

"Well, he told you not to," Mama said.

"But why?" I repeated.

"Because he told you not to."

"That's no reason," I said.

She turned swiftly on me, and said, "Young lady, if I get any more of that talk, I will tell him you were drinking iced tea."

Well, I thought, my mother could take my tea away, but she couldn't make me like that awful man. The stupid house he had brought us to live in had boards that ran along it and made ridges so I couldn't bounce a ball without it flying off at funny angles. And there was no honeysuckle like there had been in Lexington, where with Jeanne and Susan I'd spent hours breaking off the blossoms, sucking out the droplets of sweet nectar. The white spirea flowers of our hedge had no nectar. There was nothing at all to do, in fact, until I decided to become a writer.

The absolute worst thing about Daddy was that he thought Johnnie, drool, dirty knees, and all the rest, was Mr. Wonderful. Mama told him that *I* was the one who finally got Johnnie housebroken, and he never even commented. "Son," he said, just about every day, "we'll go hunting and fishing and camping and swimming," repeating the words like he was reciting a stupid poem.

Johnnie only grinned like an idiot.

Johnnie was so stupid he had not even objected to the fat smelly Mrs. Arbuck who had come to sit with us in Lexington before Daddy came home.

"I can babysit him, Mama," I had insisted, when Mama said she had to go to New York to meet Daddy's train, two weeks late because he'd stopped to visit friends in California. "You know I can!" I said. "Let me."

But Mama reckoned we needed someone else at the apartment, and wouldn't let us go to Andaddy's where she thought Johnnie wouldn't be supervised enough. Mrs. Arbuck did make waffles every morning for breakfast, three mornings in a row, and gave me the frizzy permanent, and even made me a brown corduroy skirt (for Daddy's return) on Mama's sewing machine one afternoon. But the last night she was there, we had a storm, and Mrs. Arbuck came and got in bed with me, shaking all over and praying out loud at every flash of lightning or rolling crack of thunder, pulling the bedspread up over her head and stinking of B.O. and onions. I was appalled at her ignorance, and said so, for Andaddy and I often sat on their wide front porch during thunderstorms, with lightning exploding right around our heads, thunder like laden china safes crashing down, the bent and tossing trees lit to weird blue brilliance. Andaddy always shouted at me between crashes to take deep breaths, breathe deeply, because ozone, released during the storm, was good for you! "It'll give you energy!" he'd shout, over wind and rain and cannon-fire thunder.

THE FIRST WEEK I WAS IN THE NEW SCHOOL in Norfolk, I'd written a poem called "The Present" and entered it in a school contest. It was all about how much I loved the wonderful present God had brought us, and in the final line, I'd let on that it was my father, home safe from the war. It had won first prize, five dollars, but I felt too guilty to even tell Mama, who would recognize the lie.

So I'd hidden the five-dollar bill, having decided that I could never spend it. But lately I'd seen a red bathing suit with something called a floating bra in Maxim's window on the boulevard, that the schoolbus passed by twice every day. The idea was that when you got in the water, air would get trapped in the top, making you look as if your bosoms were enormous. I was about at the point of deciding that my vow to save the money had been a foolish one. The sign said it cost five dollars. What a coincidence! I hunkered down and looked again at the page where Linda Lou's mother had fainted.

AS THE DARKNESS GREW DENSER, and the insects began to shrill in the warm night, I worried about the chewing gum. By now my back was numb from the nubby surface of the bowling alley. I tried to assess how much trouble I was in.

Here's what happened: my mother did not allow me to chew gum much, said chewing made you look like you were from the wrong side of the tracks. Of course it was not allowed at school, because, as the teacher had explained, the bottoms of all the chairs and tables and desks would be covered with it by now. But Nancy Barfield, one of the big girls, had a new kind today called Juicy Fruit, and I could smell it in her mouth while we were jumping rope out in the compound at recess, and had asked for some. She'd said no and I'd begged.

"Not a chance, Skinnybones," she said, so I'd said I'd tell what I saw her doing last week after school in the bushes at the end of the playground. Looking scared and mad, she'd given me a stick of the gum. Five minutes later the monitor had reported me to the office and didn't have the foggiest notion about Nancy Barfield, who had been chewing as hard as I had, and a lot longer.

The principal, Mr. Holly, said that though I'd been in the school only a short while, I should know the rules, and he would have to give me a Conduct Card. "We must not relax our vigilance," were his words.

Both parents had to sign it. I wished I'd thought to lie, to say Daddy was still at the war. Mama was never any problem, so after school I just had to look sorry and put up with a little bit of lip; true to form, Mama never asked where I got the gum, just sighed and rolled her eyes up, said, "What am I going to do about you?" and signed it.

But *he* was a horse of another color. I didn't have any idea how he felt about gum. I knew he spanked unexpectedly and hard. Though gum was not a subject that had ever come up, I expected he'd be lots worse than Mama, as he was in everything else. Sometime before bedtime tonight, I had to show him the big pink sheet that said "Chewing Gum," and get his signature. For an hour before supper I had tried to write his name the way it looked in the checkbook on his desk, but I couldn't come even close.

So instead, I'd fiddled some with that piece of spring, noticed it had a nice cool languid heaviness. I'd bent it into a fat curved rainbow of spiral in my hands, but it had run up on itself again, into that smug, boring cylinder.

When he was away at the war, I used to dream of the things he would bring me, like pearls, pirate coins, gold, and heavy, whole coconuts, maybe some soft jungle animal I'd never seen, for a pet. A locket that would open. From his letters, it seemed like he liked animals. But there were no presents, only his presence, threatening and disapproving. And in my own home I smelled strangeness and felt homesick. And Mama seemed so tired, so beaten down.

Why was it in the companionable darkness that I kept thinking that I heard Johnnie's baby voice between rolls and crashes, but coming from the wrong direction? I didn't want any more of the sucker, as it had become too sweet, and I could almost feel the germs sticking to my teeth, boring in, taking big bites and spitting out rot. But I had lost the waxed paper cover some time ago, so how could I save the rest of it for another day? If I put it in my pocket it would get furry again, and I might forget it and Mama would wash it and I'd get what-for, for having had it there in the first place.

It *was* Johnnie's voice, so I figured I'd better see what was going on, since it came not from our yard but from over near the Officers' Mess, on the other side of the bowling alley.

I experimented to see if the sucker would stick on the nubbly plaster on the outside of the bowling alley, but it would not. Gum would; I left gum there all the time, and came back for it the next day. Finally I laid the candy on the top board of the picket fence that enclosed the house. I hoped briefly for no rain, stuck my notebook under my arm, and followed the sound of Johnnie's voice.

In the light from the Officers' Club kitchen, I saw him outlined, saw also the shape of a sailor. Johnnie had on the sailor's white hat. "Johnnie," I said, "what are you doing?" The thing to do was ignore the sailors until they talked to you. Usually they were friendly. Like my friend Bill Nutter that I'd met at the pool. He cooked in the Mess, and every Friday they had all the oysters you could eat for a dollar. Sometimes on Friday nights I snuck over here, and he handed me hot fat deep-fried oysters on a paper towel out the back door of the Officers' Club Mess.

Johnnie didn't answer, and suddenly I saw that the sailor was staring at me, and the way he stood scared me. Johnnie at three and a half wasn't totally housebroken yet, so he sometimes had diapers on, but tonight he was standing in front of the sailor with no pants on at all and the sailor's hat on his head. It seemed that they had been having a conversation as if everything were normal. The sailor didn't say anything. "Johnnie," I said. "What are you doing over here? Where are your pants?"

"We playing ball," he said. "You got a ball?" As if in answer, a bowling ball landed in the side alley, with a muttering bumpy roll.

"No," I said. "Listen, you've got to come home."

"Don't want to, Katie," he whined.

"Where'd you leave your pants?" I asked. "He has to go home," I said, over my shoulder, to the sailor. The sailor still didn't say anything, not a word, just snatched his hat up off Johnnie's head and clamped it on his own.

When Johnnie wouldn't come by himself, I gathered him up naked-bottomed, shoving my notebook tighter up under my arm, and carried him across in back of the bowling alley toward the picket fence around our house. There was a narrow passage between the bowling alley and the fence and I had to haul Johnnie down that to the street, and along the fence to the gateway. There you could feel the bowling balls like heartbeats, as well as hear them, the rolls followed by satisfying crashes. As I turned the corner, I looked back and the sailor had disappeared. My brother's head smelled sour and grassy.

Out of the darkness nearby, Daddy called, "Katie!" Instantly I was overtaken with fear and guilt and furtiveness. How could I explain? Here I was, skulking outside the fence, lugging Johnnie around with no pants on. Daddy did not discuss things like Mama did. So I squatted down, hoping to hide from him, but forgetting to put my hand over Johnnie's mouth.

Johnnie called out, "Katie, lemme down!" and began to struggle.

And there was no explaining. I had not answered when Daddy called my name. I yelled that I hadn't heard him. He called me a liar, wanted to know where Johnnie's diaper was, wouldn't listen to the story about the sailor, put his hand down on the lollipop, came away with it stuck to his palm, somehow guessed it was mine, though I denied it emphatically. My shoulder was jerked until I felt my arm would come out of the socket, and I was hauled inside and past bright lights and up the stairs and into my room and whipped, my own bottom shamefully exposed to his big red hand until it was on fire.

I fell asleep without brushing my teeth or putting on pajamas. My sailor hat was gone, and my book. Sobbing, I wished my teeth would rot and fall out before the morning, wished my skin would fall off from dirt.

Many of Daddy's friends had been killed in the war; why not him? At that moment I hated my father and I hated my brother. And I hated my mother, too, who never showed up to make him stop.

I vowed that I would not ever do anything for Johnnie again. It would serve him right if the sailor had kidnapped him. I never saw that sailor again.

IN THE BLACK OF NIGHT I WOKE UP, and snuck downstairs and out into the dew of the summer night to find my notebook on its side in the passage between the house and the bowling alley, with some of the pages fanned out. I looked around for my sailor hat, but it had disappeared. I brushed the damp grass off my notebook, crept back up to my room, and after reading my story over, I put it under my mattress to press it flat again.

In the morning, Mama said she'd gotten Daddy to sign the Conduct Card. She said he hadn't been at all upset, that in fact he'd thought it was funny. *Funny?*

He had already gone to work and Ivy was giving Johnnie a bath and the schoolbus wasn't due for another half hour, so I sat at the kitchen table and picked up the silly piece of spring.

Slowly I began to move my hands up and down. It sank, then lifted, shifting its slick slack burden from one of my palms to the other. I liked the cat-like looseness. But when I tried to set the coiling bridge on the wooden table, it quickly gathered itself together and stood upright, again a perfect, if wobbly, cylinder. I reached over, pulled one side over into an arch again, and, strangely, the first side followed, like an inch-worm — no, more like a summersault. Now the coil was poised exactly at the edge of the table. I couldn't resist reaching for the edge of the metal curl, and pulling it over towards me. It poured, a corkscrew dryfall, into my lap, and settled down heavily, with a charming tipsiness, even trembling a little as if it had the sense to fear a stranger.

Mama let me have a cup of coffee with hot milk and sugar, and I explained everything to her, and she listened carefully, took me on her lap, and assured me she would explain everything to Daddy. She said that she was sorry, sorry, sorry, and that he, meaning Daddy, hadn't meant it, that the war had been so awful he hadn't gotten used to family life yet, and that I had done exactly right to bring Johnnie home, that sometimes grown men did hurt small children, and that Daddy had got-ten frightened himself.

I held the slinky coil until it warmed in my lap, and I did feel better. But only about Mama. And maybe about Johnnie. I guessed it wasn't his fault, really. I even gave him the last bite of doughnut when he came downstairs smelling of soap, and he hugged me around the waist. "Don't get sugar on me, Midget," I told him. "Want to see how the coil goes from the table down into your lap?" Johnnie watched, clapped his hands, and I showed him how to do it.

I felt better, but vowed not to forget, vowed I'd never again speak to my father. The last thing I said before leaving to catch the schoolbus was, "I wish he'd gotten killed in the damn war." I knew how that made Mama cringe, and I had to say it. Behind me she sighed, and rubbed her stomach, which was pooching out for some reason, but for once she did-n't tell me not to say things like that.

COMING IN FROM SCHOOL LATER THAT DAY, I shed my denim bookbag, and sat down once more at the kitchen table, this time to finish my book. It was to be the first in a long series of adventure books. I could see them on a shelf, all lined up, dark red with gold lettering.

The story had gotten exciting. In chapter 4, Linda Lou Larkspur and her father, at the end of their voyage to India, which was described in chapter 3, had stepped off the ship and into a great hole, the Black Hole of Calcutta. Her father had skinned his knee in the fall, but Linda Lou said, "Here, I'll fix it," and put a Band-Aid on it, and her father was pathetically grateful. "We must never relax our vigilance," Linda Lou scolded him sternly.

At the beginning of chapter 5, they had spotted light and begun walking. And, lo and behold, the black hole led them directly out into the garden of the Assembly Speaker! They had started for the house to ask for the bracelet back, when suddenly they were surrounded by huge fierce tigers! The best illustration yet was the head-on portrait of a tiger, fangs dripping, coming at them. Somewhere upstairs, Ivy ran the vacuum cleaner.

Mama came heavily down the stairs, asking me how school was, what we'd had for lunch, and said again that Daddy was sorry for the way he had acted the night before. Very sorry.

"I'll bet," I said, and ran my hand around the winsome spring still lying where I'd left it that morning. "Look," I said, changing the subject, "this thing will walk from the table to my lap, and from the table to the chair to the floor." When I was done, the thing lay, a dear scary weight, in my lap. Mama smiled.

"What is this thing, anyway?" I asked.

"I don't know. Something Daddy got somewhere. Ask him about it. How's your book coming?"

Mama was impressed especially with the Black Hole of Calcutta. I tilted the Blue Horse notebook into a slant and got the spring to walk two steps, to the bottom of the notebook and then on to the table.

Then Mama leaned forward. "Daddy really is sorry about last night," she said. I didn't answer, true to my vow.

"Can I have some iced tea?" I asked.

"No, but look what I got today. It's something called Ovaltine. You put it in milk, and it makes it into chocolate. Want to try it?"

Linda Lou's father, frightened, had climbed a tree in chapter 6, to get away from the tigers. "Oh, never mind," Linda Lou told him. "I'll take care of them."

While I drank the smooth sweet chocolate stuff, I tried to figure out how Linda Lou would do this.

I was still thinking about it when *he* came home.

He tossed me a grubby sailor hat. "Isn't this yours?" he asked. I watched his back as he stood at the sink washing his hands. He did a thorough job of it, sudsing front and back, and every finger, rubbing and wrenching until they were white with foam, then rinsing thoroughly. He did it every afternoon when he got home.

I put the sailor hat on. I picked up the coiled metal that shone shyly and jiggled like a fat puppy, and did tricks for me. I wished it were mine.

"What do you think we ought to call that thing?" my father asked, over his shoulder.

Startled, I said, "I don't know. What is it?"

He stood, facing me now, wiping his hands on the towel he'd gotten from the top drawer.

"Well, one of our machinists was working in the shop a week or two ago, and a piece of this spring fell off the workbench in a way that interested him, and he got to thinking that maybe he could do some things with it." He dried carefully between all his fingers. "What do you think?"

I looked at it in my lap. "It does tricks," I said. "Look at this." And I made it walk from the table into my lap, where it settled with a shifting wiggle of its own. "You can pour it back and forth between your hands, and you can walk it down stairs."

"More than one stair?" His eyes, blue, the light shade of mine, were skeptical.

"I'll show you," I said. I led him into the hall, walked up four steps. "See, you start it at the top and it goes all the way down the steps."

"Well, I'll be damned."

I watched him do it. "It'll walk a plank, too," I told him. Daddy squatted at the bottom of the stairs. "I'll be damned," he said again. "The guy who invented it wants to find a name for it."

"Why?" I asked. I climbed to the top of the stairs, and started the spring off the landing. It went nine stairs before it stopped, a couple from the bottom. I felt that the coil had a personality all its own, cheerful, chuckly. The idea of a name for it was interesting.

He handed it back up to me. "You see, it's a sort of — spring — it's used in heat generators — but he thinks it might make a good toy — and he told me to bring this piece on home."

A name! I didn't know about that. I looked down at the toy in the hammock my jumper made, and with the slightest motion of my knees it seemed to jiggle like gelatin. Merrily. A name for it? I could not imagine what.

"Is it for Johnnie?" I asked.

"What? The spring? Oh, no, you can keep it. Bill James has a warehouse full of the stuff."

Mine! I was careful not to express any emotion. *Springy* might be a good name. I watched while my father, far below, leaned forward then as if he had remembered something, reached into the back pocket of his khaki uniform, and brought out a dime. His voice went low, and he looked around like he feared someone else might be listening. Ivy, most likely. He frowned at the dime, or at his hand. "I think I owe you an ice cream cone."

At the end of my book, Linda Lou Larkspur's father was going to get down out of the tree. The way the book would end, and I had already got the last chapter in my head: Linda Lou was going to walk right in to the Assembly Speaker's house and demand her bracelet, which he would meekly give her.

I slid my bottom, still sore, down one, two, three, then four steps, carefully. Still over halfway up, I looked down at my pet lying in the cradle of my skirt. It seemed to wink up at me, waiting to play some more.

"But no more gum." I jerked my head up, to where Daddy frowned sternly, then broke into a grin, and lowered his voice. "If that's the worst thing you ever do, I'm not too worried. In fact, I chew gum now and then. It exercises your teeth. But you do what Mama says. The PX is open. If you're in a mood for ice cream, I'm heading that way."

I tried to see if he was kidding, but he slid the dime through the railings, across the riser and left it in front of me. A dime meant a double dip, exactly what Miss Edmonia had promised to the one with the highest grades.

I wanted groveling, I wanted an apology from his lips. But the more time that passed, the less likely that seemed. I shifted the floppy toy slightly back and forth in my lap.

Someday I would write lots of books, for the pleasure of naming them. I would have babies for the pleasure of naming them. And then, I couldn't help it, I had to smile, at the heft of my new unnamed toy in my lap, something like the heft of a baby, and all at once I knew what would happen at the end of my book:

After it was all over, Linda Lou's father would put his hand on her head, and say, *"Well done, my child."* The End. The cover would show a splendid drawing of the diamond bracelet, with shine lines going out in every direction, and the title written in an arch above it, on a ribbon, in fancy letters.

Pete and Betsy in Norfolk, 1947.

Fear

*Y*ou," *he roars at me, "will wash all the dishes from now on. All of
them!"*

*"I can't wash the breakfast and lunch dishes," I retort, for he is not the only
one who is mad. Nyah, nyah, I say in my heart.*

*He hits me, knocking my shoulder against the wall. "Mama is very, very
sick," he yells, red-faced and towering. "Do you want her to die? You will get up
half an hour earlier every day to do the breakfast dishes, and you will do the
lunch dishes when you get home from school."*

*Fear dries my mouth. I will wash them all, I will do everything, if only she
won't die.*

THE TWINS ARE BORN IN NORFOLK nine months after Daddy is back from
the Pacific, in May of 1946, three days before my eighth birthday. *A
birthday present,* someone says. Then someone else. They are for me? I
don't want them.

Enter Mrs. Knipe with her Bible, who leans over Mama when she
isn't changing diapers, and exhorts her to repent. Mama cries. Mrs.

Knipe tells her to throw away all the medicines by the bed, that Jesus will save her. Mama hemorrhages. Mrs. Knipe is shouted out of the house by Daddy; no one else can go near Mama. He is mad at us all. My fury at *him* is such that I determine to break every goddamned bitching dish. Of course I don't, but I do break some, as many as I dare. Just as many as I can and still turn the blank, surprised stare on him when accused. "Who, me? It was an accident."

"It will come out of your allowance."

Breathless. Months and months of trying to breathe right. Fear and resentment writhe inside me like vipers in a too-small nest. I am scared when I leave for school, scared when Mama leaves to shop. She stays tired, and her face is sad. Every afternoon I go with her when she wheels the big double carriage with the babies, for I have a deep fear that she will get lost if I don't go along, or die on the street, or just somehow never come back. I am afraid Daddy is right, that she will die. If she has already left with the babies in the afternoon when I get home, I ride my bike frantically up and down the grid streets of the naval base until I find her. Then I pretend I am just out riding, and happened to end up on the same street she's walking on. I wobble along beside her, or speed ahead half a block and circle around and back until she turns toward home. From aboard my bike I tell her about school, about whom I like and don't like, about Miss Helen Rock, the meanie who is my teacher at Meadowbrook School.

In the stew of a Sunday school on the naval base that catered to us all, Jews, Methodists, Baptists, Quakers, and even Episcopalians, Johnnie and I learned that *God was our father.* Creating God in Daddy's image, I was terrified of Him. Down the street lived Chester, Catholic; the Catholics were the only type among us with their own separate church. I asked the teacher, an ugly WAC, about that. She answered vaguely that there weren't many Catholics in the Navy because they didn't like the water.

I learned that God would punish wrongdoing (as if I hadn't already figured that out!). Whenever I snuck to a movie or swiped a candy bar or stole money out of Mama's purse to buy a Grapette at the Px, God retaliated by giving me appendicitis. Mama was so against sugar that I'd have put it at the top of the list of sins. For years after that, I was so conditioned to fearing sugar that eating or drinking anything with sugar would cause a relapse, another appendix attack. An ice-cold Seven-Up, the sunshine stunning through the beautiful green of the bottle, clutched at my insides like poison, beginning with my first sip. A banana-flavored marshmallow peanut caused instant side-ache. I lay in bed at night sweating with the fear of a hospital stay, which was described to me in the most gruesome technicolor by another girl in the neighborhood who'd had appendicitis. My left side collected the pain into a hard mass that throbbed and ached until the forgetfulness of sleep overcame me. Years later someone would convince me, with a medical dictionary, that it was the *right* side where the appendix dwelt. Somehow, I would feel betrayed by that also. Apparently I hadn't paid very close attention to *Gray's Anatomy*.

WHEN NO ONE IS WATCHING, I torment Johnnie, for I see he is not touched by my pain and anger. He sails with no cross-currents, no high winds. He doesn't seem to resent the babies at all. I can see him today, his toys an odd array of nails, dirty string, tin cans, perhaps a jar lid or a milk bottle. He plays in the bald dirt of the yards of the houses we lived in, oblivious to filth, heat, cold, hunger. His mouth is gently pursed as he makes soft machine noises to sound-track whatever mysterious experiments are hatching in his head.

How often I walked on purpose across the intricate webbing of string and bottles, knocking them down, pretending I hadn't seen them! Or kicked him when I walked behind him. I couldn't stand that he wasn't afraid for Mama.

MY DISHWASHING WAS NOT VERY SATISFACTORY, and when it wasn't, I had to stay up late into the night to redo the dishes. Daddy did laundry in the middle of the night. We often ate bread and canned applesauce, sometimes even for supper when Mama didn't have enough strength to cook. We finally had to hire a maid, then a succession of maids, for none stayed long in that house full of diapers, messy children, an exhausted mother whose directions were indifferent, even capricious, and Daddy, dangerously near the edge.

All the maids fascinated me. Ivy, the first, Carib or Cuban or something else exotic, dated an Eye-talian boy named Tony. When he was due to show up she'd splash vanilla extract out of the kitchen cabinet onto her palms and run them over her neck and ears and through her hair. She smelled wonderfully sweet. Ivy told me that when you kissed, you always turned your head sideways. I practiced on trees, walls, books, my own arm, from then on.

Once, after she went out, I took a big slug out of the vanilla bottle, and was shocked at the bitterness. Ivy didn't stay long.

Minnie had thin pinkish hair and beady eyes and looked exactly like a chicken. She often got words confused, telling my mother she couldn't work because her larnix had gotten tangled up with her pharnix. The doctor, she insisted, had told her that. She suffered from shingles and from phenaria, which she insisted was a disease. "What you want for brefkisst?" Minnie would ask. "Bacon? You lak it crips or swoft?" Daddy soon fired Minnie for being off more days than she was on. But the family never did drop her language. We still speak of our cats as being *swoft*, our bacon *crips*.

THE SUMMER OF 1946 WAS HOT AND DRY, and crawling with Japanese beetles. As the season progressed, all the compound gardens in the middle of the block behind all the houses on the Norfolk Naval Base drooped and wilted and turned to lace under the assault, and sheer

weight, of millions of the insects. Japanese beetles became the chief
topic of conversation on the street, over the children's heads among the
adults, and, for me, became the tiny Jap monsters of my dreams. I was
determined to get rid of them, for they showed up in my bed, in the
sink, on the floor, blatting mindlessly against my window screens, tumbling stupidly into my milk. How best to collect them? How best to kill
them? One neighbor put up traps, but they cost money, and Daddy
hated to spend money. Another topped buckets of water with kerosene,
and shook beetles off the vines into the buckets, where they drowned.

Daddy had an idea that would occupy the children all summer long
at useful labor, and cost him nothing. We would work for our
allowances: a dime for a pint of beetles, a quarter if you brought in an
entire quart. Every night he'd set a pot of water to boil and into it we
would dump the day's collection of the black-green beetles.

It wasn't long before a neighbor child walked through our kitchen,
noted the evening's activity, and passed the word all over the base that
the Letchers made *soup* out of *their* Japanese beetles.

Letcher kids by the Quonset hut, 1946.

Popsicle Sticks

Got a present for you, honey," Mama says.

A check for ten million dollars? A new doll? An overlooked Christmas present? An early Christmas present?

A clipping from The Saturday Evening Post she thought I'd like: a recipe for "Fut Nudge," by Mrs. Spooner. "Cake a bup of tutter, a sinch of palt, and selt them with coo tups of mugar," it starts.

"Oh," I say, not hiding my disappointment.

"If you'd expect the worst, then you wouldn't always be disappointed," Mama observes.

AFTER TWO YEARS IN NORFOLK, Daddy was transferred to the West Coast. 1947. We spent ten days in a transport ship, The LeJeune, obviously a done-over wartime troop ship, composed entirely, it seemed, of perforated, reeking, newly painted steel, a dark gray color. The ship hugged the East Coast through paling colors and warmer weather into the clear Caribbean waters. We went through the Panama Canal and saw monkeys in the jungle only yards away from the decks. All day we went through gates, and our water level was changed, and we moved on, only to repeat the process three or four times. We spent one day and a night with our relatives in Panama, Nainai's youngest brother, Seymour, and his family, and went swimming in a bay with a mesh fence across the sea opening to keep out the sharks that frequented those tropical seas. One woman I saw had no arm below the elbow. A shark, Uncle Seymour told me.

Up the West Coast we lumbered through the colder, darker Pacific, to San Diego, and Oceanside Marine Corps base, which floundered in the midst of the confusing postwar changes in the military.

The best thing about *The LeJeune* was the bar that stayed open twenty-four hours a day, and at which all nonalcoholic drinks were free. This meant that I could wake up at three in the morning and go get a chocolate ice cream soda if I could sneak out of the cabin without waking Mama and Daddy. It became the object of my life, to sternly keep myself awake until everyone else was snoring. I got away with it several nights, easing my way out of the cabin, zipping around the ship, up and down the pierced metal stairways, to that little room where bored red-eyed people seemed cranked down into slow motion by the drinks and smoke. They sat at tables, leaned on the bar, slept in deck chairs, and all of them had cigarettes, and drinks, some the color of tea, with cherries or other pieces of fruit, some clear, with olives.

Not one to let opportunity slip away, I went around to abandoned glasses with little puddles of liquor and leftover cherries and olives in them, and helped myself — at first cautiously, but then when I realized no one cared, more boldly, even inquiring occasionally of some sleepy-eyed woman if I might have her cherry. When someone told Daddy on me, my night missions were cut off cruelly. Disgraced ("Begging! You were in there *begging!*") I was put in solitary confinement in our cabin, forbidden to leave, and there I sat and stewed, becoming a better hater with every passing moment.

Above the top bunk where I slept was a large unfilled nail or screw hole in the ship's metal, and through it I watched the people in the next cabin. At night when our lights were out, all of us bedded down, I could see best. But they did these strange things. Night or day, the man and the woman took off all their clothes and wrestled, he on top of her, just for no reason at all. Then they would get up and run around the cabin, and he might pick her up and run around with her white legs gripped around his naked bottom. I thought that was neat. I asked a girl my age named Sydney that I met on the ship about that, but she seemed as baffled as I was. She was the captain's daughter, and went on trips like this all the time, and had seen whales and icebergs, northern lights and other stuff, but she said she'd never seen anything like that.

IN 1947, ONLY FOUR YEARS SINCE WE'D LEFT, California was a different country. Now it was overcrowded, panicky, long waiting lines everywhere, short tempers, air pollution, traffic jams, shortages of the very food we'd had in such abundance when we'd lived here before. Everywhere the smell of tar hung in the air. Postwar housing on the West Coast was a nightmare, and we ended up living on a base in Oceanside, a squalid dirt flat of thousands of rows of identical Quonset huts, which Daddy resented bitterly. He thought that after all he'd done for his country he deserved better.

Ours was identifiable out of the cloned acres of huts only because of the red fire extinguisher on the side. The base was flat land, not a stick of grass, just row after row of depressingly identical lined-up half-cylinders, each with two families living inside. Johnnie recalls going to play somewhere, and getting lost on the way home as darkness was falling, finally finding the red fire extinguisher, and bursting in — on another family who happened to have one on their Quonset hut.

His instant and firm assumption was that we had gone off and left him, because we didn't want him. He also remembers how thin the walls were when the wind blew, and how little room we had.

Mama and Daddy shared the one double bed, the twins slept in a playpen in the living room, with rope lashed back and forth down the middle to keep them from rolling over on each other, and Johnnie and I haggled over a daybed and the lumpy smelly sofa.

In the evenings, there was nothing much to do. Sometimes we went to movies in an ugly hall set on bare ground with benches that were so uncomfortable it didn't matter how good Humphrey Bogart or Popeye was. Daddy was home only after dark, and overwhelmed with paperwork which he had to do on the cleared kitchen table.

Sometimes we drank beer with ice in it — it amused Daddy to see me get tipsy, and to have Mama scandalized and scolding — and he amused me and himself by teaching me the Marine Corps hymn, explaining about who Montezuma was, and his halls. I thought maybe he'd be proud of me if I memorized the whole thing, so I did. I loved one verse especially, with its mixed myths and lovely absurd images of God and a bunch of gruff generals eating together out of tin cans:

When the fighting is all over, and He calls His children home,
And Tojo's hanging from the wall of Valhalla's golden dome,
God will wink at General Vandergrift as he eats his Spam and beans,
Saying, "God on High sees eye to eye, with the United States Marines!"

And I loved too the Marines marching on clouds in my head at the words: "If the Army and the Navy ever looked on Heaven's scenes, / They would find the streets all guarded by United States Marines.

That could always get a grin out of him, even in those bad tense days when the babies cried and crawled in the California dirt, and there was not enough money, and Mama was still always tired, always dragging.

The Quonset hut had laid over its bad smells a nasty fakish smell like cherry-perfume disinfectant, an odor we could never dispel in those weeks, even with our own distinct odors. Undeodorized sweat over Lifebuoy was Daddy's smell: he avoided artificial anything, and that included deodorant. Mama still trailed light breezes of L'Heure Bleue, possibly to fend off that odiferous sweat; and the smell of it still made me feel vaguely anxious. Johnnie smelled like squashed bugs; he never bathed until forced to. The twins, still babies, of course smelled of urine and dirty diapers most of the time. The quarters reeked not only with all our mingled odors and with whatever Mama was making for supper, but also what the black woman whose family lived in the other half of our Quonset hut was cooking for supper, generally featuring cabbage. There couldn't have been any ventilation, and only cardboard divided us from them.

My own smell, however, was the most interesting of all: old popsicle wrappers. The aroma that clung to me and my clothes was a comforting potpourri of chocolate, vanilla, banana, grape, cherry, and tutti-frutti, with a wistful soupçon of sour milk. . . .

With no toys except whatever would fit in one shoe box (a doll and three dresses and a tiny trove of jewelry and pretty stones), I had to devise some hobby to fill my hours. Hating the smell of the Quonset hut, I stayed away for as many hours a day as I could steal. I learned that you could send in popsicle wrappers, and get all kinds of stuff free. I learned where every trash can was on that immense base, and collected and stowed in my bureau drawers over a thousand paper wrappers in the eight weeks we lived in that sliced half-cylinder.

There were order blanks right on the wrappers. With only a hundred, you could order a yo-yo; with two hundred, an unbendable celluloid doll or a collection of three tiny bottles of perfume. With six thousand, you could get a bike. But with five hundred, you could get a bracelet with a large heart-shaped bangle that said "I love you" in fifteen languages! That was my goal. It gave purpose to the dreary days, and it was my reason to get up each morning.

Every afternoon when the bus from the Mission Road School bumbled to a stop to let the base children off, I would run like a paroled prisoner from the den of snarling big boys who menaced me, stole my bookbag, twisted my arm, or pushed their friends into me, threatening each other with a dire fate, "Last one off the bus has to kiss Kitty Letcher!" throwing my bookbag back into my face, distorting their own faces into ugly caricatures.

The school, just for starters, had got my name wrong the first day, and I had no success whatever in getting the error corrected. I was also a frequent casualty in the boys' fierce battles waged over my head, the driver of the bus stolidly pretending to be oblivious to the chaos at his back.

Fleeing the bus, I would forget the torment of school at once, free until the next morning. I would take up my search from the afternoon before, staying away from the stink of that unhome where the babies howled and the afternoon heat turned the metal hut into an oven of rude smells.

I knew if I went home I'd get roped into babysitting. Mama was tired and out of sorts, possibly still not recovered from the twins' births; today I understand that she was also probably severely depressed. Certainly she detested the ugly Quonset hut. Daddy was gone all day, and had to drive to work, so she was stuck there with the fussy twins, no car, no friends.

Though she probably never dared to allow the longing, treasonous and murderous, to articulate itself in her head, there might well have been times when she wished the outcome of Daddy's years in the Pacific had been different. In my pitiless memory, she was tired all the time, too tired for me. But she might have been brooding about what her still-young life had become. Did she think about the Countess and Prince Buffito, the glamorous Peking days, servants bowing and seeing to the tiniest detail? Did she ponder the broken promise of their lives together? She was isolated there, not even a good woman friend to unload with.

But children don't know these things in a way that makes them compassionate. Alone for the afternoon, anonymous, I allowed the obsession with my new hobby to own me. Maybe it was just another manifestation of the woodland forays I'd loved, with Daddy in California, with Andaddy in Virginia, in search of free food, but I determined I would become the world champion popsicle-wrapper collector. I was dead set on being famous, and daydreamed all the time of headlines with my name. I wasn't the first kid who thought the escape route from the horrors of school, the school bus, the Quonset hut, my infuriating brother, and mewling babies I certainly hadn't asked to join us, lay in fame.

I would roam until darkness those ugly bare rows of half-cylinders of corrugated metal. I remember thinking they must look to God like corduroy from up there in the sky. I cased the grounds around the canteens, rifled the khaki USMC-stenciled metal trash bins methodically and thoroughly. There was no playground on the base, and I never got to know any other children who lived there, so single-minded was I. Only hunger would lead me home when darkness fell, and I'd stuff my day's finds into one of my drawers, wherever there was room in the cheap dresser, among my clothes. Next day, I'd go to school perfumed by the leftover aromas of those wrappers. As far as I know, Mama didn't notice. The entire place stank.

West Coast, postwar, public schools: education was a shambles. The school system I was part of seems symbolic of the whole upturned world out there: the Mission Road School never gave homework; in fact, we were not allowed to take home any books; they belonged to the school and were on call anytime, apparently, from other classes who wanted them. It was commonplace to be interrupted halfway through an arithmetic lesson by a messenger from another teacher who needed, that very moment, the books we were using. They would immediately be collected and piled into a wagon and carted off, and we would have to think of something else to do. It was also common to arrive at your usual classroom one morning to learn that the class had been moved to another room, or that there was suddenly, for no reason you were told, a new teacher.

Children of migrant workers came and went, children who spoke no English appeared at school out of nowhere, big-eyed and solemn, and smelling, somehow, always of kerosene; military kids were there one day and gone the next. Nobody knew my name, there were no report cards, and no consistent rules or discipline. There were not enough rooms, not enough chairs.

Even as day-care, it was inadequate. I recall not one thing I learned at that school, only a few pre-adolescent snickers I didn't understand about underpants and pussies. Odd things would stick in my head, and I'd sing them or they'd turn into perseverative mantra-like jingles: *Mary Jo Moneypenny lost her Kotex* (repeat, and repeat, and repeat, until it's replaced by something else). Was there really a Mary Jo Moneypenny? The Mission Road School was a holding chamber, jostling with young humanity; some teacher there told us that Amen meant "Our man," who was, of course, God. Once when a man walked along the road by the school during recess, some girl remarked darkly, "He's a morphodyke. Not a man or a woman." At the Mission Road School I learned from a girl sitting next to me that Such Mess After Birthday Parties was how you remembered the main cities of Australia: Sydney Melbourne Adelaide Brisbane Perth.

But I learned nothing there about George Washington, or the multiplication tables. Education had hit the skids on the West Coast, that suddenly.

I remember an enormous seven-foot Pacific rattlesnake that was run over on the road high above the ocean one day near the school; the bus driver stopped and we all had to bail out to look at the monster out of a myth, with its black and gold checkerboard skin and its bloody guts smeared across the road, its foot-long set of rattles. I wanted to stay on the bus, but was scared to. What I feared most was that one of those terrible boys might pick it up and menace me with it, but of course I forgot that they were as awed as I was.

I made not a single friend. We weren't in Oceanside very long, about ten weeks, but I spent most of the day hidden behind a wrong name, in that other world. At the Mission Road School after the war, there were no naps, and I never threw up, because by then I'd learned to move into the realm of imagination, to absent myself from unpleasantness.

Each night after it got dark, satisfied that I had gathered the day's harvest of popsicle wrappers, anxious that I might have missed one, I would pull my ragged red plaid suitcase out from under the dresser and get out the shoe box and play with Jane, the one doll I had out of storage, until bedtime. Johnnie would pull out his disgusting cigar box of boring metal and filthy string and rocks, and I would make him move it away from my sweet doll. He'd of course do it without complaint.

Oh, how I detested him! Living, which was so hard for me, seemed so easy for him. I reacted and overreacted to everything. He, on the other hand, tolerated deprivation cheerfully, and always seemed to come out ahead. In this particular situation, he came out twenty-five cents a week ahead, which was his price for the favor of allowing me to sleep on the daybed all the time instead of every other night, which is what Daddy had decreed. Johnnie, always willing to suffer in the interest of obtaining money, amassed his first fortune in the months we lived in the Quonset hut. Daddy praised Johnnie's economies, and ragged me about spending foolishly and being too soft to adapt to sleeping on a sofa.

But I had my own plan for wealth and fame, and the sticky wrappers piled up in my bureau drawers. I shoved pants and socks and shirts further toward the back to make room for more. I counted them, and rearranged them.

For weeks I wanted only the elegant "I love you" bracelet, but then the wrappers became an end in themselves. Always hungry for recognition, I let it be known to all I met that I had collected, that I possessed, 610, or 722, or 1187 popsicle wrappers. People seemed politely awed. I could not for a long time bring myself to take five hundred from my hoard to order the bracelet, yet every night I fell asleep thinking of the splendid thing jingling on my wrist, and of the fame it would bring me.

Finally it occurred to me that I could as well become known as the girl with the amazing bracelet as the girl with the million popsicle wrappers, and the compensation at last seemed worth the loss. I sent off the wrappers somewhat fearfully, and arrived home breathless each day for what seemed like an eternity, only to be disappointed.

ONE NIGHT BOTH TWINS WERE CRYING with earaches. At first, Daddy told them firmly to be quiet and go to sleep. They kept up the nagging crying. Then Daddy yelled, scaring them so that they upscaled the crying.

Finally, in frustration that I understood, he threatened to spank them if they didn't stop. Mama's voice rose, and with it, the twins' cries.

They still didn't, couldn't, wouldn't stop. Daddy hauled them one by one up out of the playpen, and spanked them. They cried louder.

The black sergeant's wife from the other end of the Quonset hut banged on the thin dividing wall and hollered at Daddy to stop torturing those babies, or she would call the MP's!

Daddy grew quiet, his face a dark, dangerous color. Nobody said a word. His glance defied us to utter a sound. Even the twins, still babies, sensed that they had better stop. I guess after a while we all went to bed.

Daddy said that night that no one was going to tell him what to do, especially not a nigger. I don't know what else besides integration pushed him, but perhaps he realized, either consciously or subconsciously, that he would not progress in the peacetime Marine Corps. Perhaps he'd already been passed over for promotion, and knew he could only get to be a general by retiring. The fact that the Corps had put him and his large family into half a Quonset hut instead of moving earth and heaven to find us a house may have implied a less than superior future to him. Looking at it from my adult point of view, I think that, although he was a hell of a soldier and could stoke his anger to absolute fearlessness, he was not diplomatic enough; he could not change with the times and envision a different future; his viewpoint was invariably a negative one. But a black woman yelling at him through a wall as if they were equals — well, even if it wasn't the whole reason, it was the last straw.

WHEN I GOT UP THE NEXT MORNING, he was still sitting there at the table in his clothes. He hadn't gone to bed at all. After that, things happened very fast: I remember him coming home early that day, sitting at the round table under the bare light bulb where we did everything: wrote, chopped onions, drew, colored, shelled peas, ate, sewed — writing his letter of resignation from the Marine Corps, his rejection of the life he loved. As he wrote, he kept breaking down, and putting his head down on the table to weep. He never, ever, shed tears. Was God not God? Before the year was out, I would see him in that posture again, and both times, it scared me to death.

JUST BEFORE WE LEFT CALIFORNIA, my bracelet arrived. It was divinely heavy, shiny gold, and indeed it did say "I love you" in fifteen languages. I counted them over and over, like toes on a new baby.

With the bracelet on, I felt complete, beautiful, and graceful, as a woman with a new dress will feel closer to her perfect image of herself. I went around to all the strangers at Oceanside and at Mission Road School and showed them the bracelet, and related its costliness. On that one day, I was at home on that dreary base, at home in that dreadful school.

But almost at once, one face of the golden heart began to peel, and underneath the thin shell of gold metal was ugly zinc and no statements of love at all. At Mama's suggestion, I painted it over with clear nail polish, but that too began to fall away in a leprous betrayal.

Did I take a lesson in that disillusionment? No, I never seemed to learn, remained optimistic no matter how fate swatted me down. Each time it happened, I'd be shocked with loss, then emerge from whatever wreckage still expectant. When I got up to six thousand wrappers, I was going to order the bicycle.

Me pretending to drive the old Ford, c. 1950.

Transcontinental

Somewhere in the Deep South we stop to eat at a real restaurant: next to me at the counter, an enormous monster of a man with red hair and pink eyebrows tells the counter girl that he wants pigs' ears, and I watch fascinated as the waitress plunges a long fork down into a big pot and brings out impaled dangling gray flaps of flesh, and slaps them down, repeats the action until there are six of them, on a white plate, in front of him.

"Vineguhotsauce," he says, all one word in his mean voice. Two bottles quickly come to rest near his plate. He stares at the plate. "Where mah bread is?" he demands warningly, shaking vinegar all over the gray triangles, sprinkling my arm. Six slices of white bread stacked on a little plate appear as he splatters the red sauce over what obviously really are the ears of pigs. Then, using a piece of the bread as a kind of potholder, like he doesn't want to touch the thing, he grabs a dripping ear in it, and eats, the whole thing going into his mouth at one time.

After the first one is gone, he turns to me and rumbles, "What you staring at, girl?"

WE HAD DRIVEN EAST IN THE CAR IN 1939 WHEN IT WAS NEW, a million years ago right after we got back from China, so that my grandparents could clap eyes on the firstborn grandchild. Then we drove it back to the West Coast for our years in California. Then Mama and Johnnie and Harriet and I had driven it again to Virginia in 1943. It had taken us to Norfolk after the war. It had floated through the Panama Canal with us, stowed in the ship's belly. Now, in 1947, Johnnie, Daddy, and I headed east across the postwar continent for what would be the last time. The car was distinctly in its decline. Having never been washed or polished, its once shiny black paint was now faded to an uneven purply-blue-gray.

The trip was like a bad dream, without Mama my buffer, who had gone east on the train with the twins. We had to take her to the train amid huge milling crowds, steam hissing from the enormous wheels. "Oh, please let me go with you," I begged. "I could help!" I was terrified of her leaving, terrified we'd never find her again in the wide world. I thought if I'd been more help with the babies, I might have gotten to go with her. (We were treated to her tales later: three days of her own hell on crowded trains, not enough diapers, no places to change the babies, the three of them crammed into filthy spaces elbow to elbow with servicemen smoking like chimneys trying to sleep while the babies grew progressively crosser and smellier.)

As for the rest of us, money was scarce, Daddy was not in good spirits, and the trip was tense. Mama, with no spare time at all, had still managed to fix Johnnie and me each a surprise box: mine was a pink overnight case with ten individually wrapped presents. We were carefully instructed that we were to open one a day for each day on the road. Naturally I opened them all in the first ten minutes. Johnnie, always honorable, damn him, slowly and deliberately opened one each morning, dawdling with the paper, making cats' cradles out of the string, sniffing the package, feeling it tenderly all over, guessing endlessly before he finally opened it. He didn't realize that he got even with me for my meanness every day of our lives just by being his easy, placid self.

On the road, the old car broke down continually. Pieces of the body would detach and drag behind us, striking sparks on the road. We'd tie them up with rope. The engine groaned and made terrible noises. The radiator was so unreliable that we carried three or four gallon jugs of water to pour in when steam began to rise from it. We still carried my baby potty, for Daddy didn't want to stop just because Johnnie or I had to pee. We were supposed to pee when he did. We made scarcely three hundred miles a day, driving from daybreak until nightfall.

The car made such racket while running that hardly any noise caused much alarm, though on one occasion it made such awful sounds that we pulled over to the side and got out and had a look. There was a dead chicken in the grill, caught by the neck, its feathers all standing out at messy angles, whose squawking we had for an hour or more taken for just more cantankerous engine sounds.

Daddy for years regretted out loud not having been able to figure a way to cook and eat that bird.

Daddy lectured us on health matters all the time, though he himself ate chocolates by the pound, Hershey Bars, Peter Paul Mounds, and Baby Ruths — and ice cream, often as much as a quart at a time. Driving through New Mexico he lectured us on piles, which were caused (he said) by bad eating habits, sitting on the wet ground, straining on the toilet, or all three. Johnnie and I were told, in lurid detail, about some friend's egregious eating habits, and the terrible piles that were the result. The lecture was prompted by a stop we were going to make at Carlsbad to see this friend of his.

When we met him, and I shook his hand, I stared long and hard at this man whose rectal tissue had pushed out four inches once on Guam, and who could not bear to this day to sit on a hard surface.

But Johnnie, only six, as he was shaking hands with the man, said politely, "I hope your piles are better."

I don't recall the rest of the visit, which was very short, but the minute we got away, Daddy stopped the car by the roadside and beat Johnnie within an inch of his life. I felt a great injustice had been done, but Daddy's temper was something you didn't stand up against. I didn't say a word, just tried to disappear into the corner of the back seat so he wouldn't turn, notice me, and decide *I'd* had something to do with it.

I DIDN'T LEARN UNTIL I WAS OVER FIFTY that the only thing I fear is violence. It was an interesting test: on a scale of 1 to 5, how afraid are you of heights, snakes, death, insects, enclosed spaces, people's opinions, darkness, deep water, ghosts, violence, the Devil, God? I had nothing above 1 on any of them except for a 2 for insects, until I came to violence, when my hand of its own volition veered sharply over to 5 and circled it firmly.

THE CAR, OLD THERMOSES WHOSE CORKS smell of sour milk, bad motels reeking of the dead-mouse smell of gas, terrible food of Daddy's choosing. Daddy's idea of a good lunch is still sardines and saltines, and milk with blackstrap molasses stirred in. He repeats to Johnnie and me over and over that it "tastes exactly like chocolate milk," which is so patent a lie it makes me boil. I dare not contradict him. Mentally I am brave, but physically I am a sissy.

At night we stop at the cheapest tourist court we can find and go into a room with iron beds, usually two, which means I have to sleep with Johnnie. Always there is a gas heater, and what we do for supper is heat water in our all-purpose pan: an old tomato juice tin propped against the heater. Daddy has drilled two holes right at the top, and hung a piece of wire through them for a handle. When the water begins to boil, we drop eggs in and leave them awhile. Then we scoop the eggs out of the water, and add to the water cocoa powder and condensed milk. We eat apples while the rest of supper is cooking, then hardboiled eggs, and finally cocoa. Every night.

Eight days or so into the trip, eight days of the same menu — "What's the matter, don't you like eggs?" Daddy asked Johnnie, who was frowning down at one on the tin plate before him.

"I like 'em okay," Johnnie said mildly. "But not well enough to eat anymore."

Johnnie has a most vivid memory from the cross-continental trip on narrow roads, depression highways that had not been repaired throughout the war years. As Mama could not take much with her on the train, we had most of our possessions crammed in the trunk, piled on top of the car, and secured with ropes. We wore the same clothes for ten days. Johnnie, told there would be no extra space for toys, had consolidated all of his treasures — all of them — into a used Hershey's cocoa can. There were a pocket knife, some neat pieces of metal he had from a boat someone was building, some marbles, his wad of filthy string, a few special nails, which he played with constantly. I was allowed the usual shoe box.

One day while we were bumping along eating lunch in the car instead of as usual on the side of the highway, Johnnie somehow spilled his molasses milk into the cocoa can.

Daddy had to stop the car to clean up the mess. Mad at Johnnie for spilling his milk, which Daddy already knew Johnnie didn't like (and therefore suspected Johnnie had spilled on purpose), and irritated to have to go into the trunk after a towel, Daddy made Johnnie abandon the entire can, all his worldly treasures, in a trash bin.

Johnnie felt he might as well die. Everything he had loved best in the world he had carefully chosen so it would fit into that small and inoffensive container, and not take up precious space in the car, and not bother anyone! It was all snatched from him in an instant with no apology. It took a lot to make me feel sorry for Johnnie, but I did, as he wept silently and inconsolably the rest of the afternoon, his nose red and his mouth blubbery.

We took a southern detour to Vicksburg, Mississippi, where there was a Civil War museum Daddy wanted to see, and then for a day or so passed through fields of cotton, the white bolls being picked and bagged on either side of the road by Negroes with huge puffy sacks on their backs. We stopped and plucked a stem or two, and I picked out the black oily seeds from the fluffy plants, and Daddy told us about Eli Whitney and his cotton engine that could separate seeds from fibers so fast.

I collected and wrote down red Burma Shave signs: BIG BLUE TUBE IS LIKE LOUISE, YOU GET A THRILL FROM EVERY SQUEEZE, BURMA SHAVE. And, DRUNKEN DRIVERS, NOTHING WORSE, THEY PUT THE QUART BEFORE THE HEARSE. BURMA SHAVE. On billboards, pretty girls in flirty positions urged us to Drink Grapette, Drink Coca-Cola, Drink Dr. Pepper at 10, 2, and 4, directions we never followed.

One day on that cross-continental trip Daddy, in a generous mood, allowed himself to be talked into a box of assorted Nabisco cookies, some of which had creme filling. I, bored, began to separate the filled cookies, scrape out the filling, and form an icing ball with it, which of course I had every intention of eating at some point. I don't know how long I'd been at it when Daddy turned around to the back seat and saw what I was up to. He demanded the candy ball, vanilla chocolate and strawberry icing, saved for last, which was about golf-ball size by then — saying I was playing with my food. I gave it the briefest thought, and popped it in my mouth. He stopped the car, jumped out, yanked open the back door, stuck his finger in my mouth to retrieve it. I bit him, hard, surely out of sheer excitement, for I was far too terrified of him to openly defy his commands. Quickly I swallowed the stuff. I got a terrific whipping, right there on the roadside.

All in all, it was a sad and desperate trip. Embittered and disillusioned, Daddy felt the Marine Corps, to which he'd committed his whole life, had let him down miserably. He'd always told us the United States Marine Corps was the cream of the crop: the best men, the best training, the toughest officers, the most elegant fighting force the world had ever known.

It wasn't in his nature to ever stand outside himself long enough to consider the misery and stupidity of taking out his hurt and anger on two helpless kids. At least I got to eat the icing.

AT THE END OF THE TRIP, late in September, we left Johnnie in Norfolk with Mama and the twins at her parents' new house, and we went on to Lexington so that I could be enrolled in school before the year got any older and I missed any more of fourth grade.

I imagine it was a bad time for the Norfolk contingent of the family. Boppie and Laolo had experienced their own upheaval: an abrupt enforced early retirement for my grandfather, who had expected to see three more years' service. At Camp Lejeune, where Boppie had been the CO, Laolo had her own chauffeur-driven car, and everyone had kowtowed, which she loved. Now, in postwar Norfolk, they were just two more aging civilians, and here came their daughter with year-old twins! I think the idea was that Mama and Laolo would help each other, with the retirement, with the twins, with those *husbands* of theirs. They must have been desperate. Nobody knew a thing about psychology in those days. And Laolo didn't like children.

But for years, one of us occasionally would frown and growl, "Where mah bread is?" at the table, cracking up everybody else, doing what we did a lot of, making even terrible times seem funny.

House Mountain, Rockbridge County's central landmark,
near the farm Daddy chose.

Farm

arch 9, 1943. "A beautiful Valentine received by your old frumpy Daddy who loves you very much. Do you think Santa Claus will come next year? Are you taking good care of Mommy and Johnnie and helping Harriet in the kitchen? Are you as frumpish as ever? Do you still love your Daddy? Won't we have a good time when we get back to our farm? We'll have rabbits and kitties and dogs and horses and ducks, and you can have dogs in your room, and when Johnnie's older we'll go hunting and fishing and camping and swimming. . . .. You can sleep with the skunks if you want to. You can have the pigs in your room. The sheep will keep you warm. Love every minute to you and Mommy and Johnnie. Your frumpy Daddy."

ONCE WE WERE BACK EAST and Daddy was out of the Marine Corps, we had to decide where to live. I wasn't invited to contribute to the discussions. Naturally Daddy wanted to return to Lexington, where he'd grown up. Mama had made some women friends there during the war. It felt to me like the only real home I'd known, and I did adore my grandparents.

But Daddy had to get a job. Marine Corps retirement pay, even for a tombstone general, which he was made when he retired, wouldn't stretch to feed a family of six.

Lexington it would be. A fresh start, a return to the house where I'd been so happy and so adored! This time I *wanted* to go with him. We would get to live, really live, with Andaddy and Nainai again, and they would protect me. I knew Daddy would never treat me badly in the presence of his parents, because they wouldn't let him. If they had been hard on him growing up, they were wonderfully easy on me.

And the fall of 1947 back in Lexington became in some ways the happiest period of my life: I was in a stable school with my old friends from the used-to-be, and some new ones, and teachers who called me by my right name. I basked in the admiration of my adoring grandparents who were just delighted to have me back. Daddy, relieved of whatever it was he left the Marine Corps for at last, was charming and funny, full of hope for his future, and he had big plans.

He didn't want to work for somebody else. He made up his mind. Finally we were going to get our farm!

The autumn itself was achingly gorgeous: slow and golden, sunny and fragrant, the trees like torches of flame, everyone saying it was the most beautiful autumn any of them could remember.

Eager to prove myself, I forgave and forgot the two years since his return. Somehow it made sense to me to launch a peculiar campaign to reenact Daddy's boyhood, as I thought that would win his approval. I slept outside as Daddy had done when he was my age, on the upstairs back porch with only a tarp lashed to the porch posts between me and the wind that swooped down off House Mountain and across the endless back ridge. Really cold nights, I'd start out on those icy sheets balled up like a wad of cold chewed gum, only gradually softening out as my body warmth made the bed bearable. Sometimes in the night I'd wake up and Nainai would be adjusting the covers high around my neck, standing on the freezing porch in a gigantic white flannel nightgown hanging and billowing like a fat ghost. Her hands were soft as kidskin gloves. Those nights, the end of my nose was numb with cold.

Determined to be a good buddy, I cheerfully accompanied Daddy on long walks to survey land he was considering buying, to nearby towns where he asked about various kinds of jobs, to look at farms he thought we might buy. I got so I could squat and pee by the side of the road, no problem. I didn't even worry if a car passed. As Daddy said, if they hadn't ever seen a bottom before, it was high time.

He was excited and genial during that time, getting ready to start a new life, still young — only in his early forties — and eager to try his hand at civilian life. He was bitter about the Marine Corps, but he seemed to look forward to maybe being a forest ranger, and to farming, which he'd been dreaming of doing ever since I could remember.

He told stories that usually had a terrifying retributive quality: there was one about the time when he was out driving, and a big expensive luxury car came up behind him, honking and running all over the road. The driver hollered and cursed, and passed him at high speed, forcing him off into a muddy ditch in his little sturdy economical car (one he'd had before marrying Mama). The driver of the big car tore on, weaving drunkenly, hogging the road.

After the dust cleared, Daddy had to get out, and pull and shove his car, and dig dirt away, and go through all sorts of tricks to get back up the bank and on to the road again. But he straightened his shoulders and went on.

But then, ten miles down the highway, ta-dah! there lay the big cruising car, smoking and hissing, its front crumpled like tinfoil against a tree, its driver forever silenced.

"This one time when Gee and I were kids," he'd start, and there would come a parable from which we were to learn how to behave. Like the story of his first financial investment, a lesson in *caveat emptor*: he and Gee saved their money for a long time, with a grand scheme in mind. They were going to buy a goat, sell its milk to the neighbors, and get rich.

They came home with a goat, all full of themselves. It had cost much less than their mother had said it would. Weren't they smart to have gotten a goat so cheap? they crowed to Nainai. "That's fine," their mother said mildly, "but it's a *billy* goat."

I DISCOVERED THAT DADDY CONSIDERED TUNA a reasonable substitute for sardines, so I'd hasten to make us tuna sandwiches for our forays before we left. I proudly did not mention gashes, hunger, thirst, my nervous bladder. I asked him what everything was, concentrated on learning the names of flowers, trees, and animal prints, learned the outline shapes of all the leaves, chewed teaberry leaves and dug Indian cucumber that we'd wash off in a stream and eat like Indians in the woods.

Having Daddy to myself, I was absolutely determined to win back his lost love. He was a sparkling and agreeable companion, anecdotal and observant, as long as I was willing to nearly kill myself to keep up. So, cheerfully, that's what I did.

And he was capable of dramatically redeeming actions: one day, after we'd both talked about how much we loved chocolate sodas, miles from nowhere he pulled up at a country store, went in, and bought a square pint of vanilla ice cream, a can of Hershey's chocolate syrup, a big bottle of soda water, and asked the storekeeper for two paper cups, and if we could borrow a can opener. Then he proceeded to mix us up chocolate ice cream sodas, in the dirt parking lot of a tiny country store that couldn't, not by the wildest stretch of imagination, have produced an ice cream soda!

Perhaps missing Johnnie and the twins, I even figured a way to make and save money, which Daddy was big on doing. I began to babysit in the neighborhood, and soon had a thriving business, making ten cents an hour. I took care of another set of twins named Barbara and Doug Miller every day after school, and their mother paid me a handsome twenty-five cents an hour, and told everyone on the block that nobody but me could do a *thing* with them. I sat for other neighborhood children, too.

For a whole weekend spent with a child whose parents had gone to a football game out of town, I once got five dollars, a fortune. Daddy was impressed, I could tell from his face. He paid me for A's on my report cards, fifty cents each. He insisted that I save the money (for it was not natural to me to hoard and he knew it, and it worried him to death, how like his profligate uncle Letcher Harrison I might become), and save it I did for a while. But the truth was, with me it was always easy come, easy go.

I knew how when he was sick as a child, Nainai paid him a nickel every time he'd take his castor oil, and how once the doctor came, and saw him with the purse full of coins, and said, "Buzz, what you going to do with all that money?" And how he'd replied, "I likes to watch it *bulge*." I got a barrel bank free from the Rockbridge Bank, with a slotted top and a key that would open the bottom up for my weekly tallies. I wanted *my* money to bulge, too.

So I sold scented stationery, and Christmas cards, all over town. I approached the school superintendent, and he ordered five hundred cards with his name (Jake) and his wife's (Vida) printed on them. I was ecstatic, bragging to everyone about how I was making twenty-five dollars, as I got a dollar for every twenty cards I sold.

The only problem was, somehow I misunderstood, and therefore misspelled, the wife's name, which turned out to be Vada. I had to pay for the cards myself, so by Christmas I was dead broke and discouraged. I remember trying to figure out how I could keep part of the cards, use the envelopes, and make some kind of note papers out of them. For years those damn boxes sat in my closet, and I never could figure out anything creative to do with them.

From then on, Jake ("Mr. Samples to you") didn't like me. I'd ruined his Christmas cards. Way later, at the end of my junior year, I'd taken summer school for three years, gotten into Hollins a year early, and went to Mr. Samples' office to claim my high school degree, having completed all the requirements. Jake refused, and to this day I don't have a high school diploma. He said you had to spend four years, and in those days, a student had no recourse.

Anyway, I begged Andaddy and Nainai not to tell Daddy about the cards. I don't think they did, figuring I'd suffered enough. Andaddy saw no reason to save very much, and gave things away impulsively, so I took it that it was okay to do that. Andaddy gave to every cause, even ones he didn't know about. He had this notion that bread cast upon the waters would return. He gave lots of money to his careless but hardworking grand-daughter, including five hush-hush five-dollar bills that Christmas.

Nobody monitored my bedtime that fall. Instead, at night we'd sit in the dim forty-watt light and talk, Nainai, Andaddy, Daddy, and I, about how it was going to be. The economy was going up, they'd conquered most dis-eases with penicillin, they were inventing new things all the time, and we were all going to be around to see them, for the next hundred years!

But no jobs materialized, and Daddy decided that a farm was the thing: it would be healthy, fun, and productive. I agreed enthusiastically, he made it sound so great. We made lists, and maps, and drove around to see every farm on the market. We had to find a stream with watercress. Good river-bottom soil. Daddy planned to support us by commercially raising Kentucky Wonder beans and Silver Queen corn, his and my favorites. Big Boy tomatoes. Our winter garden would have kale and chard, which we also loved. In addition, we'd raise sheep, horses, chickens, cows, dogs — well, maybe the dogs would stay outdoors because of Mama — and lots of cats! Peacocks, he opined, would be good to guard the place. They'd had peacocks in Rockbridge County when he was a boy. There'd be sleigh-rides in the winter, hay-rides in the summer!

Of course the river would have a swimming hole. We'd have a fireplace, and toast marshmallows. I could have friends out for the weekend, and we'd gallop around on the horses. I could hardly wait!

He delighted me and amused himself that fall with descriptions of all my future boyfriends, and how I'd come to grief with them all. I relished the stories, for already I had crushes that Daddy teased me about. On Letcher Avenue, I was surrounded by cadets and students, three thousand of them, and they got my hormones going early.

Garlic Joe would be scrawny and Italian, with Brillcreamed hair and a big diamond ring on his little finger, and would always be making some slick deal. "Make you a deal, sweet-hot," Daddy would mince, with his little finger raised, and the other hand pretending to slick back his greasy hair. Garlic Joe would offer me a hot diamond for an engagement ring — and when the police came after him, he'd take it back with the promise of a bigger one next week. In the end, he'd go to jail and I'd end up working in the sewing machine factory.

Sleepy Sam would be countrified, uncouth, and barefoot, and he'd make us keep hogs in the kitchen when we were married. He was so lazy he'd sleep his life away, so we'd never have any money, and I'd have to go to work again in the sewing machine factory. We had no money for firewood, so when we'd sit down for dinner (Sam in his undershirt), the hogs would lie on our feet to keep them warm. And when it got really cold, he'd throw the kitchen chairs in the fire to keep warm, so we'd never have any furniture and just have to end up sleeping on the floor with the hogs.

Muscles Charlie was huge, dumb, and muscle-bound, and would show off by lifting me up onto the garage roof. Wandering off, he would forget about me. "Ah'm strong!" Muscles would brag. Then he'd raise up a cow to join me on the roof, and maybe the car after a while, and the garage roof would of course eventually cave in under all that weight. Muscles had a terrible car that wouldn't run, but that was no problem. He'd come courting me *carrying* his car.

Alphonse was the poet, the worst of them all, the way Daddy told it, making me listen all day to incomprehensible things like Shakespeare, which Daddy had little tolerance for. Alphonse would wear his hair long, and sprinkle himself with cologne, and write endless stupid poetry. Also he would be hopeless about making a living. So of course I would have to go work in the sewing machine factory to keep us alive and to get away from having to listen all day to "Wherefore the bodkin harmeth him that doth? Oh, let me clutch thee, firkin . . ." or, "The fairy leaves tramp to and fro. . .". He loved inventing the silly poetry, and I helped gleefully.

Fairy Harry wore lace shirts and perfume, and had his hair curled at the beauty parlor, and manicured his nails like a girl! He would come to call on me, but then, distracted, forget and ask one of the boys for a date.

Finally there was Boho Bo, who went barefoot, and wore black turtleneck sweaters and banged on drums in the smoky dives where he hung out. Bo drank coffee all night to stay awake, and was really depressed at the state of the world, just everything made him sad. Then, because he'd been up all night, Bo would sleep all day while I, as usual, had to go trudging off to support us by working at the sewing machine factory again.

I loved those stories, and Daddy, egged on, made that endless string of suitors come alive. He was a terrific and entertaining companion when he was in a good mood.

THAT FALL WE GOT ALONG SO WELL he even intervened with my teacher when we clashed over how often I might be allowed to go to the girls' room. My bladder got nervous when I was told I could go only twice a day, though twice a day would have been enough if no one had *told* me I couldn't go. Maybe I suffered from one of Mama's maxims: *always* go to the bathroom before you leave home, because you never know when the next opportunity will come. Maybe I was nervous because normally Daddy would not stop the car to let me pee. At any rate we clashed, Miss Hazel Flynn and I, and I was verbally accused of loitering, voyeurism, and general laziness, and finally chastised in a mildly worded note home.

Katie is not lazy, my father fired back, *she just needs to use the toilet. Sincerely, J. S. Letcher.* Indelicate, maybe, but its point was clear.

After that Miss Flynn allowed me to go when I asked, but I reported to Daddy on her grudging reluctance. I trotted back with another note, this one written in threatening capitals: YOU WILL ALLOW KATIE TO USE THE TOILET ANY DAMN TIME SHE WANTS, AND YOU WILL NOT HUMILIATE HER FOR IT. — J. S. LETCHER, BRIG. GEN., USMC.

My hero was on the job. He also called up Miss Nettie, the seventh-grade teacher and principal, who'd taught him many years before, and had a chat with her on the phone. Miss Hazel Flynn tightened her lips and glared at me from then on, but she certainly never said another thing about my going to the bathroom. She was not from around Lexington, and Daddy made up a sardonic song about her that we could sing in the car: "Miss Hazel Flynn, from sunny Tennessee, You'll love her when you see Sweet Hazel!" Apparently she was not up on her local genealogy, and did not know who the Letchers *were*.

EVERY SUNDAY NOON THAT FALL we had vanilla ice cream with brandied peaches for dessert. Nannie made them according to an old method: *in July or August, you pack the Mason jars tight with whole peeled ripe peaches, add sugar to the top, add 2 tablespoons of fine brandy to every quart, then put on the heavy zinc and porcelain tops and stow them in the cellar. By Christmas they will be ready.*

What the directions didn't tell you is that, in Indian summer when it got hot again for the last time, usually in the middle of October, the pressure of fermentation would build up and some of the brandied peaches would explode, startling us day or night with their detonations followed by the tinkling crashes of falling glass. It was an annual event. Indian summer, you stayed out of the cellar, which was fine because nothing was down there at all that needed human contact except the furnace, which wouldn't be turned on until past cold weather.

Any jar that didn't explode by cold weather was safe to fetch and eat, and had become frightfully alcoholic.

Nothing in the world was as good with vanilla ice cream as those heady brandied peaches. I spent most Sunday afternoons that fall in boozy slumber after consuming enormous quantities of them at lunch. Mother would have put the brakes on that fast, but Daddy and Nainai and Andaddy gobbled them, too, an entire quart after a Sunday dinner, and nobody singled me out as a child in that second, brief Eden.

I'd sleep off the drunks in the southwest sitting room on one of the horsehair stuffed velvet couches, and when the sliding autumnal sun played across my face, the light through my eyelids was peachy pink.

I took jars of those peaches to the old ladies in the neighborhood, and won them all over, so that when Halloween came, and I sashayed up and down Letcher Avenue in a gypsy costume built out of the attic trunks, plenty of jewelry, scarves, shawls, and makeup, and a huge beauty mark just above my lip, they all loaded me down with cookies and brownies and homemade popcorn-caramel balls. Mrs. Bates, Miss Ellis Archer and her sister Miss Marie, Miss Catherine Mann: they were all my pals.

In November, Daddy and Andaddy and I went on several outings to abandoned orchards where we collected apples and brought them home. The world was golden, and smelled of the boxes of ripe apples stored in the back hall. At an auction we bought a wooden cider mill for a dollar, and painted it red. We made cider and stored it in the bathtub, which wasn't used, actually, much at all. We drank it immoderately. After a while, it got fizzy and heady, and we kept drinking it. We had to drain away the last of it, just before Christmas, when it suddenly turned into vinegar.

NO MATTER HOW LOVELY THE WEATHER, it's bound to rain sometime. Outside, I am climbing trees with two neighborhood boys who live on Letcher Avenue. I am panting and sweaty, in shorts and no top, and have beat both of them to the highest safe branch, when Daddy, coming home from somewhere, strides over and stomps around beneath me, at the base of the fir's trunk, and yells up to go inside and put on a shirt.

Why? I call down.

Because I said to, he yells, right in front of the boys. Below me I see their heads, stopped to listen. *Never come out again without a shirt on!* Daddy hollers up.

Angry as I was, I somehow knew it meant I was growing up, and I wanted none of it, and I wanted all of it, and I wanted no one to notice, and I wanted everyone to, maybe even David, who sat silently on branches halfway up and moved over to let me by and watched me slink down out of the tree.

BUT LORD, WE TALKED THAT FALL! The three growns discussed everything freely in front of me, without Mama's forbidding looks. Daddy and his parents all had a fascination for any immoral behavior, especially all shades of fornication, people who were of odd sexual orientation, and untimely births. (It was a long time before I could see the absurdity, not to mention the cruelty, of blaming the poor people who had the bad luck to be born out of wedlock, as though the immorality of the circumstance were the fault of the bearer.) I knew every graying banker in town who had been born before his parents had been married long enough, knew who drove like a bat out of hell to Roanoke to frequent whorehouses, knew who was really old Ann Baker's daughter even though she'd been raised by the Doolittles, because Ann Baker had gotten pregnant while she was still in high school in 1914.

I knew what the undertaker did with the corpses (though how Daddy knew is an interesting thing I didn't wonder about until many years later). Daddy's favorite story about the man he called "Digger" was that someone had asked him one spring how business was, and that he replied, "Terrible. Cherry-blossom time passed, and we never buried a single child."

I knew that Dean Carter and Frank Fields had flipped a coin to decide which one of them would marry Gertrude Ann Stevens Fields, because either might have fathered the child she was pregnant with, and how the baby, a boy, was a dead ringer for Dean Carter. They talked just as if I were a grown, too, nodding at me, listening if I had an opinion.

I digested these stories along with the fried chicken and rice and peas, the stewed tomatoes and gingered pear conserve, the lamb roasts, the deep-dish apple pies and pork chops and cheese sandwiches we ate.

I can still pass a blue-haired arthritic widow on the street today, and remember that she reportedly messed around with other men while her husband was overseas. I know who is a lifelong closet alcoholic, and I know who, long dead, was a kleptomaniac. I knew who was "adopted," but was really the natural son of the unmarried sister of the one who adopted him. To this day I don't know if everyone in town knows these things and doesn't mention them, or even if they are true at all, or whether they all occurred only in Daddy's suspicious imagination, in Andaddy's storyteller mind, or in Nainai's starvation and loneliness and suspicion of other women.

Yet I did know that no one could really keep their natures a secret: I had long known my other grandmother, Laolo, did not like me, just as I knew Nainai adored me; I saw and knew what they felt, those tall growns. I knew Mildred, who was my friend Susan's mother, didn't like me. I knew Tut's mother found me appalling, unkempt and rough-edged, wanting in every way. And I knew that Jeanne's mother found me interesting; she liked my costumes especially, for she herself had been an actress. With a sideways sense that was not ever a word-knowing, I knew I had a smart mouth, and that some people didn't like that I moved quickly. Yet try as I might, I could not make myself move more slowly, or speak more cautiously, for more than a few moments at a time when I concentrated absolutely on doing exactly that. I even knew that a certain neediness on my part put people off, but I didn't know how to change it. I knew to some degree what about me made Daddy mad, but I seemed unable to do anything about it except by the most determined effort, and only for the briefest spans of time.

We idle at a corner, waiting for the light to change. "You see that man?" Daddy asks.

"Which one?"

"That one." He points.

I nod.

"You stay away from him," Daddy says.

"Why?"

"Because he's a lesbian."

"What's that?" I ask.

"You'll have to ask Mama when she comes."

It was apparently okay to hear, but not to ask for more than was given.

COME SUNDAYS, ANDADDY'D ALWAYS ROUND UP the cadet and student sons and grandsons of his old friends or state legislators he'd known, and they'd come to dinner and devour fried chicken and mashed potatoes, hot rolls and green peas, cherry cobbler and ice cream, like all those foods were going out of style. Carters, Byrds, Taylors, Barrons, LeContes, LePrades, Lewises, Jacksons, Lees, Catletts: they were all there, handsome and embarrassed, in their stiff uniforms or navy blue suits.

Nainai was never ungracious, but she didn't see the point of it. I sympathized with her, but I loved having cadets to dinner. I thought the boys were interesting, the ones we could get to talk. In fact, for awhile, I thought the Presbyterians' Lord's Prayer had in it the line, "Forgive us our cadets, as we forgive cadetters . . ." which made as much sense as most of the words I heard or repeated in church.

LIVING AT NAINAI AND ANDADDY'S WITH DADDY, I was even freer than when Mama alone had been in charge.

I was allowed to go by myself to the only department store in town and charge a winter coat. I chose the only interesting one in the store, in a luscious shade somewhere between pink and red, the color bursting forth from the rack of gray and navy, black and brown, wool coats, like a peony out of winter soil. It had rhinestone buttons and a fake mink collar. Nobody said a thing, except Nainai, who said, peering at its deep fuschia color through one of her thick magnifying glasses, that it was lovely. It was what Mama and her friends would have called a Sunday Coat, but nobody kept me from wearing it to school from then on, and I felt beautiful in it.

After school during those autumn months of 1947, Daddy and I cooked a lot. Nainai and Andaddy ate their big meal at one o'clock, and Nannie left around three, so the kitchen was empty after that, and of course Nannie would return next morning to clean up whatever mess "Mista Seymo" made. (Daddy had changed his name to John S. Letcher, disliking his birth name of Seymour. But Nannie couldn't change.)

If I liked what Daddy was making, I'd help, and we'd listen to "Straight Arrow" or the local "Hi Neighbor!" hillbilly music program, and, on

Saturdays, to "The Grand Ole Opry." Weekday evenings a couple of years later we'd tune in eagerly to hear Lowell Thomas broadcasting by short-wave radio from Tibet, and after that someone named John Nesbitt, who told fifteen-minute stories about ghosts and lost treasure.

With none to say we couldn't do it, we invented Brackers, a cornmeal cracker that, although delicious, was so brittle it broke your teeth and gouged holes in your gums. Daddy thought them excellent exercise for the jaws and wonderfully cleansing for the teeth — sort of like pumice. To each cup of cornmeal was added 1 teaspoon salt, 1 tablespoon corn oil, 1/2 cup water. This watery batter was spread evenly and thinly on a greased cookie sheet and baked at 325 degrees for about 40 minutes, allowed to cool in the oven, then broken into odd-sized chunks to nibble on. The cornmeal we made in the hand grinder Daddy got for fifty cents at an auction sale, from windfall corn gathered as we hiked through some farmer's field in late autumn.

Daddy hated the way bacon cooked unevenly, parts of each piece getting burnt while other parts curled up or bubbled away from the pan and stayed raw. So he and I, over some weeks, and with various experiments, devised a sensational new method which cooked the bacon in the oven in matching pie pans with the bacon in between them, the top pan weighted down with a brick — so that bubbles of raw bacon could not form. He tried to patent the idea, but, like so many others, it came to nothing.

I, spurred on by Daddy and Andaddy, invented Paradise Pie, which was wildly popular with my grandparents, Daddy, and my friends. In a raw pie crust, I put a mixture of melted butter, brown sugar and white, lots of vanilla, 2 eggs, a can of coconut, a cup of chocolate chips, a cup of almonds. This lumpy goo was baked for an hour, and got served topped with lots of whipped cream. My grandfather said, as he did of many of my creations, "Little Sweetheart, you ought to write that up and send it in!" I would've, but I didn't know how, and our plans never got beyond the dream stage. He said it about the bloated poems I composed, the essays I wrote for English class, and the songs I sang. But the fame I longed for continued to elude my grasp.

MAMA AND THE OTHER KIDS WERE COMING FOR CHRISTMAS. Nainai provided me with more money than I'd ever seen, and I went uptown and bought everyone presents. I brought them home, where Nainai was full of praise at my choices as we wrapped them and discussed over our hot chocolate and cheese sandwiches how delicious Christmas was going to be.

At the slightest hint on my part, more dollar bills fluttered down from her hands like green confetti, and back uptown I'd go for another haul!

Daddy came home one day, his face shining like a cranberry. He had a secret; he'd found a farm he liked, several miles out of town. It had a spring with watercress, hills, outbuildings, a small river with a wooden bridge, room for the animals, a house for us to live in with a garden behind. All the things on our wish-list! The fifteen hundred dollars was a price he could afford; it needed work, but he was going to surprise Mama with it for Christmas!

Daddy and Andaddy and I drove out to look at how the old farmhouse rested, nestled in a hollow in the swan-neck curve of the pleasant creek, its tin roof in need of paint, its log sides still plumb 150 years after the house-raising, its massive stone chimney with an outside fireplace as well as a huge one inside, a framed ell out the back for the bathroom. Daddy pointed out the barn where the animals would stay, all but the cats, who were going to stay inside, in my room. He showed us the apple trees we'd pick from next fall. I was sworn to secrecy. That night we described it to Nainai in great detail.

At night after Nannie had gone home for the day, Daddy and I made applesauce cakes. Daddy, in a generous frame of mind, thought they'd be nice for us and the neighbors for Christmas. The recipe was as expansive as Daddy, a pound of butter, 2 pounds of sugar, a dozen eggs, 2 pounds of applesauce, 3 pounds of flour with 4 tablespoons of soda, 2 big jars of cherry preserves, a pound each of yellow raisins, black raisins, currants, and dates, a pound of pecans or walnuts, a 4-ounce bottle of vanilla, all mixed in a big washtub. I grated ten, twenty, nutmegs into a brown pile, hammered cloves (a small pile) and cinnamon (a medium pile) to powder in a double paper bag while Daddy squinted through the flour-clouded room over the mountains of sugar in great bowls, beating eggs into yellow froth with Nannie's old green-handled beater, urging, "Do more, Chick. We need lots!"

All the time, we discussed our wonderful Christmas surprise. I greased up containers, and we poured that sweet batter into loaf pans and baking tins, coffee cans and pie pans, anything we could find. Nannie would clean up in the morning.

One time that fall, Andaddy was offered, in pay for some legal work in West Virginia, his choice of a barrel of speckled beans or a rosewood piano. He and Nainai wrangled over the offer: he thought the beans were the more sensible choice, but Miss Katie wanted the piano, which, he made the mistake of telling her, had rose satin backing behind delicate carving above the keyboard. Daddy and Andaddy and I went to Lewisburg and got the piano, driving in the Model A Ford Andaddy owned but hardly ever drove, and referred to as "that confounded contraption." Daddy and another man hoisted the petite upright piano into the backseat of the open car, upside down, and we drove it home to Lexington over the mountains along the old Midland Trail, and I played it from that day on. "You're the spit and image of yo' daddy," that man told me all the way over in West Virginia, and Daddy grinned with pleasure. I probably did, too.

Buzz, Gee, and Katie (Nainai), c. 1910.

Death

10

*I*t's impossible to remember a single time Nainai ever left the house. She hadn't attended her only son's wedding, which was not more than two hundred miles from home. She didn't go uptown; she didn't even go to church. She supported the church, but believed a person's deeds were the thing God would go on.

Only rarely did another woman visit her. She thought other women were fools, and talked about boring things like children and cooking. Disdaining housework, Nainai listened to books for the blind on large round records, sometimes to operas, and she soon snared me into winding the Victrola up for her when it ran down. Her hair was long and white and soft, bunned or braided, and Nainai was herself fat and soft and lavender-smelling.

Slowly she shuffled through the old house, weaving and reweaving the rooms, a tired, old Penelope, leaving teapots and teacups of fine china, and thermoses of tepid coffee and their cups in her wake. Her whole adult life she had an incurable thyroid disease (which I have inherited, and control simply with one tiny pill a day) that made her fat. She had been a Suffragette when young, and liked to talk about politics, which she felt other women didn't know anything about.

She had always had terrible eyesight, and by the time I knew her she was nearly blind. She peered at the world through giant magnifying glasses that lay on every table in the house so that she could read what she wanted or needed to. Today, I wonder if she didn't also suffer from agoraphobia, and if a lot of what she said wasn't just to avoid going into a world that, for whatever reasons, terrified her.

From the first, she had a wonderful way of trusting whatever I did, and often said things like, "You just go on and do it your way. It'll turn out fine." She took my side against everyone: "Nannie, if she wants to cook, let her." "Betty, she's just being a child" — and later, after the war, "Buzz, don't you touch that child!"

And, despite believing in being a good hater, she had lists of people she thought very highly of, often for some long-past deed she admired especially. Like a woman she knew of named Ida Mae, who'd got herself engaged to a fellow when they were young, and Ida Mae was ripe for the picking. There wasn't a boy in Harrisonburg who didn't want to marry her.

Then tragedy struck. Ida Mae's fiancé got hit by lightning walking home through a field one night after leaving her; he was totally paralyzed, and his brains got fried. But he didn't die. He lived on in his body, not recognizing her or anybody, for sixty years. Now, that would stop most people, but Ida Mae didn't flinch; she went and moved right into his house and took care of him.

Years went by. After his parents died, Ida Mae stayed on, an old maid, ignoring all the other fellows who courted her, turning up her nose at the gossip about an unmarried woman living alone in the house with an unmarried man.

Finally, when she was old, Ida Mae took sick and died, and the neighbors noticed because there was no activity around the house. They found her dead body slumped on the floor by his bed, him still alive in the bed but nearly starved. As they were moving him out of the house where he'd been a patient for sixty long years to take him somewhere, probably the poorhouse, he expired coming down off his own front porch. Some figured it was the sunshine hitting him, like the lightning had so many years before, that finally killed him.

Nainai thought that was the greatest story she'd ever heard, all that loyalty. Ida Mae was high on her list of Most Admired.

Her laws were few and fervid: "Don't let down" was one (by which she might be *referring to anything from gaining too much weight to getting into the sherry or whiskey before five, from letting your slip show to telling someone something when it was supposed to be a secret). "Stand up when older folks come in the room," "Keep your skirt down," "Don't talk about the cat's titties in front of company," and "Be a good hater."*

I DAY-DREAMED EXTRAVAGANTLY OF OUR FARM: I would have all the animals I wanted: lambs and rabbits, a horse maybe, if I could choose it myself, though I really didn't like them much. I could have as many cats as I wanted, a deodorized skunk, a baby fox maybe — and they would all be friends. My room was going to be painted and decorated in turquoise! Mama and Johnnie and the twins (darling twins!) were coming in a few days, and we had this wonderful surprise for them for Christmas! It was all going to be wonderful. Now we would live happily ever after.

DECEMBER 22, 1947. WE ARE AT THE DINNER TABLE, all of us together for the first time in months. School is over for Christmas, and Mama and Johnnie and Betsy and Pete have arrived in Laolo and Boppie's black Buick bursting with boxes, bags, presents! We plan to go tomorrow out to the country to cut a Christmas tree. The twins are barely recognizable, they've grown so, but I am secretly pleased when Betsy holds out her little arms and cries, "Kiki!" — her version of my baby nickname, Chickie.

My Mama has come back, and I am so proud of everything, how I've cooked, done the shopping, held the place together, how I filled two closets with wonderful presents for everybody! Daddy has made a roast leg of lamb, and I have made the famous Paradise Pie for dessert, and am itchy with anticipation of the cries of admiration I will hear when they all taste it.

I am bursting inside with the secret about the farm Daddy is going to buy us for Christmas, have already chosen for myself an upstairs room under the eaves, now open with trash and leaves blowing through its frail unplastered lathing, but fixable.

Suddenly, seeing me sipping a cup of coffee for supper, Mama is horrified, and tells me I will never be able to go to sleep.

"I drink it every night and I go right to sleep every night," I tell her.

"What?" she asks, and turns to Nainai. "Miss Katie, is that true?" There's a sort of silence, in which all you can hear is silver, and chewing.

"Pass the chutney," Daddy says.

Mama glances at it, but doesn't move to touch it. She stares at me. "You drink coffee every night? When did you last have a bath?"

I can't answer.

"It's obvious you haven't had a bath for the entire three months since you've been here."

"That's not true," I say, adding that I can remember at least two, before the cider. We eat on, and in the uncomfortable silence Andaddy begins to tell about my poetry recitations, and my singing.

As Andaddy is singing my praises, Nainai simply falls sideways out of her chair, with a quiet rustling, onto the floor. Her silver clatters to the floor after her, dislodged by her descent. The growns all rush to lift and drag her considerable bulk back onto the chair, but she will not stay propped, and so they instead raise her floppy soft body up, and ease her over and onto the nearby sofa.

All is hushed, the Christmas euphoria is sucked away in the tense phone call to the doctor, the subdued conversations outside the dining room door, the blankets rushed in, the kids told to scram. Including me. The doctor comes with his black bag swinging.

She has had a stroke, a massive one. Twenty-four hours later, when she has awakened only enough to mumble confusedly, she will have another, and die. For the second time in my life, the second time that year, I see my father put his head down on the table and cry inconsolably.

I HAVE BEEN SLEEPING, BUT AWAKEN TO INTENSE VOICES. The dim bell-shaped light hangs off the wall, and the linens of the bed have the wonderful herby, musty odor I have come to love. "You will help me," I hear him say, and it is Daddy's voice, angry.

"I can't do that. It's not civilized. You call —"

"I will wash her myself, and you'll help. Get a pan of hot water and some soap and towels."

"I won't do it," Mama replies. "I never heard of such a thing. I've never even seen her without clothes."

"It's the least you can do —"

"I won't touch a dead body."

"You will."

I cover my ears, pile on the dusty pillows, the cold smooth covers, the dozen thin layers of flannel and wool, cotton and linsey-woolsey, still peeking out at the graceful dim night-light like a flower. I need to pee but don't dare get up. Outside the dark stretches so far that light may never come again.

A COFFIN, DENIM BLUE, appears on a stand in the middle of the parlor, next morning.

Is Nainai in there? I ask.

My father shakes his head. No, just her shell.

I am puzzled, as I didn't know she had a shell. Then where is she?

Heaven.

Oh.

ON CHRISTMAS EVE, I am hustled away early from the house to Susan's house to make Christmas fondant, boiled then colored and flavored with almond, peppermint, vanilla. We stuff dates, surround nuts, make balls which we dip in chocolate or roll in coconut. A lovely day, even though I can tell that Susan's mother resents my intrusion upon their Christmas, and thinks I eat up too much of what she calls "the profits." She's right; I do. I can't stop eating the candy. Their tree is gorgeous, with bubbling lights and something called angel hair that surrounds each light with a glowing halo.

The day ends in the gray-green cemetery with the blue coffin being put into the ground, me holding Mama's hand in my new beautiful fuschia coat that Nainai had admired so, peering intently through a heavy magnifying glass at its color with her blind eyes, reaching to touch it with her soft fingers.

Tomorrow is Christmas, but we will have no tree. Mama has already said, Don't mention it.

The Letchers, 1899.

Family Portrait

11

In the dining room, on the wall . . . always staring out solemnly. Only now, years later, do I know who they all are, and the sad end of the story I am part of.

I BRUSH AWAY THE DIRTY FLAKES of art-gum eraser, and they emerge from the oily film of coal dust and years of warming, cooling, wetting, drying. In chiaroscuro I see that they have the sun in their faces and are trying not to squint. The Letchers near the turn of the twentieth century in Lexington, Virginia, gaze unflinchingly out of the Michael Miley photograph, fourteen of them. The word that leaps to mind is candor: they do not smile for the camera, but just stare out at me, with disconcerting clarity. It is summer, for the leaves are in full bloom; the year 1899 I have come to by deduction.

They are not a particularly good-looking lot; there is not a one of them whose looks one would *want* to inherit. Their ears are big, their chins in general somewhat too strong. The men are slender, even slight, but the women! — alas, not only are they generally taller than the men and bigger-boned, but also their bodies run to flesh, as my grandmother put it, and as I am unhappily aware.

I know, however, that they are mentally strong, what a sympathetic friend might call *interesting*, but what in fact my mother called *peculiar*. They were an idiosyncratic lot.

They appear neither happy nor unhappy, with the exception of my grandmother, Katie, whose namesake I am: she is twenty-three in the picture, and, though she is hidden modestly behind the rest, I know that in two months she will deliver her firstborn, a son, who will die of influenza at seventeen months, when her second son (whom she also will lose, tragically, just in the flowering of his manhood) is only two months old. She looks stoic and sad, as if she knows already that her pregnancy — and indeed her life — will come to grief, her round black Paul-family eyes the darkest thing in the picture, her mouth held down at the corners. She is even dressed all in black. In contrast, leaning easily and jauntily on her chair is my grandfather, youngest of the governor's children, full of good will and confidence. His bow tie is askew, and his jacket flaps open casually. He looks more — modern — than the rest.

The grim-faced woman in front of Katie, her mother-in-law, widow of the Civil War governor who was my great-grandfather, still wears widow's weeds, as my father says she did until she died. Some sort of tiara tops her white hair. No wonder she looks solemn: while the South was losing the war, ex-Governor Letcher had to go into hiding when the Federal troops occupied Lexington in June of 1864, as a reward had been offered for his capture. She, Susan Holt Letcher, called Sue, was awakened before dawn on June 12 by soldiers delivering a verbal order from General David Hunter that her house was to be burned down, and told she had ten minutes to rouse the family, get dressed, and leave the house. While she waked them all, Union soldiers poured flammable fluid over carpets and furniture. Sue stood in the yard and watched with baby Fannie in her arms, while the Yankees burned her home to the ground with everything in it except what the bluecoats could carry away as their own. By bayonetting the yard, the soldiers found the buried silver and took even that. In the entire town, they burnt only the Virginia Military Institute, which was training soldiers to fight against the Union, and Governor Letcher's house. Him they saw as a turncoat, once a strong abolitionist, who later saw it his duty to represent his constituency, though he was at heart always a Unionist. He is not in the 1899 photograph, having died in 1884, after ten years of disability following a stroke. But Sue Letcher had to build her life up piece by piece after the War, a good deal of it by accepting the charity of neighbors and distant relatives.

Mrs. Letcher, née Mary Susan Holt, had been a doctor's daughter from Middlebrook, a town thirty miles away down the valley.[1] Susan Holt and John Letcher met when she was eighteen, he twenty. Immediately, the affable and energetic John Letcher began a vigorous campaign for her hand. Off, then on again, then off again, with his friends predicting their marriage a full three years before it took place. She appears to have wavered, uncertain, at least once breaking their relationship off totally. He evidently persisted until she agreed. What I want to know, of course, is why she held out for so long: what was it in his personality, or family, or in her own life or nature, that took three long years to resolve? There really are no clues. There were no family crises to prevent their marrying during those years. She and John Letcher were not far apart geographically. He might have chosen someone else, and probably could have, for the accounts of him paint the portrait of a bright, sociable, fun-loving, hardworking fellow — charming in the way that politicians have to be to get elected, and eminently eligible.

But once she accepted his suit, and they were wed, all wavering was over; she committed herself to running his house, wherever that might be, Lexington, Richmond, or Washington, and to bringing up to responsible adulthood their flock of children. Seven survived to relatively old ages.

---

[1] On the map it's up, but the Shendandoah River flows north, and so when you go north, you go "down" the valley.

When she married John Letcher and came to Lexington, Sue could not brook her husband's family's Methodism, and spearheaded the building of Grace Episcopal Church, which stood on the site of the present day Robert E. Lee Memorial Episcopal Church, at the edge of the Washington and Lee campus.

The union must have been happy, as romantic anniversary letters from the governor to his wife survive. Letters from many of the children show a lively interest in politics, and more than a modicum of humor. Mrs. Letcher was regarded as an "exceptional hostess" while they lived in Washington, where her husband was a congressman, and in Richmond during his term as governor of the state. She was known, along with my great-grandfather, as a true democrat, an oddity in the stratified Virginia culture of the times. Of course the Letchers were not aristocrats; they were bourgeois through and through.

Historians and Letcher's biographer tell that no one was a stranger at the governor's mansion, no matter his background or station. The Letchers entertained the Prince of Wales, the son of Albert and Victoria, in Richmond, just before the Civil War. The young man who would become Edward VII of England gave young Lizzie Letcher a watch during the visit. The Letchers also entertained country folk from western Virginia; anyone who was a constituent got an audience. Among the governor's papers is a note from the White House inviting the Letchers to dine with President and Mrs. Buchanan.

Among the surviving letters is one marked "Private," and not in an envelope, addressed only to "My Dear Sir," dated January 5, 1860, immediately before John Letcher's inauguration. It reads, "I received your letter of the 3rd instant, this evening. My duty in this trying time will be discharged fearlessly and independently. My friends have not been deceived in me heretofore, and I feel persuaded they will not be now. I have written my message to suit myself, and will trust to the people for their approval. It will be long, but I have no fears of the popular verdict, upon the views it will embody, in this crisis of public affairs. Kind regards to

Martha, In haste, I am truly, Yr Friend, John Letcher." I don't know how it came to be back in his possession, or whether it was ever sent.

In his excellent biography of Letcher, F. Nash Boney characterizes him as self-taught (he disliked school, and learned the law by reading it in another lawyer's office), witty, open, gregarious and hospitable, sociable and political, a devoted husband and father, whom his constituency affectionately dubbed "Honest John Letcher, Watchdog of the Treasury." The son of a storekeeper and carpenter, John left the formal church early and energetically applied himself to politics once he'd decided that was what he wanted to do. He was criticized for his use of tobacco and for serving bourbon while in the state house. Because John Letcher was florid of complexion, he was accused often of drinking more than he should; family lore has it that this criticism infuriated Mrs. Letcher, who, in spite of her Episcopalianism, did not imbibe at all. Though her husband died in 1884, Mrs. Letcher nearly got to peek into the twentieth century, dying in October of 1899 surrounded by her seven surviving children. Only one, Margaret, lived away, but she visited often.

Sitting to Mrs. Letcher's left in the portrait is Aunt Mag, Margaret Catherine Holt, Sue's younger spinster sister, who moved in with John Letcher and Sue at the time of their marriage, when Mag was a young teenager. She lived her entire life with them, helping to care for their eleven children. Aunt Mag was apparently a docile and pallid lady, properly deferential, loving with the children but never intrusive. My father knew nothing of her personhood except an impression of a quiet presence. He believed his grandfather, the governor, was very fond of her. She died only seven months after her sister did. (Also a former member of the household but no longer alive at the time of the portrait was Elizabeth Yount, Mary Susan and Mag's mother, who had a second marriage early in life, then came to live with her daughters, and died at age eighty-eight in 1889.)

One cannot help wondering why sister Margaret never sought to make a life for herself beyond her sister's household, but that course was common in the nineteenth century. Her life is a reminder to us today that a life of one's own appears to be our concept, not theirs, as does the notion of a right to happiness. Life in the nineteenth century was regarded as a workhouse, often a vale of tears, and certainly not the current smorgasbord of pleasure whence one's right and duty is to grab whatever he can in the way of personal fulfillment. Certainly, from his papers, one can gather that my great-grandfather thought in terms of a life only of service to others, and to his beloved state and country.

John Davidson Letcher is the tall long-faced man standing behind Aunt Mag, and he was always described (even by his own family) as eccentric. In this merely conventionally religious family, John D. was *really* religious, but he didn't get that way until he was past grown. He was a distinguished VMI graduate, married late, and had no children.

In his youth, he went west like so many other single men of his generation, and landed up in Eugene, Oregon, where he decided to become a professor and college administrator. In 1895, he wrote a wonderful letter back to his youngest brother, Greenlee (my Andaddy), who had just opened his law practice, saying "Green, go see Colonel Nichols and tell him to get me a Ph.D. out here immediately. I'm acting President now. There's a Harvard man coming, and if I don't get a Ph.D. he'll get the job." Colonel Nichols was his mathematics teacher who later became the VMI superintendent. Fifteen long letters to Colonel Nichols on the subject went ignored (though filed forever at VMI for eyes like mine to see), and Uncle John lost the job to the Harvard man, noting in one of the last letters that "there are six members of the Board, three mine, and three his. But on the day of the election, all three of mine were absent, one due to death, one sick, and one in the East, and he was unanimously named President." Uncle John later claimed he lost the position because he was a Southern Democrat.

Uncle John, feeling hampered by a mere B.S. in engineering, moved quickly on to jobs in Alabama, Texas, Arkansas, Ohio, Oregon again, Iowa, North Carolina, and finally Norfolk, Virginia. During those years he held positions as a teacher, a construction engineer, and a building engineer for two railroads. Somewhere along the way, he got religion. In Norfolk, in 1908, he had the good luck to meet and marry a religious socialite, Louise Taylor. Aunt Loulie shared Uncle John's passion for the foreign missions of the Episcopal Church, and got him settled down. They lived in Norfolk until her death eight years later.

When Loulie died, Uncle John returned to live out his life in Lexington with his sister Jennie, by then a widow. Family lore claims that he designed the first curved railroad trestle in the world, just below Lexington. Everyone said you couldn't curve a trestle, but Uncle John went right on and did it, and the trestle was built and lasted until the terrible night of August 22, 1969, when the infamous hurricane Camille took it out. Uncle John was the first of the family I know of to wear two hats to church on the coldest days, because (reasoned he) two would be twice as warm as one. Later Andaddy adopted that eminently sensible behavior, crediting his older brother as its originator.

Uncle John's avid interest in the church infuriated the rest of the Letchers, not a particularly churchy lot with the exception of their mother, Sue. His zeal led him when he died to leave all but a small amount of his estate to foreign missions; this so incensed my father that he wrote from Peking to his father as follows: "I was sorry to hear of Uncle John's death, but I was glad that he hadn't suffered at the end. . . . I'm glad I never wrote to him because I would have had to say something about the missionaries and it would have disturbed him I'm afraid. I don't believe anyone who has ever spent any time in China believes that missionaries ever make one convert. . . .The missionaries have a racket and an excellent one. They live well, do little work and must soon realize that they can't really convert a single Chinese. They get pictures of hoards of converts by giving away food, free medical treatment, shelter in cold weather, an opportunity to learn English, but stop these things and they will never get a single convert. The Chinese surpass all people in realism and in absolute realism they have no room for religion as we know it. I received your letter about

Uncle John's death and his will leaving most of his estate to Bible societies, charitable organizations etc. I'm afraid that I don't quite agree with you in your idea that such a disposal of his estate was all right because it was his to do with as he liked. I believe that most of his estate came from Aunt Fannie's and Uncle Hootie's estate didn't it and that such being the case he should have left his property to his relations. To leave them the little that he did seems to me to have been a very wrong thing to do. . . . Feeling as I do about it I would rather not take the money left to me. I want $750 of mine to go to Houston Showell to help him with his boys' education and the remaining $250 to go to Margaret Showell. They both need the money a great deal more than I do and as I say I personally feel that Uncle John did a very wrong thing and feeling that way I'd rather not have any of his money. The clock belonged to the family and not to him so I'll be glad to have that when it comes to me. I'll be able to feel that it came from my grandfather and great grandfather and not from him." In fact, the clock stayed at Andaddy and Nainai's, Mama not wanting to give space to antiques, especially those that did not work.

Aunt Fan, Fannie Wilson Letcher, the huskiest one, the one standing on the right, was born in 1864. She seems to have been, in today's parlance, developmentally delayed. She was sent to Stuart Hall in Staunton, an exclusive boarding school, which is in itself odd for this apotropaically democratic clan, who hardly believed in school at all, and *certainly* not private school — but my father recalled there was something not quite right about Fan, and sending her away may be proof of the Letchers' efforts at correction. Daddy recalled that Fan was reclusive, never married, was shy, and mostly worked in the kitchen. She always retreated to the kitchen when company came. According to Daddy, Fan was always nice to him (she called him Bucky) and his older brother Greenlee (Gee), making them sweets for after-school treats, and baby-sitting for them when their parents went out. Fan herself never went out. But she wouldn't read to them, did not "believe in" stories. She took a special dislike to their favorite book, the *Just So Stories* by Kipling, said the stories were terrible and untrue, and refused to read them. (I wonder now if perhaps she could not read them, and so made their "untruth" her excuse; there is not a single notebook or letter from her at all among the papers.) Aunt Fan, once grown, kept house for her brother Hootie, Sam Houston Letcher, for the rest of their lives.

Margaret, the youngest of the governor's daughters, seated to the viewer's far right just below Fannie, was obviously home from Maryland for a visit on the occasion of the family portrait.

Maggie had married a fellow named Rob Showell, who came to Washington and Lee after the Civil War. His letters to her during their courtship are deliriously eloquent: "Before I knew you I lived entirely in the present, or if I ever thought of the future at all, it was over a misty hiatus of years into a shadowy land of phantoms; but now there is no gap. . . my past is not entirely dead, but will be like the flowers and insects, die in reproducing a future, which can only have birth on the 26th" [their wedding day].

Maggie responds, "A week today since you left, — and it seems an eternity, — you say my letters are short, — I could make them each a volume, I believe, — but somehow the warmth of my feeling seems cold in expression. . . ."

Late in January 1884, she wrote, "Father died last night, quietly, like a child falling asleep. He left the world as unconsciously as he had entered it. He had such strong physical life that I was afraid there would be a terrible struggle when the end came, — but my prayers were answered and we were spared such a harrowing distress."

He took her to White House Farm, in Millsboro, Maryland, to live. In later years, my father said, they were always hard up, and Maggie Letcher Showell, needing the money, worked for many years as postmistress at Ocean City, Maryland.

Maggie's daughter Margaret sits in the forefront of the portrait, looking like a younger version of her mother. She grew up as a Marylander, and today I keep up with her granddaughter.

My father recalled that Maggie and her family visited often, and spent time each summer in Lexington. After Rob died, she returned to Lexington, where she spent the last ten years of her life. She is buried in Lexington with all of her sisters and brothers except Uncle John, who wished to rest in Norfolk beside his wife, even though he lived in Lexington with his widowed sister Jennie for his last seventeen years.

Sam Houston Showell, Maggie's son, a barefoot child of two or three, is leaning on his uncle's knee at the left, in an uncomfortable-looking get-up. In 1916, he will attend Washington and Lee University from his Maryland home. He will live until 1986, the successful proprietor of a mobile home community built on his family's land.

Aunt Jennie, Virginia Lee Letcher (the one in the Hat), was born in Richmond in 1863 while Letcher was governor. She was the only god-daughter Robert E. Lee ever had, by a formal prearrangement. Lee apparently took this duty most seriously. If the baby had been a boy, she was to have been named Robert E. Lee Letcher. She is the one my father always said I take after, and she is hands-down the ugliest of the lot: plump, with a moony, thin-lipped face no less stern than those of the rest, her head topped with an amazing hat that looks more like a whorehouse lampshade than anything else I can think of. At the age of thirty-seven, a year after the portrait, she married Walter le Conte Stevens (1847–1927) from Savannah, Georgia, a diminutive professor of astronomy and physics at Washington and Lee, born of an aristocratic Georgia family. They had two stillborn children and no others, yet the big house they had just built on Letcher Avenue became the central gathering place for the family after Mrs. John Letcher's death, for holiday dinners, weddings, and funerals.

According to my father, Aunt Jennie sang and played the piano, and later the ukelele,[2] was a schoolteacher for most of her life, loved cooking,

---

[2] To my intense delight, I came across Aunt Jennie's own songbook in the four cubic feet of papers I inherited: in it are a dozen songs that I, too, have in my repertoire, including "Lorena," "I'll Remember You, Love, in My Prayers," "Juanita," and "Will You Love Me When I'm Old?"

and adored having dinner parties and big gatherings at her house — all of which I have to admit sound like me.

Though you wouldn't call them snooty, the Stevenses were perhaps a bit more lofty in their tastes than the rest of the family. Uncle Steve, as he was called, boasted openly and often, my father remembered, of his five hundred opera records, and on Sunday afternoons the Stevenses would hold opera parties, with friends gathering in their big living room to listen to *Aida* or *La Bohème* on the windup Victrola. It grieved Uncle Steve that he was prevented from fighting in the Civil War because he had gotten measles. Aunt Jennie's obituary called her "a leader of social activity in Lexington" whose home was "a mecca for college boys and faculty gatherings."

The only story that Daddy could remember about Uncle Steve is rather unfortunate: it seems Dr. Stevens did not believe in tipping, and he once took the train to Lynchburg to hear Frieda Hemple sing, and on the way there he refused to tip the porter. Returning the next day, he fell asleep and slept through his stop, and was outraged that the porter (the same one from the day before) hadn't waked him, thus forcing him to spend another several hours backtracking to get home. Uncle Steve acknowledged that a tip would have saved him money in the end, but refused to see the lesson as anything but a fluke, and certainly no reason to adopt a habit he viewed as evil.

There on the far left holding his nephew is genial Sam Houston Letcher, Uncle Hootie. He seems to have been the all-round pet of the family. A newspaperman and lawyer, he was named for General Sam Houston of Texas, a near kinsman. (The governor's father and Sam Houston were first cousins.) My grandmother Katie, who never warmed up entirely to the rest of the family, adored Hootie. Who fought at fifteen in the Battle of New Market, and lived to tell about it. Who never married, though he attracted and was attracted to women. Who loved good whiskey, Havana cigars, and freedom from marital ties. Who became a circuit judge and a frequent legislator in Richmond. Daddy said that though Hootie liked pretty women, classy women, well-dressed women, he was extremely wary of ever getting mixed up with one on any kind of permanent basis.

Hootie was a favorite of his nephews Buzz and Gee, and used to pay them handsomely to pull the wild onions that sprang up in his lawn each spring.

"Yankees brought 'em," claimed Uncle Hootie, going on to say that there had never been any wild onions in Lexington before the war. "Brought it in the horsefeed," he'd say, clamping his teeth down on his cigar, directing from the porch. "Pull 'em up! Pull 'em up, boys!"

Hootie, who favored whiskey and good living, took it upon himself to get my Daddy and his brother Gee drunk, as a useful lesson, when they were about eight and ten. Gee died before he could make use of Hootie's lesson, but Daddy ignored it, if the tales are true, until one day in his forties when he suddenly decided that drinking was no longer fun, and was causing him to waste large pieces of his life.

There is Aunt Lizzie (Elizabeth Stuart) in the middle, the eldest living child, who as a girl in Richmond during the Civil War corresponded often with her cousin J.E.B. Stuart. She regarded this epistolary relationship as her war effort, a duty she willingly attended to, to cheer up the fellows in the field. Perhaps somewhere those letters still exist. I have never seen them, though my father says she was famous for them. She finally married, when she was forty, a Dr. James Harrison from Louisiana, who taught history and Spanish at Washington and Lee, and wrote at least one book about Spain. He is the little bespectacled man with the droopy moustache, and it was on their front porch, 305 Letcher Avenue, that the photograph was taken. They traveled every summer to Europe, and therefore were in a position to bring to Lexington the cutting edge of European style and chic. In the portrait, Lizzie has a contented and self-confident air, and modish spit curls around her face, perhaps a style she picked up in Europe. My father recalled his Aunt Lizzie as a good cook and housekeeper, with a flair for decorating and a fascination for furniture. Lizzie had, amazingly, three children when she was past forty. The first two were stillborn, but the third, born when she was forty-seven, survived.

In front of Lizzie is that child, age seven, with stick-out ears, frowning as the photographer tells them all to be still. After such trials and this miracle, Lizzie and James doted on that child, and in the picture he leans back familiarly against his Mama's ample lap. His name was John Letcher Harrison, known as Letcher, and there is more of him to come.

Four children born to the Letchers are not in the portrait: the first son, William Holt, was born ailing, and died at six months. Susan Holt died at birth. Mary Davidson died at three, and Andrew Holt died of lockjaw caused by an infected splinter wound when he was ten. Perhaps their little ghosts hover in the foliage of the creeper that surrounds the solemn family posed there on the threshold of the new century.

But in my heart, I want to take after my grandmother Miss Katie, Greenlee's (Andaddy's) young wife, prettier — or at least a lot more delicate-looking — than the rest of them. She was, of course, from another family: the Pauls. No one would have told me, but I think the Pauls were classier folk, closer to *nice* people than to the *good* people that the Letchers were. Her father and brother were both judges, as is her nephew, my first cousin once-removed.

Katie Paul Letcher's first baby, John Paul Letcher, the one she would deliver soon after this portrait, would die, but not before her second son was born (who also would be snatched from her when he was only sixteen). Finally, my father would be born four years hence to this young woman in black in the family portrait, for whom I was named thirty-nine years after this portrait was made. Thirty-nine years after *that*, I named our last child, our daughter, Virginia Letcher Lyle, for Aunt Jennie (the one I was supposed to be so much like).

These are the people who shaped my father. The Letchers are arranged for their portrait spilling off of a porch that still exists. One can see that it was a special occasion: they are all dressed and coiffed carefully. Perhaps they planned it for the time when Maggie would visit with her children, so that they could all be in the picture. Maybe afterwards, they all had lemonade as a sort of celebration.

The abundant Virginia creeper, now of course an unfashionable weed, is long gone. In the foreground of the group portrait is a big century plant, four or five feet across. Perhaps the Letchers saw themselves just on the brink of the new century, and placed the potted plant there as a symbol. Or perhaps the famous photographer of Robert E. Lee, Michael Miley, who took this portrait, dragged the huge agave around in his horse-drawn buggy for sittings, the *prop extraordinaire* for the turning of the twentieth century.

If you have been paying attention, you will have realized that of the seven living children, only one, my grandfather, produced Letchers to carry on into the next generation. He sired three sons, surely enough to assure perpetuity of the name!

But luck was against us, and two of his sons died before they could produce offspring. My father, always aware of his mission (for he talked about it), and the only Letcher to survive to adulthood, dutifully produced four children, including two boys.

But neither of my brothers has sons, though they have fathered five daughters between them. This was something of a concern to our father in his declining years, though on this subject he was as stolidly philosophical as he was on other unalterable events. Daddy, as Mama often said, choked on gnats, but swallowed camels with ease.

Both my sister and I have sons, but their *names* are other than Letcher. And so this is the end of the line, not for our genes, but for our name. I suppose that is one reason why I wanted to write this book. For Daddy was first and foremost a Letcher, and quite capable of giving as the reason why I was not allowed to wear a backless dress, or take a waitressing job, or date certain boys — that I was a *Letcher*. Though I didn't want to hear that, I am sure that it smoothed down the roughest of my edges. I am proud of my family and my name, and it saddens me that the Virginia branch of the Letchers stops here.

Easter, 1949, in front of Andaddy's house.

Misery

*M*y grandparents had no washing machine in 1942, and they must have reckoned that a rough washboard in the bathtub was adequate laundry equipment for a woman with two children, one of them in diapers, the other none too neat. With little money of her own, Mama was more or less their guest, and didn't feel free to protest. It was apparently not in the job description of Nannie, their housekeeper, to do laundry. My grandparents sent theirs out, and it came back in a week or so starched, banded, the sheets perfectly ironed, each shirt folded around cardboard, and all of it beautifully wrapped in big crackly warm brown-paper bundles with string.

Mama declined to do that, feeling it was extravagant, and consequently she spent a lot of time on her knees over the tub resentfully but self-righteously scrubbing diapers. Now I wonder if she weren't making her situation impossible to give us a compelling reason to move.

Mama once wondered aloud to our next-door neighbor Prissy Flournoy if the socks and nightgowns, shirts and long johns, Andaddy and Nainai sent to be laundered came back from the Lexington Steam Laundry monogrammed. I did not understand why they both laughed.

I knew how Mama loathed living at Nainai and Andaddy's, but I didn't care; I loved it.

But move we did, to an apartment half a mile away. Until Daddy's return from the War, Mama would maintain a separate residence. I knew Andaddy felt that she was wasting money, and it made Nainai unhappy. But they couldn't do anything about it.

IN 1947 I GUESS NONE OF US REALLY KNEW we were in Lexington to stay until Nainai's death made moving impossible. After her funeral when Daddy finally mentioned our big plans, Mama refused, point blank, to even discuss moving to the farm. It was short-sighted of her, but she wouldn't even go out and look at it. If she was going to have to live here, she wanted to be in town, where her friends were, and she didn't want mud tracked in the house, and she wasn't going to live in the mess of farm animals, and the house was unlivable, he'd already admitted that. She wouldn't tolerate being cold. That was that.

Daddy said fine, we would live in town, all right, *in this house.* He prevailed over Mama's adamant protests. We would arrange the house, he declared, so that we would have the entire second floor, except for Andaddy's bedroom. We would take one room on the first floor as our living room. Andaddy had Nannie but still needed looking out for now that Nainai was gone. Rent was free, Daddy couldn't find any other work than farming that he wanted to do, and since Mama wouldn't even talk about the farm, we'd stay right here.

At that point, Mama agreed to go look at the farm, for she was caught between a rock and a hard place. She minded Andaddy's house, its darkness, its dirt, its space that would never be hers. Her father-in-law offended her. Though she dreamed of a Spanish-style bungalow in town, maybe she relented, given the alternatives.

But then suddenly someone else bought the farm for cash, and the choice was made for her. Daddy ranted and raged about the son of a bitch who'd do a thing like that, and then blamed Mama. If he'd bought it when *he* wanted, we'd have it now. Day and night they wrangled about it. She took the others and went back to Norfolk.

DARKNESS HAS DESCENDED. Daddy can't sit at the table, and gets up and paces the floor, swearing. "We don't have any other choice," he says. "This is a perfectly good house. It's almost empty."

Andaddy nods, chewing a mouthful of cold roast pork left over from lunch. "It's only sensible to stay right here, Buzz. Don't worry, she'll be back. It's silly to think of moving anywhere else, and think of all the money you can save living here. You're perfectly welcome here. Here, come on, Buzz, eat your supper." Nannie goes home at three, and we have to make do for supper unless we cook it ourselves.

Late into the night after Andaddy's gone to bed, Daddy talks to me, to himself. "Mama hates this house. I guess she's not used to houses like this. But she ought to be grateful. Dammit to hell, she could be out on the street. A lot of people don't have any place to live."

"I love it," I say, both because I do and because I want to win his approval. But he doesn't notice.

"You should have seen some of the places I had to live in the south Pacific," he says.

I nod.

"This house was good enough for Mudder and Pop," he says.

It seems in the end of no consequence to him that Mama hates that Victorian house with its horsehair chaises, its fringed purple velvet couches, its busts of the governor and dreary dark law books and nineteenth-century landscapes and unsmiling portraits, some of them of *saints*. "It's a roof over our heads," Daddy says, "and we're damn lucky to have it!"

I CULTIVATED MY FUTURE: I still planned to be a famous anything, bonne *vivante, femme fatale*, actress, singer, poet. I must have been an odd sight: tall for my age, blonde and pale, riddled with infected flea or mosquito bites half the year, no idea at all what to do about myself. I was crazy about chiffon scarves, and devised ways to wear them as belts or necklaces or headgear. Mama was big on nice manners, so all her children were carefully schooled in how to act at the table, when we met a grown, when someone older entered a room. She ordinarily made us bathe every other day.

But in matters of beauty and glamour, I had no teachers. I emulated, as best I could, Kitty Wells, Dinah Shore, Doris Day. I owned dozens of lipsticks, bought or stolen, eye makeup, and dark tan leg lotion which I liked to think camouflaged the runny sores from the tormented mosquito bites on my legs. I pinned socks inside my dresses and sweaters to simulate the swelling breasts of my idols. My hair, always long and thin and stringy, I could never, no matter how many hours I spent on it, get to approach whatever upsweep or mass of curl I was trying to achieve.

I roamed hours and hours alone in the vast woods behind my grandfather's house and sometimes consorted with the hoboes that camped along the tracks, who might tell me a ghost story about an engineer who saved a train *after* he had been killed. . . . *Of course after he was killed they got a new engineer. On the third day of the green engineer's run, a man appeared suddenly, out of the twilight, waving a lantern frantically in front of his train. The new engineer slowed down, thanked him, and watched as he appeared to vanish in thin air. Just ahead the track had washed out in a heavy downpour. Without doubt, it would have wrecked his train without the warning.*

When the new engineer got safely back to the roundhouse and described his savior, down to the length and color of his beard, and the plaid bandanna he wore, everyone was amazed, and recognized it as the engineer who'd been killed several days before.

AND SOMETIME IN THE MISERY OF FEBRUARY, MAMA CAME BACK, BRINGING Johnnie and Betsy and Pete. This time there was no fanfare. Daddy put a chicken-wire fence around the big front yard, built a wonderful sandbox with benches at both ends for the babies. But the twins used to stand jammed together in the corner nearest the house, yelling, "We don't have anybody to play with!"

Daddy never did find another job, though he didn't stop looking. He did some freelance surveying, a skill he'd learned at VMI. He still wanted to farm, and from time to time would come home excited and animated about a lovely one he'd seen that day, but Mama pricked his bucolic balloon every time.

"A dirt road? Absolutely not."

"Twenty miles from town? Never."

"No heat? Are you crazy?"

"An outhouse? An *outhouse*?" She, city girl, would have none of it: not the dirt, not the distance, certainly not the cows and horses and sheep and inconvenience, absolutely not a dog. I spent a lot of time in my room practicing the ukelele they'd bought me for my ninth birthday.

Coming back to live in Lexington stressed us almost to the breaking point. Daddy, bereft of his ten zillion spiffy obedient soldiers, tried to replace them with the small Marine Corps of his family. He was hell-bent on rules. As wonderful as she'd been to me, Nainai had failed to teach her son to temper rules with compassion.

As Mama said, Daddy strained at gnats. All I saw on a day-to-day basis was his fury at Lord knows what. At anything. All the gnats. I think he felt out of control. We lived with his father, in a house owned by his father, that he hadn't earned. There was never enough money. Mama was too tired to companion him. He tried to spiff us up, everything from square corners on our beds to cleanliness inspections at meals. Hell, we didn't even *make* our beds until he came back. *Square corners?*

Sullenly we mutinied. In little ways, we got even. We dawdled, we "forgot." None of us shaped up. None of us passed inspection. None of us ever got promoted. And his mother, supremely gentle for all her fierce protests about being a good hater, the only one he ever really heeded, was gone.

Daddy predicted darkly that we would never see adulthood, being so untoughened, so soft, preferring hamburger to venison, cowering in our overheated rooms, in our disgusting beds with soft mattresses and feather comforters, whining about rides to school on rainy days.

But he didn't leave; he never abandoned us; he didn't crack up from the strain of a huge family after the strain of war; he never again took up the alcohol they'd left behind in Peking, nor the cigarettes; and he never looked at another woman. It was things like the square corners on the beds of his six- or ten-year olds that got to him.

A SOLITARY ISLAND IN THIS SOUTHERN SEA of Appalachian small-town culture, Mama often sat alone, sewing or quilting, later painting with a mayonnaise jar of water streaked with sunset or sky colors, listening to soft classical music on the radio or the Victrola, a modern one she'd bought herself after the war that played the new slowed-down, long-play records.

When Daddy discovered the pleasures of the Victrola, he bought Sousa marches, German drinking songs, Jimmy Rodgers singing railroad songs, and some funny monologues he adored by an illiterate racist preacher called Brother Dave Gardner. Mama shuddered at them all. But Daddy didn't notice. He moved right in on her machine. If he was playing it, she couldn't. She sighed, moved into a back room, but held in her anger for the most part.

AT SOME POINT, MAMA ANNOUNCED that she could not and would not go on without a washing machine.

Daddy said Andaddy thought washing machines were frivolous confounded contraptions.

Mama said she didn't give a damn what Andaddy thought. Daddy said they were living in Andaddy's house, and had to observe his wishes.

The row went on for weeks, and the outcome was bizarre. Mama had something like a nervous breakdown, and had to go away for several weeks for a rest, to some center somewhere. I couldn't do the laundry in addition to everything else I did, all the cooking, much of the baby care, plus my schoolwork. Johnnie was too little. Daddy tried it, but the diapers got to be too much, and his disposition deteriorated. He'd rise from bending over the stinky diapers and rippled washboard down in the bathtub, his face red as a beet, suds dripping down his elbows, swearing. And the twins got rashes on their bottoms, which he took as a personal insult.

Daddy saw what Mama was up against, but was still reluctant or afraid to go against his father's wishes.

He fretted with me about it while we cleaned up the kitchen at night, and finally took a coward's way out.

How he arranged it I don't know, but one night at midnight, a wringer washing machine was delivered, hoisted on ropes all the way to the second story, over the porch rail, and into a window over the back porch, all while Andaddy slumbered in his bedroom at the front of the house. It was imperative that Andaddy not find out we had a washing machine.

As far as I know, he never did. It was very secret and exciting, and my job was to feed the diapers through the wringer. Soon after the washing machine arrived, Mama came home again.

Now I wonder if she got the idea from Nainai.

Extended family was the norm for Greenlee, whose aunt had lived with them all his life, in addition to all his doting older brothers and sisters who were in and out of each other's houses and pockets all the time. Aunt Mag apparently lived happily and helpfully with her sister's family for her entire life.

But in 1898 when Greenlee Letcher and Katie Seymour Paul were married, and they moved in with Lizzie, his oldest sister who by then lived alone in a big house, this did not sit well with my grandmother, who wanted her own house. After her first child died and she had a second baby, she urged to her husband her sister-in-law's removal, first gently, then more firmly.

When my grandfather, vaguely promising her a house "soon," appeared to be not tak-

ing her seriously, Katie Paul Letcher took herself and tiny Gee to Philadelphia on the train to visit some friends, and once there, wrote back to her husband that when the promised house was complete, she would return. That was in the spring of 1902, and it got his attention.

While she sojourned in Philadelphia, her husband got the sixteen-room house planned and drawn up, the foundation and cellar dug, the house built, all three stories of it, pocket doors, hand-carved woodwork, four porches, eight fireplaces, formal front staircase and narrow hidden rear staircase — in three months. Katie returned serenely to her new, own house with her gorgeous red-cheeked curly-headed, black-eyed baby, and was soon pregnant again, this time with my father, who was born in December of 1903, and named for her brother Seymour Paul.

MAMA TRIED AFTER THE WAR to take up her war-time friendships where they'd left off, but Daddy disapproved of all her friends for one reason or another. She'd associated mostly with newcomers like herself, people from elsewhere who, like her, were forced to be in this off-the-beaten-track cultural backwater.

Almost all of the women Mama liked were artsy-craftsy for the time, wore loopy earrings, bright lipstick, permed hair, and sewed patchwork quilts or painted flowers or landscapes; none was pale or meek; every single one of them had made it through the war without their husbands, and they were a sassy lot.

Mama would have liked to continue to move in that liberated direction, but plainly she could not; Daddy would have killed her rather than let her become outspoken and independent. He accused her of letting her radical friends put ideas into her head; and when a couple of them actually got involved in local politics, he ranted and raged that running for office was something no womanly woman would ever do. It was easy to discount them all as stupid: the fact that none of them made their own money was enough. But if they had made their own money, they would have been uppity. His own mother seemed to be the only woman he ever readily admitted to admiring. Perversely, he admired his mother for the edge she had: he loved the story about her going off until the house got built. But if Mama had tried it, he would probably have had a fit. Mama just got sick; he couldn't touch her then.

Some of her women friends Mama had over anyhow, when he went fishing, for she needed to talk, and she loved sewing and embroidery, later quilting and painting.

"He needs a job," Mama said. "If he would just get a job!" She'd talk to her friends to relieve her mind, and they all urged her to insist on more independence. Mama's salvation was her ability to talk out her problems. She fumed about his taking over the kitchen or making her friends feel unwelcome. They just came when he was not home.

Daddy, in addition to putting every spare dollar into the burgeoning stock market, had struck on land acquisition as a way of passing time; he amused himself with buying up parcels of mountain land on which ownership had become unclear and taxes had not been paid for several years. He became skilled at tracing deeds in the courthouse, running down lost relations and right-of-ways. Sometimes he and I would walk those tracts, picking blackberries or just seeing what was there. Mostly it was useless inaccessible steeps choked with boulders and laurel thicks and scrubby juniper trees that wouldn't support mountain goats. But he couldn't resist the prices, nearly free, and accumulated lots of mountain land. On one piece, he put a drive-in theater, and on another, a stock-car race track. Both made him right much money but caused him continual aggravation. And he followed the stock market, bought and traded stocks wisely, and began to accumulate a fortune. He also wrote; he worked on the story of his Marine Corps years, and on another recollection of how Lexington had been when he was a boy. Both efforts led to self-published books. A third manuscript, a novel about his adventures in Nicaragua, never got finished.

I both wanted to go on walks with him, and at the same time did not. I loved the woods, and found everything in them of interest: the flowers, the trees, the mushrooms, the streams, with crawfish and mint, the smells, the tracks, the droppings of different animals. I loved nothing better than to piddle around in a creek, turning rocks over to try to catch crawfish. We'd dig wild ginger root and take it home and candy it by boiling it for hours with sugar. We made sassafras tea, pink and pungent. We'd hardly ever go out that we didn't arrive home with a hatful of berries, or ten crawfish in a coffee can that we'd boil at home to lobstery redness, shell, and dip the tails in mayonnaise. In the spring, we'd come home with pockets full of morels.

On these trips, I might hear about someone who lived off down that road who killed his wife and kept her body in the house for twenty years, or Selim the Algerian who'd been found wandering naked right near where we were, during the French and Indian War. How this view was called Buena Vista because Lee had fought in the Battle of Buena Vista during the Mexican War, and this view later reminded him of the hills of Buena Vista, Mexico. Or how George Washington himself had once owned the very land we were tramping on!

I was as crazy as Daddy was about the heady summer perfume of Rockbridge County: cows, spearmint, faint ghost of skunk, the sweet heart-breaking smell of honeysuckle. There wasn't a plant Daddy didn't know, a trick he couldn't do — blowing a harsh green-heron rasp on a grass blade held taut between the heels of both hands, the plump of both thumbs. He knew just how to pinch off a honeysuckle blossom, draw the stamen down carefully through the tube of petals backwards, forcing the nectar into a fat drop at the base of the flower, that you could catch on your tongue. He could skim a rock so many times you'd lose count. He'd produce a paper bag from one back pocket, a pocket knife from the other, and hold me down over a creekbed by my heels so I could cut watercress, and we'd take it home, muddy triumphant hunters and gatherers.

But trips with Daddy had once more become dangerous: if I did not walk fast enough, or hold my water long enough, he might (or, unpredictably, sometimes might not) grow irritated. If I whined that my eyes were full of spiderwebs, or asked him to wait while I untied my shoe and got a rock or a cleaving burr out, it might put him in a mood for the rest of the trip. If I dared to complain of hunger or thirst, I'd likely call down a lecture on the subject of spoiled modern children. If a crawfish pinched me, and I let it go with a yell, I was a sissy.

WE ARE IN THIS CREEK, in it, both of us, and he is brandishing a black net, showing me how to hold it. The water is too swift to see what's coming. I'm braced against two rocks, and it is my job to position the net to catch the hellgrammites, the awful larvae with sharp pincers, that could come tumbling down into my net. He is going to flush them out by upending and turning over rocks. He will use the hellgrammites for fish bait, piercing the squirming bodies with a fishhook as though they were not alive, not suffering.

I can't get out of this, and only hope no hellgrammites will appear. But of course they do, and a big one tries to crawl up toward my hand, and so I drop the net, jerk my leg away from something brushing it underwater, and collapse into the cold stream hollering. Shrieking, I grab for the net half-heartedly, and it too disappears in the tumbling current.

His anger flares like a brushfire; he stands over me and tells me I am the most disappointing child in the world, a total failure. *What?* he demands, not expecting an answer, *is wrong with you?* Wet and miserable, shaking from fear and cold, I tremble below his rage. I will have to walk all the way back to the car wet.

DADDY HAD A FEW FRIENDS he fished and hunted with, but they never came to the house. One time, he persuaded Mama to invite some fishing buddy of his and the buddy's wife to dinner; before the dinner, he'd told us excitedly about how lovely Mrs. X was, what a wonderful housekeeper, mother, wife, et cetera, and how we all were going to like her so much!

But, perhaps predictably, Mama and the other lady had nothing in common, and the dinner party went badly, with long stiff silences between mouthfuls.

And for months afterwards, Mama would tell us how *awful* the other wife was, how *boring*, and how she *put out her cigarette in the middle of that expensive steak!* It was Mama's only way of getting even.

When I was twelve, I won a Keep Virginia Green poster contest, a trip to a banquet in Roanoke, and a check for the unbelievable amount of sixty dollars. Joyously, I bought presents for the entire family while I was in Roanoke for the banquet where I was given the check. I was so sure they would love everything: a chemistry set for Johnnie, a beautiful blue silk scarf with flowers for Mama, leather gloves for Daddy, an expensive doll for Betsy, a fire engine for Pete. For myself, I bought a new trash can for my newly coordinated bedroom, thirty-nine cents. I felt full of bounty and generosity with all my packages, and could not wait to get home and bestow them.

But Daddy's eyebrows rose in alarm, and I had to endure once again the story of Letcher Harrison, Daddy's profligate uncle. Daddy never even opened the gloves.

When I was about thirteen, Daddy was persuaded to take on the junior wardenship of the Episcopal church, but he came home and complained that the preacher and the choir were all wife-swapping on the sly. I was indignant; I was in the choir, and I wasn't aware of any of the shenanigans he was so sure about.

On that one, I made up my own mind. I couldn't see any wife-swapping (though I was aware of flirtations in the choir between people who weren't married to each other). I was sure he was wrong. I began to wonder what else he might be wrong about, and that didn't help our relationship much.

The house Daddy built for Mama.

New House

13

ndaddy teaches me Las Vegas Solitaire, so that I will never gamble. I have to keep track. I "pay" fifty-two dollars for a shuffled deck, or a dollar a card, and get five dollars back for every card I can retrieve out of the deck by only going through the cards once. It looks like great odds: really, all I need to retrieve are eleven cards out of fifty-two to come out ahead. If I can get them all, I of course get a whopping $260. But soon, according to my notebook entries, I am hundreds of dollars in arrears, and then thousands. Though I occasionally come out ahead (with twelve or thirteen cards), never once in all these years, thousands and thousands of games, have I ever won back the whole deck. I still play Las Vegas Solitaire, and I know that no matter how good the odds look, a gambler is bound to lose.

FINALLY MAMA PUT HER FOOT DOWN, demanded her own house. Andaddy's house was filthy, and she couldn't clean it the way she liked. She couldn't bear the damn furniture. The stairs hurt her back. She couldn't see to sew. She couldn't entertain. She wanted a place where she could do what she liked.

The arguments raged night and day; there was no sense, Daddy said, in moving from that big old house that everyone loved except Mama, unless we got a farm, and raised our own food.

She wouldn't move to a farm, she said, repeating for the umpteenth time that she didn't want chickens in the hall, mud tracked in, children clamoring to get driven to town every minute. What she really wanted was a tropical beach with a Spanish bungalow. "I followed you around in the service; now I want a house of my own, is that too much to ask?"

It was indeed. Daddy said, mustering support at the supper table, that we could have lots of pets on a farm, and we all cried, "Oh, please, please let's get a farm!" Mama rose angrily from the table, and swept off to the sink, dishes in both hands. Once I reminded her how she'd loved animals when she was young, in Haiti and Nicaragua; she ran out of the room crying. I went after her, to try to apologize, but she locked her door and wouldn't speak to any of us until the next day.

And their furniture arguments stretched out over months. Mama would announce she wanted a new sofa, that the old one was unsightly. She would tell Daddy she'd found the one she wanted at Schewel's, for three hundred dollars.

"Three hundred dollars!" he'd thunder. "That's ridiculous. We have an attic full of sofas. I'll get you down one of them."

"You know I hate antiques," she'd say categorically. "I don't want anything antique. I want the one at Schewel's." She was going to stand firm, let him know what she thought of the dark, carved, and overstuffed Victorian bad-taste junk his family had.

"You find one for one hundred dollars," he'd retort, stung at her rejection of his family's furniture. "We're not made of money." Mama's fury surprised him, hurt him, miffed him, then finally angered him.

Weeks might go by with variations of this conversation. Eventually, a new sofa would appear that had cost what he gave her to spend, but which she disliked because it was a cheaper sofa than the one she'd wanted, and which he disliked because it was such a waste of money.

I hated their bickering, and actively tried to think of ways to block it. "Mama," I'd say, "help me make a suit for church." "Daddy," I'd say. "Let's go on a walk. Aren't the persimmons ripe?"

MAMA GOT SICK AGAIN, AND WENT AWAY TO SOME HOSPITAL, THIS TIME FOR several weeks, and when she came back, the house was going up in the back yard, twenty-five feet behind Andaddy's. Perhaps she was copying Nainai's trick from a half-century before.

The new house cost under nine thousand dollars and was as cut-cornered and ugly a box as could be imagined. Mama hated it from the outset. Grimly she demanded modern furniture, and got the absolute cheapest. She had wanted a house all on one floor. This one had three, if you counted the basement. Mama wanted airy Spanish style with rounded arches; this house had no style at all. There would be no landscaping, because Daddy said roots would undermine the foundation. A giant black walnut tree left standing in the side yard assured that there would be nothing but roots and bald ground anywhere near the house on that side.

Mama, not liking the house, did little or nothing to it, tending to line up seashells from their winter trips to Florida on the plain mantelpiece. That was it for embellishment. Not one chair or bedstead, not one dish or linen towel, from Andaddy's, was in that house. Chinese plates and lamps she'd bought in Peking made their way back from the packing crates into the house.

Daddy moved beehives into the front yard, down along the fence that had disappeared under honeysuckle. He fooled with them all the time, hanging the huge combs in cheesecloth from pulleys rigged up in the kitchen, so that the honey dripped silently down into brown-gold pools, and the cellar shelves groaned with quarts of dark fragrant honey, more every year.

He used to treat his single fig tree like a baby: he built a stone terrace for it, and planted it in a protected southwest-facing ell of the house (which I suspect he planned with that fig tree in mind) right up close to the house.

On winter nights, he'd haul out mountains of old quilts, parkas, and tarps, and wrap blankets over and around its low spreading limbs. He'd make charcoal fires and set them in buckets near it, and go out in the night to worry over the shrub. If you looked out an upper window, you could see his breath in great puffs in the air, and his bare feet sticking out from under his overcoat as he patted and pushed and tucked that tree around. Most years he succeeded in getting a pretty good crop of figs, which he kept count of and did not really like to share. He adored figs, and they were unobtainable around here. Today, I understand that: there are hard-to-get things that I don't like to share either. But at the time, I felt it was terrible.

MAMA HAD LONG DESIRED A FUR COAT, which Daddy took to be an extravagant and foolish notion. Mama's Chinese rabbit coat had shed all its hair after a few years in the Occident, and now was balding in patches.

For a long time this Platonic fur coat she wanted had been a point of mutual irritation and acrimonious suppertime discussion. Mama said she didn't see why she couldn't have one. Daddy said a fur coat was a waste of money, that the winters weren't cold enough to warrant spending such an amount. One day, after some brilliant burst of inspiration, Daddy announced he was going to make her one, a beaver coat. She said absolutely not.

But that didn't make any difference to Daddy. Undampened, he drew a pattern on brown paper; four hides for the back sewn together to make a large squarish rectangle; four for the front, the two lefts sewn together, the two rights sewn together. Out from the top hides would go two under, two over, for each sleeve. The pattern, which would take sixteen beaver skins, looked like a fat letter T.

My mother walked by the pattern lying out on the dining room table, turned up her nose in disgust, and refused to show any interest at all, which in no way deterred Daddy. "You'll see," he said confidently. "It'll be beautiful, just wait."

He bought a book called *Beaver and Otter Trapping*, and ordered up some pungent herby-smelling perfume called Hawbaker's Beaver Lures, which must have worked fantastically, for soon he had trapped the requisite sixteen fat beavers. Carefully, he skinned them, leaving them without more than four holes in each hide.

We had roast beaver, Daddy extolling the virtues of those clean-living animals while consuming the pile of greasy meat. The rest of us piled our plates with cabbage and potatoes and *Hmmmed!* and nodded agreeably when he exclaimed how wonderful it was. I couldn't make the single mouthful go past my throat. I don't think anyone else even tried.

Then he read up on tanning, and concluded that human urine was the cheapest available tanning agent. Urine was used worldwide, too, and he liked being associated with the Chinese, the Indians, and all those fine folks back there in history. He liked talking about his project, too.

Cheerfully, for an entire summer, he loaded up on water at night, quaffing several quarts before going to bed, and all night he made the trips down the steps, out into the back yard, where the vat of beaver hides stood against the wood shed, where we could hear him urinating voluminously and volubly onto those sixteen hides. Everyone else in the neighborhood heard him, too. It gave them something to *tsk* about over coffee. I was a little horrified, but I also thought it was funny, and regaled my friends with the story.

The rest is anticlimax; the coat, while marginally serviceable, had exactly the same shape as his pattern: a fat T. Thus it had no shape a woman would want, as well as no lining. Daddy sewed the seams by hand. It had brown leather buttons with loops of black thread opposite them. And it never stopped smelling of urine at the least hint of moisture or body heat, so of course Mama wouldn't have anything to do with it.

MAMA WANTED THE FRONT PORCH SCREENED so she could watch the sunset without getting mosquito-bitten. Instead, Daddy closed in the front porch with some aluminum siding halfway up, and cheap aluminum windows all around that were supposed to open to screen windows, but would not, as Daddy somehow put them in backwards. The room that resulted was hot as the hinges in summer, gelid and damp in winter. Mama naturally loathed it.

Daddy or I brought home a succession of scroungy flea-ridden cats that lived with us a while before getting run over or succumbing to worms, or mostly just disappearing. Soot, Blackie, Pinky, Tiger, Snowball, or Smokey, it was up to me to name them. No question of taking one to a vet; if they got sick, they died. Cats Mama would tolerate; they looked sleek and pretty lying in the sun, and they were clean.

Daddy knew better than to even bring up the possibility of a dog, though occasionally he'd admit to me a longing for one. He thought a dog would be a good woods-tramping companion. Mama's disdain for dogs was magnificent and famous, and she could make anyone dislike them. "They lick their privates in public!" she'd point out, "and then they come lick you." "They eat their own upchuck!" she'd say. "As soon as you get them clean, they go out and roll in other dogs' BM's!" she'd go on. Of course by then none of us wanted a dog.

Daddy bought two lambs each year. The front yard of the house stretched a quarter mile down to the creek between VMI and Washington and Lee, and Daddy hating mowing. The lambs were the answer: they cropped the lawn. To keep them from roaming, he fenced in the whole sloping front yard in mesh wire, just as he'd earlier fenced in the yard in front of Andaddy's. We'd name the sheep, and play with them until the novelty wore off. In the fall, Daddy would butcher them.

And every fall one of the children would ask mournfully, over the first leg of lamb of the season, "Is this Mimi or Ewe-ewe?" or "Who is this, Blackie or Whitie?"

THE NEW HOUSE HAD A HALF-BASEMENT intended optimistically as a playroom for the children, which quickly got taken over with Daddy's collectibles, Daddy's Japanese telescope, Daddy's surveying instruments, Daddy's canned goods, Daddy's workshop, Daddy's hunting and fishing gear. And woe to the child who broke anything of his while playing in the basement. So we never did. It was dark and smelly anyway, with a sump pump smack in the middle of the floor, just behind the concrete post which kept the dining room from falling in.

I tried once in junior high school to turn it to its intended use, that is, to have a teenage record hop down there. I cleaned up and stacked things carefully. We danced to a record, "The Stars Will Remember," and I leaned on Ronnie Ordel's shoulder, smelling his Mennen's and dreaming my way to grownhood.

"Turn those lights back on!" Daddy roared down the stairs. "What's all that jumping around? Stop it!" "Chick! Get up here. Who's car's that blocking mine?" "Coca-Cola? I told you never to bring Coca-Cola into this house!"

I barged up the stairs to try to shush him, turned up the lights, and we went on. I assured him I wasn't having any Coca-Cola. I went back down and made everyone put out their cigarettes, knowing that would be the next thing he'd yell about.

Daddy, as unembarrassed as he'd been peeing on the beaver hides or riding the trolley in his baggy wool bathing trunks, ended the evening of my party doing what he did every winter night; he drained the water out of the car radiator, so the engine would not freeze. Anti-freeze was available, but it seemed to him ridiculous to spend money on it. He preferred spending hours under the car watching the water drip out. In the morning he'd carry out two gallons of hot water from the kitchen and refill the radiator. His odd economies were already the bread and butter of Mama's sewing and quilting friends, but on that night, I remember all the boys at my dance huddled open-mouthed at the little cellar window that gave on to the gravel lot where General Letcher was actually *doing* what everyone said he did. That and the beaver coat made his reputation among my friends.

Later in the evening, a boy pulled his date over into the dark part of the basement behind the concrete post for a kiss, and stumbled into the well that held the sump pump in the darkness. Daddy came charging down as the sump pump started up, ranting and grumbling, demanding to know who had done what. The boy held his ankle and moaned, while the girl put on a marvelous display of Bereft Girlfriend. Mama and I drove the boy (and the weepy girl) to Dr. Brush's house, where the ankle was decreed to be sprained. We then took the boy home, and drove the girl back to the party. But when we got back to our house, the basement was all cleared out. Silence, the ghost of cigarette smoke, and nothing else. Daddy had gone to bed.

Me at 10.

King Lear

*T*he second day we were in Lexington, May 12, 1943, just in the middle of the war, was my fifth birthday. Nainai invited the two boys my age, David Foster and Cabell Flournoy, who lived on either side of my grandparents' house, to come for ice cream and cake. David, a gentle solemn kid with glasses, brought me a toy that had been his: a realistic stuffed bear on wheels. I loved that bear wildly, fiercely, until its skin was rubbed hairless, and it got a hole and all its sawdust drizzled out. The other boy, Cabell, was not to my liking. He sneered, seeming impolite and unsporting. He wouldn't play house. And he said, "If you come in my yard, my dog will eat you up!"

"Don't be scared of him," Nainai told me later. "You have to learn to be a good hater. Just hold your head up, and go on. Stare him down. Bullies are cowards. He won't do anything to you. And neither will that loudmouth cur of theirs."

I turned summersaults for everyone by way of entertainment. This shocked Andaddy, who started in that first day with his maxims: "Horses sweat and men perspire, but Little Sweetheart, ladies don't do either!"

I DID ALL I COULD TO LIVE UP TO MY IMAGE OF MYSELF AS POET, movie star, fairy or druid princess, clad in gossamer, moss, peacock feathers, fog, and cloth of gold. The best I could do on my allowance was collect and wear, as ingeniously as I was permitted, those Japanese silk scarves available at Newberry's for twenty-nine cents apiece. When I lacked money, I stole them. Mostly, I was a writer.

I never had much competition. It just so happened that I was the only person in my grade interested in being a writer. So whenever there was a class play to be written, or a May Day skit, I was automatically elected. It was early assumed by teachers and peers alike that I would edit any publication there was to be edited.

I'd slid easily back into that quartet of girls I'd met in first grade, unstable as a hydrogen atom, in which I jockeyed for top position. I longed fiercely to be as pretty as Tut, as sweet as Susan, as smart as Jeanne. Tut's hair was soft, brown, and naturally wavy, and her ways were ladylike, as mine never were. Susan genuinely loved her dolls, her animals, and her mother, and grieved for a younger sister's death at birth; I secretly admired her compassion and pure heart, for I possessed neither. Jeanne simply didn't notice or care if someone didn't like her, or might be mad at her, and I wanted for myself the lofty strength of her unconcern. In addition, Jeanne's enthusiasm for reading *Lamb's Tales* from Shakespeare and Rumer Godden novels and whole long Victorian novels I could not even fake. It especially galled me that Jeanne, who didn't care at all, made consistently higher grades than I did.

For myself, I was a tangled net of monsters dragged up from the sea depths and examined in the light of my friends' superior personalities: I was homely, had straight hair and limbs as cratered with mosquito bites as the full moon, knew my heart was evil, wished mortal harm on my mild brother, was always mad at my father, and was daily in agony over what people thought of me. It seemed I was a lightweight in every department that mattered.

A lady named Mrs. Lee advertised that she would motor up from

Roanoke to teach ballet to the young ladies of Lexington on Saturday mornings, in the Pine Room at the Mayflower Hotel. On the first day, standing in a dirty white tutu with her hair twisted back into a mean knot, she said to me, in the foreign accent she faked, "Mees Letcher, you have zee grace of the zee wounded water-buffalo."

Of course I never went back for the second lesson, though I followed for two years, feigning scorn, every *plié* and *develope*, every tutu, every fluff of lamb's-wool shoe stuffing of the others who stuck it out, grace or none. They had recitals for the parents, followed by parties with ginger ale and lime sherbet punch, and I was as green as that punch with envy and frustration. I got invited to the recitals, but I'd rather have died than shown any interest.

EACH AFTERNOON AFTER SCHOOL, I'd go to Jeanne's or she'd come home with me, and we'd draw paper-doll dresses and listen to Clyde Beatty, or Bobby Benson and the B-Bar-B Ranch, or Straight Arrow. And I practiced singing songs and playing the ukelele. I was going to be a famous singer, like Dinah Shore (as well as a famous writer). Jeanne, a fine musician, was tolerant of my pitiful talents, and was glad to pick out tunes for me on the piano, as well as teach me both parts of Chopsticks so we could play it together.

Thus was I more or less channeled by circumstance into my future. Since I had no interest in sports, especially horseback riding, where the serious competition raged, I wandered around in the woods a lot, feeling poetic, and wrote things like, "The music o'er the Sunday rock/ Made hymns more beautiful than Bach." The fascination the others had with horses was to me kind of like the virgin birth; maybe someday I'd understand it, but so far it didn't make any sense.

I'D LEARNED EARLY TO BE A SECRET LISTENER, learned to look up from my books with an idiotic stare to assure the growns that I wasn't in the least aware of what they were talking about. I learned not to answer when called by name until the second time. Learned to lie on the floor pretending to draw, as still, as invisible as a cat. For only that way did I get to hear interesting stuff. Mama, unlike Nainai and Andaddy and Daddy, didn't think children ought to hear everything. A lot of the most interesting stuff turned out to be about our next-door neighbor, Fitz Flournoy, Cabell's father.

In a town where the phone numbers were still in two digits, there was not much that everybody didn't know. For instance, when someone would call Central, and ask for five-eight, Mary Poke Hatwell's number, Central was likely to say, "Oh, Mary Poke isn't home today. Her car conked out this morning, and she's over at Lloyd Bowling's garage getting it fixed."

So that was one thing: listening. Another was that, early on, my writing brought me fame, and people politely asked me about it. My mother carried home this intelligence from what Andaddy called The Chatting and Tatting Club. They'd started during the war, a loose-knit group of women doing what they could for the war effort, and had such a grand time gossiping and knitting neck scarves and sweaters for the GI's that any excuse now served: quilts, their own mending, bootees for orphans, bandages for leper colonies, socks for Indians on reservations. (In the postwar years as the country grew more affluent, this loose and changing group evolved into an art coterie, making quilts and wall hangings, ever more artistic than utilitarian.)

I made certain everyone knew that I'd won that prize in Norfolk (I'd eventually bought the bathing suit with the floating bra), and that a second poem of mine, actually a rewrite of my other success, about a twin shooting star, was accepted and printed in a children's magazine when I was eight. "A sibilant light/ Plunged out of the night," it began. It rhymed and was dramatic, and ended the same way the other one had, with the surprise that the stars were really the precious gifts of a baby brother and sister. I kept it conspicuously around the house until the magazine grew as tattered and spotted as an old man's necktie. Both times I had lied, or at least falsified my feelings; and both times I won fame, and money. What did it mean?

The poems that I composed later on were occasional: the birthdays of friends, for instance. Jeanne and I wrote an epic entitled *The Tomb of Nusherwan* about a mummified Pharoah who came back to life and killed everybody who had been mean to him. With Jeanne and Tut and Susan I invented a game without a name in which secret notes were hidden, found, exchanged, acted upon. I could zip off a masterpiece at the drop of a hat:

Whereto a bloody stream doth flo?
Into the life of Man!
Where ghostly spirits fond and true
Are ruled by a Squamous Hand!

The game was the making of the game, the writing of those notes, often including the invention of words; through the years I'd come across our tightly folded poems or notes, sometimes illustrated with flowers, or drawn as scrolls, in the bottoms of Chinese vases, behind some carved ivory on a mantel in my parents' house, in a mothball-scented old coat pocket: "Meet Phillip at midnight where the limpid willows lean." Another might read, "In the darkness of the Prairie in the Dairy of the Mind / Is a haunted gaunted castle where Destruction thou canst find!"

My models were horror comics, the stories and verse of Edgar Allan Poe, Robert Service's story-poems, and hillbilly music. The results of mixing them indiscriminately with W. S. Gilbert's Bab Ballads, and Rudyard Kipling's poetry, were something like the casseroles my father sneered at.

In the mornings, I still like to go over and eat breakfast with Andaddy — those lace-edged hotcakes, greasy and topped with bacon and swimming in syrup. When we are done, Andaddy works the crosswords — *conundrums*, he calls them — with pencil stubs he brings from the office and sharpens up with his penknife.

He quizzes me on the words, making me keep lists so that my vocabulary will improve. He likes *aloe, Erse, ted, alee,* while I prefer fancy, loopy words, like *panacea, teratoid,* and *inviolate,* which never come up in the crosswords. "A Norse folktale," he'll call out, and I am supposed to holler out "Saga!" just as fast.

I test him back: "Demulcent!" I'll say. "Meretricious!" "Sibilant!"

We keep score, a point for knowing, a point subtracted for not knowing. I have a hard time getting ahead of him. I catch him on *crepuscular,* though, and right after, he gets me on "entrance to a mine," which I do not know is *adit.* He believes in learning a new word every day, so I do, keeping them neatly in a notebook. "Use a word three times, Little Sweetheart, and it's yours forever," he says.

I MEMORIZED HUNDREDS OF LINES OF POETRY, and it pleased both Andaddy and Daddy to have me recite "Soldier of Fortune" or "The Cremation of Sam McGee" to their friends. My own favorite was a long poem by Langston Smith entitled "Evolution," that balled up survival of the fittest with reincarnation but had wonderful words that rolled off my tongue like balls of lightning: *coralline, caudal, Cambrian, thewed, amain, rife, ebbing, scarp, fen, jet, Paleozoic* and *Purbeck, fronded* and *amphibian.* I started my first of many vocabulary notebooks with that poem, and got my friends in on the game. I recited the poem for classes, talent shows, Girl Scout programs. I even recited it once in Sunday school.

Because of the three-time-use rule, we'd say things like, "That tomato-bacon-cheese sandwich was an *apotheosis!*" "Her scarf makes me want to *regurgitate,*" and "Isn't Harry Gerber the most *rebarbative* person you've ever in your life met?"

We also invented and redefined words: *couth* was something elegant people had; *lert* was an adjective applied to people who didn't pay as much attention in school as we did. *Coolth* was obviously the opposite of *warmth.* If *contraception* meant being against having children, then *proception* meant trying to have them. *Overbaring* (spelled erroneously by some lert class-mate) was, we decided, a wicked girl we knew named Sharlene Rawley who wore too-small, too-tight bathing suits; *intertrude* was what you did if you got between two people. *Congress* must be the opposite of *progress*, we said, and *pervious* had to mean *wide open* or *vulnerable*.

When a sixth-grade teacher pronounced the Holy Roman Emperor "Charley-magny" we referred to *her* ever after as Miss Charley Magny. She was the same one that pronounced abdomen "abodome." It made us hysterical. We had a teacher who told us we all should be more "eloguent," so we institutionalized her error, and used it from then on out.

"Quote me if I'm wrong," one teacher said, so boy, did we.

OUR SEVENTH-GRADE TEACHER appreciated our word-play, and taught us charades. To this day, I know what *ingratiate* means because Miss Nettie wrote on the board "to do something that makes someone else like you," while sitting at her desk, in a chosen-for-the-occasion *gray* dress, and eating an apple. *In - gray - she - ate.*

Andaddy kept the game alive, and made me recite. Captive growns continued to marvel politely at my phenomenal memory, but only when Mama wasn't around. She disapproved of that kind of showing off.

MAMA'S PREVIOUS SERENE STRENGTH seemed shattered, and somehow I knew she had been better off when Daddy was at war. She didn't cope well with me, with the twins. Daddy made her mad. Johnnie was never any trouble; he just disappeared, except at dinner time, when he ate quietly and solemnly.

At recess at school, we played complicated games of hopscotch, tossing our collections of keys and charms into far squares, learning to twist in midair over the double squares, inventing and reinventing the rules. And we collected cards, the cast-off jokers or logo cards of all the decks the growns played bridge with. (We called them Congress Cards, but they were actually many brands.) We traded jewelry and spun-glass animals, silk scarves and candy, but mostly we traded the cards for each other. *Two horse cards for one angel card. Trade you the cafe one for the Paris river one. I got Betty Grable; will you trade for those neat diamond designs? You want these two flower garden ones for Old Faithful?* Landscape cards were my favorites, and I could go in my mind right into those scenes and imagine whole stories, always romantic, and always with myself in the starring role. We all had cigar boxes and index cards, and learned how to file the cards, discussing categories as we went.

As childhoods go, mine was much more good than bad.

I KNEW ABOUT OUR NEIGHBOR Fitz Flournoy because his wife, Prissy, was my mother's friend, and used to come running across the yard, "Betty? Betty!" And from the tone, you knew it was something awful. Once inside, she would lower her soft bulk heavily, settling to stay, sobbing out her latest woe, dramatically reporting the latest on the long list of offenses on Fitz's part, unaware of the child pretending to play or read nearby on her stomach on the floor.

Prissy wore an apron, which was often hauled up over her face, mopping her tears. When she cried into it, she actually said, "Boo hoo," so it was nearly impossible to take her seriously, though I found the things she said fascinating. Her husband, who taught English at Washington and Lee, had overturned the table again, displeased that the bacon was too crisp, or that the popovers had sagged. Fitz had come crawling home at six aye-em, and fallen asleep on the front porch. Fitz had been gone again, this time for two days. The police had to bring Fitz home last night.

Later in the day Mama would sometimes relate it all to Daddy, so I heard many of the episodes twice. The only time I forgot myself, looked up and asked some question related to the episode under discussion, I was punished by not hearing a thing for over six months. And so I rehearsed the blank stare once more.

These stories I heard, wondering only occasionally what it must be like to live with such a monster. But it was not any different to me than some fairy tale. Fitz was not any more real than a character in a book.

I never questioned or repeated Prissy's stories. Some went back years: once he'd stolen all the lightbulbs in the house and sold them for a bottle of whiskey, and Prissy did not discover the theft until the hardware and both groceries were closed for the day, so she had to borrow, one bulb from us, one from someone else down the street, to get through the night. Johnnie and I giggled over that until our stomachs hurt and we had headaches.

Inevitably I would pass Fitz himself on the sidewalk, on my way to school, or flash by him on my skates, scarves trembling in my breeze. On the surface, he was merely a shuffling fat man who wore an enormous white suit in summer, a huge burgundy woolen cape in winter, who would tip his Panama or fur hat silently to me when we chanced to encounter each other on the street.

Compared to him, my own blustrous father seemed mild. Daddy certainly spanked; he lost his temper, he'd broken Joe Richardson's beebee gun across a tree, and once he'd kicked out a screen door in a rage at something Mama said. But he'd never come home drunk, and he'd never overturned the dinner table. I was used to keeping secrets, and so I kept those, too.

I felt mildly sorry for Prissy who had to put up with it all, yet her constant sorrows that took so much of my mother's time and energy soon irritated me. Their son was a pill in my opinion, a boy a year older than I who'd failed so often he was now behind me. Then, we had no knowledge of dyslexia or other learning disabilities; no wonder he acted out what must have been major frustrations. His main joys, it seemed to me, were wrecking my reading treehouse, throwing green apples or walnuts at me, or taunting me when I had the gall to cross a corner of their back yard.

So I came to feel it mildly disloyal of Mama to spend so much time sympathizing with Prissy, the mother of that bully.

One day in early summer while wandering around in the woods down behind the campus and Andaddy's house, I met my neighbor Fitz Flournoy coming toward me in a garb so strange even I, no stranger to odd getups, was startled: his enormous onion-pale chest and belly bare of hair or clothing formed the northern hemisphere. The southern half of him sported a pair of outsized plaid bermuda shorts. He had on black socks and long thin white tennis shoes. Around his middle was woven a thick leafy girdle of honeysuckle, redolent yellow and white-blossomed. His nose and shoulders were pink with sunburn or embarrassment, and he cradled in front of him, like a baby, a big red thermos bottle.

He hesitated, stopped, looked distressed, and shrank inward upon himself. I got the impression that he was trying to disappear. When he could not, he heaved a sigh, and instead, waxed gallant: he bowed from the waist, picked a sprig of honeysuckle off his belt, and offered it to me with a flourish. I didn't know what else to do, so I took it and said, "Thank you."

"I hear you are a poet," were his first words.

I could not have been more startled that someone so distant, so unreal, someone who did the things I had heard he did, should know anything at all about me. But I didn't run. I waited, not answering.

He cocked his head to one side. "You are Miss Katie Paul Letcher, are you not?"

"Yes," I said.

"Are you married?" he asked.

"Oh, no!" I whispered in horror. "I'm only ten."

"Hmm. Just so. No children, then, I suppose?"

"No!" The man was crazy, just as Prissy told it.

"Do you drink?" he asked.

Did I drink? What in the world was he talking about? But I said, "Well, sure."

"Good," he said, smiling, "now we're getting somewhere. You choose — bourbon straight up, martini, or iced tea."

"Iced tea," I said quickly, wondering how he could have all those things in one thermos.

"Excellent," he said, gesturing clearly that I was to sit down on the grass at the edge of the woods. The thermos had three nested metal tops; he handed me the middle-sized one, and poured me out some iced tea, delicately redolent of lemon and mint. I decided the different drinks must have something to do with the different sized tops.

We sat in the grass all the rest of that early summer afternoon, until twilight chill drove us to our separate dwellings. He referred to his "dear" wife, and his "precious" son, always with those adjectives. He did not seem to realize that I knew his son. He seemed unaware that Prissy spent most morning hours in our kitchen.

He told me that day the story of a king who had three daughters, two false and one true, though only at the end when the good daughter was dead was the king able to tell the difference.

Fitz Flournoy loved the woods as much as I did, and had discovered the same lightning-struck fallen willow that I thought no one knew about but me. He, too, knew where the phoebe built her nest every year, and was ecstatic when I showed him the dell where the showy orchis had been blooming for nearly a month. He confessed his disappointment with the drabness of modern dress, admitted to a yearning for silks and satins, with which I, of course, passionately agreed. "Ah," he promised, gesturing grandly at the blue sky, "those days will return, for variation is the theme of time!"

Though English was his field, what he loved was the stage: he trod the boards, as he put it, in every play he could.

He said he wished he had a plumed hat: red hat, purple plume.

By next morning he had left me a copy of *King Lear* to read, and a book of poems by Lizette Woodsworth Reese, in a discreet corner of the front porch, delivered in the black of night.

All summer I walked out in the afternoons and we met up near the edge of the woods; together we walked or sat under the mild skies, and talked and drank iced tea.

Something warned me not to say anything about our friendship to my parents. I showed him Key Island, and The Cave, actually an unused railroad culvert that floods and mudslides had closed one end of. He brought me Peter Ibbetson to read, and *Hamlet*, and poetry by Emily Dickinson.

I listened to him read parts of Shakespeare's plays, as he paced and gesticulated before me. In my turn, I recited poems for him, both my own and others I had memorized. He agreed with me that "Evolution" was the best of the lot. He believed in evolution, and it was part of what he taught. I tried to, and he tried to explain it all to me, but it was confusing, and the poem had rather cemented my own ideas: I could not remember having been a monkey, though I rather liked the idea, and it was hard to think much about changing later into something else, for that is how I understood the process to work. He brought me Sara Teasdale and Edna St. Vincent Millay, and *Winesburg, Ohio*, by Sherwood Anderson. He brought me *Origin of Species*, but I did not read it then.

Though I felt guilty going to meet him, he quenched a thirst I had never known I had. I showed him some of my poems, which he read gravely, folded, and put carefully into his pockets. Later he might refer to something I'd written. We never talked about anything but literature.

At ten I came to a murky understanding that he felt unloved and lonely.

I continued to hear in our kitchen that he'd gotten angry, and smashed a lamp, that he'd driven the car up on the sidewalk in front of the drugstore, nearly breaking the plate glass window. One day Prissy told my mother that she thought he was a *homo*. From my mother's eyes, round with shock, her hands flying to her mouth, I knew I could not ask what that was. The dictionary was no help; *mankind*, it said, and *having the same center*. I knew that wasn't even close to whatever Prissy had meant. I guessed it must be so terrible it wasn't even in the dictionary.

He called me Miss Letcher, but I never had a name for him. In the sun his nose would turn bright red, and his pale cascading flesh, modestly covered over with a shirt after that first day, would shake beneath its tent when he laughed.

The summer turned toward autumn. His son failed another grade. He, like his mother, had no interest in things of the mind. The boy seemed to me skilled only in sullenness. His mother was isolated in a bad marriage. And, to be fair, my friend probably did all the things Prissy told my mother he did.

As events transpired, I was no Cordelia. And he was no Lear with a happy ending, finding a breathing, loving daughter to lend companionship to his old age. Given the discrepancy between what the growns knew and what I knew, I had not the courage of my convictions.

On one of the first fall days uptown in Newberry's, while fingering some blown glass figurines and wondering if I could manange to slip one into my pocket, I tuned in to a conversation between two women across the counter from me, in square gray coats the same color as their hair. The gist of their talk was that Fitz Flournoy had been thrown out of the movie theater for unruly drunkenness. He had torn the sparkling white screen, and God knew what it was going to cost to have it fixed!

With the smell of baking gingerbread in my nose, I heard an hour later Prissy's version of the same story to my mother, as I pretended to write in my notebook lying on my stomach on the kitchen floor. He had thrown his shoe, from the first row, hard into the screen, protesting modern movies.

With school beginning, I took the cold weather as an excuse to end our meetings, and I knew better than to ever reveal at home that I even knew him.

He continued to move slowly between his house and his classes, always courtly when we met, but with his eyes moving quickly beyond me, fixing on some ideal not of this time, this place.

General Pershing (front left) visiting Lexington in 1920.
Captain Letcher (Andaddy) stands in the foreground
at the general's left.

Fame

Andaddy and Nainai both were a little like Daddy in their admiration and tolerance for unconventional behavior. From the beginning, they thought I was the cat's pajamas. It might have been that I was a girl, a different sort of child than any they had known. Or it might have been that I was very like their only living child; definite, determined, energetic, stubborn, outrageous; maybe I reminded them of Daddy.

And sometimes, when I sang or played, I reminded them of their other son, Greenlee, called Gee, who had died of influenza as a teenager.

Andaddy, the youngest of eleven children, arrived on the scene when his mother was forty-four, his father forty-nine. The child of the governor's old age and decline, Greenlee had grown up in Lexington fussed over by that bevy of doting older sisters married and unmarried, with few children of their own, and no one anywhere near my grandfather's age.

The young Green, as they called him, who was smart, always passionate about politics and the law, entered VMI at fifteen, and won a seat in the state legislature for the first time at the age of nineteen, in 1892, while still studying and reading law. In those days, state legislators had free passes on all Virginia railroads, but more than once my grandfather was forced to pay by conductors who would not believe he could be old enough to be who he said he was, and would not honor his pass.

Andaddy, following in the governor's footsteps, was a social fellow. He was a "joiner," a member of Woodmen of the World, the Oddfellows, the Fortnightly Club, the Masons, the Shriners, the Lexington Volunteer Firemen, the Graham Literary Society, and probably others I don't recall. Of course a politician knows the necessity of knowing lots of people, but I watched Andaddy's already-florid face grow flushed with anticipation for those meetings. He actually liked all those clubs.

When he wasn't in Richmond, Andaddy practiced law out of his tiny messy office down the hill, and partway uptown, from the house. But mostly he stood out in the sun, the wind, the rain, the cold, talking to folks on the street. He was a frequent visitor, a great jokester, a merry comrade, a raconteur. He visited sick people. He was interested in everything in the world. Most nights of the week he had meetings to go to, things to see about, contacts to make.

His wife, Miss Katie, my Nainai, stayed home. She'd buried her first son at a year and a half, her second when he was sixteen.

From babyhood they called their third, and last, son "Buzz." He always disliked the name "Seymour." He added John, the name of the governor, his grandfather, and of his dead brother, to the front of it when he went in the Marine Corps, and so became John S. Letcher. It didn't much matter, as everyone always knew him as Buzz.

Andaddy inherited some of Hootie's money when he died in 1914, and some of Aunt Jennie's money when she died childless in 1941. With shrewd foresight he bought some cheap land near the river in downtown Richmond at the end of the Depression. Richmond grew up around it, and when he finally sold it after World War II, it secured the future and set an example for his son and grandchildren who, to this day, all buy bits of land when we can get the cash together, which investments have served us well.

Andaddy loved the sessions of the legislature, loved later reminiscing about the good company, the good talk, the good food, the good bourbon, in Richmond. At

*home in Lexington he loved to surround himself with cadets with whom he had
some connection; as he'd gone to VMI, it wasn't hard to find the sons of classmates, cousins, friends' friends, and occasionally even a French cadet. Anyone
French coming to or through Lexington on any errand at all was automatically
invited to their house, as Andaddy had spearheaded a battery of cavalry to France
during World War I, where he'd made many friends, and earned the lifetime nickname of "Cap'n."*

*One of the French visitors, Lily de Montague, is buried in the Letcher plot.
Andaddy had enjoyed her hospitality in France while her husband was off at the
war. In 1924, Andaddy arranged for her husband, the Comte de Montague, to
come to VMI to teach French. Lily, my grandfather's friend, preceded her husband
by two weeks to look for a place for them to stay. She fell ill, died, and because it
was summer, had to be buried right away. There was no question: she was interred
in the Letcher plot.*

*Then along came her husband a few days later, and my grandfather had the
task of informing the man he'd never met of his wife's death.*

ANDADDY WAS FULL OF LESSONS AND LORE, most of which I found tolerable,
sometimes even likeable. "Don't sit on the wet ground," he'd warn me.
"You'll get piles." "Look, Little Sweetheart. See this woolly bear caterpillar?
It's going to be a mild winter, because the stripe is narrow." He knew that
locust wings would foretell the war's outcome: a P predominating meant
peace, and a W, war. The summer of '44 must have been a seventeenth year,
for locusts were everywhere. Quite seriously, we collected and counted the
wings all during the war while Daddy was away, but especially that
summer. The wars and peaces ran about neck and neck, I think.

Andaddy stood me up on the dining room table and got me to sing
"The Wreck of the Old 97" to his friends when they dropped by. He
thought it was a scream when I "played" the guitar or, later, my Sears
Hawaiian ukelele. "Sing the 'Old Flying U,' Little Sweetheart," he'd say.
"Listen to her," he'd insist, making them all attend and seeing that they
applauded.

I wrote nature poems, too, at Andaddy's suggestion. Invariably, he and Nainai thought they were great, and he even thought the ideas I had for poems were wonderful. Once he got the local paper to publish a description of fall woods that I wrote, several hundred overblown words.

Right after we came to Lexington the first time, in 1943, I'd appropriated the old windup Victrola in the parlor for at least part of every day. I quickly chose favorites out of the record collection that had been growing since the birth of recording. I was drawn especially to the Vernon Dalhart railroad ballads and other long songs of tragedy, some mellifluous old Hawaiian songs, and cowboy songs. I sang quavery versions of the deaths of railroad men scalded to death by steam, crushed in derailments, beheaded by mail cranes.

No new steel needles were available in the war years, so Andaddy gave me a rasp and taught me how to sharpen and repoint the old needles. I'd use them until the sounds were so blurred you couldn't understand the words to the "Ballad of Sydney Allen," or the "Wreck of the 1256." Andaddy, hearing me sing along, encouraged me.

I found an old guitar in the attic with four strings, and learned to plunk out chords to accompany myself — badly. But I began then to consciously memorize the words to songs, often one a day, and to sing them everywhere I could think of: school, Sunday school, Girl Scout meetings, and later, at camp, at parties. Andaddy often remarked that Daddy loved those songs; so among my dreams of glory were visions of singing them to him when he came home.

In Lexington in 1947, the ukelele I'd gotten for my ninth birthday became an obsession, and the minute Daddy and I got back to town, I began listening to the new radio station that had opened, WREL (for Robert E. Lee), memorizing and singing the local country music, and scheming to get on the air. A boy ("Little Eddie Hostetter") and his father from the nearby town of Buena Vista had their own weekly fifteen-minute show, sponsored by a local business. I didn't see why I couldn't have the same thing. Daddy was all for it. Andaddy and Nainai, too.

I found out that WREL sponsored a program on Saturdays at noon called Kiddie's Karnival, a noisy free-for-all held in Schewel's furniture store, as the studio itself was merely two tiny rooms over the First National Bank lined with records and earphones and a big turntable, with no room for contestants and an audience.

I cased the show. There were little tiny kids with guitars bigger than they were, country boys who could play the hell out of their banjos or mandolins, a skinny boy a year younger than I was who lived down in the hollow named John Starling, with a big guitar and a twangy voice, a girl named Roberta Sensabaugh with red cheeks and a tight yellow dress warbling songs about bluebirds, a tiny pair of twins who did sweet gospel harmonies. Everyone was under twelve. One needed only to sign up, in order to join the kids who brought along their own cheering sections made up of aunts and grandmas, fathers and mothers, scrappy younger sisters and brothers.

I got prepared. Already, I'd worked my way through books of Irish songs, Negro spirituals, cowboy songs, Hawaiian songs, folksongs. If I heard a song once or twice, I could usually work out the tune by myself, then the act of writing down the words imprinted them into my brain. My friend Jeanne, who took piano and could read music and play like a pro, was happy to oblige me by playing the melody of a song from a book or sheet music until I got it.

The songs on WREL were country, bluegrass, and gospel. I loved the most bloodthirsty and tragic ones, with thousands of people crying to God for mercy as the *Titanic* sank, or the drunkard's child dying of starvation in a tenement attic, or engineers bleeding to death by the railroad, or little coffins being sent home on the 7:29.

Daddy egged me on; his big favorites were one called "Traced Her Little Footprints in the Snow," in which the loved one, named Nellie, was now "up in Heaven, with the Angel band . . ." and one called "Don't Sell Daddy Any More Whiskey," in which a baby in the background cried, "Wah! Wah! Wah!"

And I joined them, standing in line with my Sears ukelele, whacking out the chords and singing loudly.

There was an instrument that measured the loudness of the applause after each number, and the winner, whoever could rouse the most noise on the Applause Meter, got a three-dollar gift certificate to some store in town. John Starling, the boy from the hollow, and I both won occasionally; I went to Oder's shoe store with my winning certificate one Saturday and came home with the most gorgeous shoes I had ever seen — high-heeled red patent leather pumps, with peekholes in the front. John went on to perfect his instrument and his voice, and to found the Seldom Scene two decades later. My own pitiful talents were put to use years later when I sang folksongs at Peabody's Bookshop in Baltimore two nights a week during the three years I lived there. That was the time of what was called the "urban folk renewal," and I struck them as the genuine article — bad voice and poor accompaniment. "Woodnotes warbled wild," as Milton had put it. If I'd been any good, I'd never have gotten the job.

Mama, who was a classical music fan, really couldn't understand anyone's wanting to sing on the radio. Hillbilly singers, with whom I was aligning myself, were just not people you wanted to be associated with. But all I knew of classical music was Mama during the war, sitting and sewing, listening to her records alone and weeping. To this day, classical music, most of it, gives me a lump in my throat and makes me feel like crying.

Andaddy and Nainai were my cheering section, and even Daddy was tickled when I won — though he'd sometimes warn, "Now don't be getting big-headed . . .".

Mama later said that it was all well and good to know a million songs, but why did every one of them have to be so horrible? and for God's sakes, please don't wear those red high heels out of this house again!

But that was okay: here at last was the fame I sought: knowing that my voice was being broadcast all over Rockbridge County, even into our kitchen, where Nainai was waiting for me to come home and make my famous cheese sandwiches for lunch, and into Nannie's Saturday kitchen, where she assured me that she and her son Tom listened to every word! I imagined my friends and all their families listening, as well as total strangers hearing me, admiring fans everywhere, maybe even as far away as Natural Bridge.

Letcher Harrison.

Bad Genes

⊰ 16 ⊱

In my grandfather's dining room, Nannie has made me a pot of tea, which my sixth-grade teacher, unbalanced on the subject of health, is against. Miss Beatrice Miley makes us all keep a health chart, and show our "health banners" (her term for handkerchiefs), on demand. We have to stay in at recess if we don't have one. We are on our honor. One of the things we have to check off each day is "consumed no stimulating beverage in the last twenty-four hours," so I get it worked out that for breakfast on Saturdays, and the rest of the day, and sometimes early on Sundays, I can have tea without cheating. In fact, Miss Miley's conviction that coffee and tea will stunt one's growth is very appealing, for already I am taller than anyone in the class, and growing serious bosoms. In this area, Andaddy is a co-conspirator; he finds tea comforting and is always up for a cup.

THERE WAS, AS THERE MUST BE IN MOST FAMILIES, a notorious relative we heard about often. Uncle Letcher Harrison, the only son of Andaddy's sister Lizzie, was the most puzzling example of Daddy's youth. For he was the apple of his parents' eyes, brilliant, debonair, and charming, a graduate of Washington and Lee *and* the University of Virginia. "He was what was called a 90-day wonder," Daddy would say, of his cousin's comet-bright academic distinctions. He was best friends with Alan Thurman, a famous football player whose father had run for president.

Letcher Harrison got a Ph.D. in English, and taught English at the University of Virginia, and I would hear more about that later in my life, as I stumbled along a similar path. As he had visited Europe often since childhood, Letcher Harrison was fluent enough in French to serve on Pershing's staff as an ambulance driver during World War I. He distinguished himself socially, too, as the first University of Virginia student to own a car, a Stutz-Bearcat.

He was the promise of the family, but alas! he was the one our father warned us about at every opportunity. Letcher Harrision had no sense about money. That, thought Daddy, would ruin a man quicker than whiskey or women.

When he came home after World War I (my father related), Letcher Harrison got a job as personal secretary to a big banker in New York named Vanderlip, but then was fired for "mishandling" money. He could not seem to get along on his own, and no job he had lasted for long. He wrote with small success for regular newspapers, then tabloid newspapers, but he was always hard up.

Yet whenever the charismatic Uncle Letcher would visit Lexington from first Charlottesville and later New York, he'd arrive like the proverbial young Rajah, slinging money around as if it were grass seed. Gee loved Hawaiian music, while Buzz liked marches. No problem: Cousin Letcher would buy each boy a record, and then, to top it off, buy each a big box of Hershey bars. He'd take his cousins to baseball games, and, the ultimate thrill, for fast rides in his autos, zipping around Rockbridge County at horrifying speeds of up to thirty miles an hour!

My father had occasion, in 1927, en route to Nicaragua, his first station in the Marines, to spend a couple of nights in New York. He called on Cousin Letcher, who greeted him joyfully and gave him a wonderful two-day tour of the big city, visiting extravagant restaurants, the

Ziegfield Follies, a show by Will Rogers, and several of the best speakeasies in town.

On the third day my hung-over father sailed out of New York for Panama. He always said that for once it was a good thing he'd paid the seventy dollars for a first-class ticket; it took him the whole ten days to recover from his dissipation, and he was glad to have a nice cabin to do it in.

After young Letcher Harrison's parents had both died, and he'd run through his substantial inheritance in record time (Daddy would go on), Letcher Harrison would write to Aunt Jennie, another of my grandfather's sisters, who'd married well but had no children, and ask her for money. She would send her nephew a check for ten dollars, and he would doctor it to make the amount a hundred, and once a thousand. Poor Aunt Jennie was consequently always in dutch with the bank. But she wouldn't prosecute, and she wouldn't stop payment. Family was family.

His end was like the rest of my father's moralistic tales: John Letcher Harrison died a bum in 1950, his body shipped COD to Lexington in a cardboard coffin for burial in the Letcher plot of the Stonewall Jackson Cemetery. I never met him, but I remember the pathetic, sodden, sagging box we had to meet at the train in that raw wet January. The fakey woodgrain look to it wouldn't have fooled anybody.

His cousin Letcher's Roman-candle rise and fall were a deeply etched lesson, for Daddy never spent a nickel he didn't have to, and hammered into his children the importance of frugality. Warmth, generosity, and compassion weren't worth cultivating; empathy and kindness were mostly wasted on undeserving people; but frugality was golden.

Daddy also believed in an almost superstitious way that family characteristics were inherited, and it scared him that such a low-life spendthrift had been his blood-kin. He expected the trait to show up in all of us, and would later grow alarmed at my leanings toward an English major in college. He felt sure the entire syndrome would develop: English major, profligacy, alcoholism, dependency. And that was one reason he feared my life choices. And perhaps I made those choices at least part knowingly, for I had a need to get even with Daddy.

I learned much later that, after Letcher's untimely death, my grandfather undertook the payment of all his nephew's considerable debts. In the settlement of Letcher Harrison's affairs, it grew apparent that he was a drug addict. He had borrowed from literally hundreds of people. Andaddy used to pore over a several-page document someone in New York had put together, a list of name after name, and the amount Letcher Harrison had owed them when he died: usually under a thousand dollars, sometimes under a hundred.

I don't know how Andaddy did it, for he had limited liquid assets, but little by little he paid off those debts. Certainly he was not legally responsible; it was a sense of morality that propelled him. When Andaddy died, there was that much less left for Daddy and us, but Andaddy surely felt, though I never heard him say it, that being poor was not half as bad as living with guilt.

The choir at R. E. Lee Memorial Episcopal Church.
I am in the third row, third from left.

Pigeons

≪ 17 ≫

ndaddy was a great trader, accepting almost anything by way of barter for his legal services, and the Depression, when nobody had any cash, had made him a great collector — though he never filed or arranged anything. He had boxes of coins and stamps, stuffed foxes and mounted deer heads, shelves and piles and crates of books, furniture and tools, even food, that he got instead of money. Daddy and Nainai fussed at him, felt that he was not a good bargainer; that he was cheated more times than not out of what was rightfully his.

Andaddy didn't seem to care, and he was interested in everything: people, coins, books, food, history, crossword puzzles, the supernatural, anatomy, botany, music, Shakespeare. It suited him fine to be given an old Encyclopedia Britannica with three volumes missing instead of fifty dollars owed him. Once someone "paid" Andaddy a box of cards with every post office in Virginia on them, and I loved going through those: Love, Lovekill, Lovingston, Lowmoor. . . . I later learned they were a teaching device: new sorters at the post office had to memorize which county in the state every post office was in, and there were one hundred counties and thousands of towns.

Two chickens were perfectly all right with Andaddy instead of cash payment for a deed traced. There was no distance in him. As Nainai and Daddy thought being a good hater was a most important thing in the world, Andaddy I think was a good lover.

Nainai would fret at her husband for taking somebody's old arrowhead collection or a fruitcake in lieu of a fee, but he'd frown, and say, "Miss Katie, this just might be worth a lot of money someday," or, "With Christmas coming, this fruitcake will come in handy."

Nainai would fume to me that he gave himself away. And Daddy would say, "Pop, you ought not to put up with that," about some perceived short-change. Andaddy would just chuckle, shake his head, and change the subject.

WHEN NANNIE FAILS TO COME TO WORK one day, and dies a week later, and Daddy no longer even pretends to be looking for a job, he announces that we will close up Andaddy's house on Letcher Avenue just between VMI and Washington and Lee, and bring Andaddy over the twenty-five feet of back yard to live with us in our tiny house out back.

Of course Mama squawks, but Daddy says we need to save money, and it costs too much to heat the big house. Andaddy takes over the den with his bed and night table and radio and slop jar; he takes up our downstairs bathroom, leaving all six of us to pile into the upstairs one, as tangled in each other's privacy as the Laocoön with the sea serpent.

Andaddy continues to make his way downtown most days, collecting up friends on the street and inviting them by, but they do not feel welcome, and fewer and fewer come. Mama goes on yearning for a house on one floor, with a screened-in porch. A neat, clean house.

I continue to haunt the old house, wandering in its forlorn abandoned rooms, which are muggy with a still, dusty heat in summer, mournfully cold and gloomy in winter, yet I let myself in, listen to old records, often fall asleep somewhere, only to wake disoriented. The sheet-draped furniture crouches in the gloom like a bunch of exhausted ghosts. I still to this day dream of the old house several times a week. It is a variable landscape, sometimes locked up tight, sometimes empty, or changed, inside. I am likely to be any age in these dreams, or many ages at once, both adolescent and talking to my grown son at the same time, for instance, or married to my husband but still excitedly getting ready to go out on a date with some sexy stranger. Occasionally I dream of a room I never knew was there appearing through a familiar door, or on the other side of a wall. The dreams are invariably suffused with loss; they are never happy dreams.

SCHOOL CONSOLIDATION BECOMES A HOT LOCAL ISSUE In the early fifties. Daddy is against it. It will bring in all sorts of riff-raff, according to Daddy, and he has heard that they intend to teach Russian, and to have Negroes in the regular classes. Daddy continues to rail at the disintegration of the world he fought to save, runs for school board on the premise that schools must answer to the taxpayers who have children in those schools. We nail up posters all over town. He loses miserably, I think because he is such a good hater. There are comments in the paper and in the air about his negativity.

Once, when I ask him how come Negroes are so bad, he stares angrily at me and shakes his head as if I had gone mad or been brainwashed, but he has no answer. Nannie's son, his friend Tommy whom he used to go fishing with, no longer comes to the back door, rod in his hand, looking for Daddy.

In the mid-fifties, when the church invited our town's black people to join the congregation shortly after *Brown vs. Board of Education*, that gave Daddy the excuse he was looking for to leave entirely. He did it in his usual flamboyant manner, walking out during a sermon in which we were enjoined to "embrace our colored brothers," and slamming the big double church doors hard behind him. He remained adamant on the subject, and never went back.

It was typical of his odd but ferocious morality that, twenty years later when he was approached (by some young eager fund-raiser who obviously wasn't aware of my father's stormy history with the R. E. Lee

Episcopal Church) to give some money for some renovations, he is reported to have said, "I won't give you a penny, not a damned penny. Of course my mother didn't feel that way, so here's a check for five thousand dollars in her memory. But you ain't getting a damn cent of my money." Daddy firmly believed what his mother had: in the end, God would tote up your life, your deeds, and not how many Sunday mornings you'd spent listening to boring sermons. And God certainly didn't believe in integration, and the "lesbian priesthood" Daddy liked to rant about.

Meanwhile, I grow acutely, uncomfortably, deliciously, aware of the succulent maleflesh teeming on either side of me, Virginia Military Institute at one end, and Washington and Lee University at the other, of our street. Three thousand lucious boys, half of them in blue uniforms, half in crisp white or pink button-down shirts, seersucker jackets, and, this season, white hushpuppies with white socks — or, most daring of all, hushpuppies with no socks. A VMI cadet walking by one day pulls a nickel out from somewhere in his tight blue uniform, flips it to me, and says, "Honey, give me a call in a year or so."

Through a process somewhat like osmosis, or however it is that boys learn astonishing obscure baseball stats without effort, I absorb the names, faces, and vital statistics of scores of college boys: Bob, from Tulsa, is an Econ major; Walt, a junior from Memphis, is a Southern Conference champion pole-vaulter; Ben, from Baltimore, is Jewish and president of Fancy Dress. Courtney, a second-classman from Lynchburg, also called Bubba by his friends, is the nephew of Jan Garber, the big-band leader. Elton, a cadet who is at church all the time, is going to be an Episcopal minister, and he rooms with Guthrie Moon, from Charlotte, who drinks like a fish, and once got so drunk that he ran his Nash into the front of Buffalo Creek Motel on purpose when they refused to serve him any more beer. Lacey Dandridge is the captain, the Company Commander, of Company A, the tallest company (the cadets are arranged in companies A through E, tallest to shortest and back to tallest, so you don't accept blind dates from Company C), and Lacey Dandridge is the handsomest cadet of them all.

We hear (and discuss at slumber parties or in lowered voices at the drugstore) that Paul "Gross" Phillips, an alarming drunk, actually peed in a lady's soup in a local restaurant when she complained about the soup in his hearing. "That'll give you something to complain about," he told her.

We repeat that story for weeks, and Phillips, whose other claims to fame include responsibility for entire rolls of toilet paper draped from local trees just for the hell of it, becomes for a time the most notorious person we know.

Quiz me, I know what fraternities they all belong to. They are my major subject, and I am an A-plus student. Friday afternoons I never miss the VMI parades. Nights, I scout out strategic positions in the Washington and Lee library for my so-called studying — and my surreptitious andrology.

Boys occasionally call from barracks or dorm pay phones, announcing in advance with the hollow metal-on-metal drop of the dime, that they are cadets or students, and invite me out. My father says no. If he'd just find a job and get out of the house, I could grind Mama down easily. "There will be plenty of time for that," Daddy says. When? I want to cry. Hell, life was passing me by. I was over twelve!

So I WENT UPTOWN CHAPERONED BY MY GRANDFATHER, and I walked to church with him every Sunday, where I could watch, and even talk to, students and cadets. We were kin in our Episcopalianism, so it could be no worse, really, I reasoned, than talking to, say, cousins. I told myself and others, especially Daddy, that it was the stained glass, the glorious language, the uplifting sermons, and the magnificent music that drew me to church, and to sing in the choir. It was those things, it may even have been the erratic odd conversations I had with God in those days, or the obvious pleasure Andaddy had in having me along, to show me off to everyone, or even the fact that my parents were not at all religious — but mostly it was the presence of all those promising God-like males.

My hormones leapt and rampaged like water drops in a hot frying pan, like wild horses stampeding. On Letcher Avenue, with VMI at one end, and Washington and Lee at the other, I was a diabetic living between two candy stores.

IT IS SPRING, AND I AM NEARLY FOURTEEN. Andaddy — right in the middle of the Washington and Lee Campus — on a Sunday morning, shuffles along in his carpet slippers, his threadbare jacket flapping out around him. We are on our way home from church. The slippers are wine-red, wool, and filthy — frayed at the edges, threadbare on the sides, soles flapping away from the bottoms like grotesque cartoon mouths when I follow him back up the hill toward home. He has bunions, and his lawyer shoes, thick with black paste polish, hurt his feet, he has explained, and he can't concentrate on God when his feet hurt. God appreciates the carpet slippers as a sensible solution to the problem.

This particular Sunday he is saying, "Little Sweetheart, now don't you ever let anyone kiss you," and I am thinking, Oh please just once . . . please let someone kiss me. For somewhere inside, I have determined that I want to be a good lover, as opposed to a good hater — and kissing seems a good place to start.

We are passing in front of Lee Chapel, headed for home and the Sunday dinner Nannie used to make, and Mama has now taken over: fried chicken peas mashed potatoes milk gravy and two pints of vanilla ice cream with hot chocolate sauce on it, when we are greeted by one of Andaddy's cronies named Willie Shields, who my mother says is a ne'er-do-well.

Mr. Shields, whenever we meet him on the street, spouts passages of Shakespeare at the drop of a hat. He seems to have no home, no wife, and he tends to show up just in time for Sunday dinner, hanging around until someone invites him to stay, inquiring of me whether I have yet learned "The Shooting of Dan McGrew" or "Barefoot Boy with Cheeks of Tan."

Before I can even answer, he's off on some hypnotic passage from

"Hiawatha" or "Evangeline." He writes his own poems, too, and used to work for a newspaper in New York. Willie reads poetry all the time, and he loves to recite it.

Andaddy always invited him to stay when he still lived in the big house. My mother is not so welcoming. She claims Willie broke one of her Chinese vases swinging his black cloak around.

There are pigeons everywhere, swooping up in the brisk March wind just inches from our three faces, walking about like stout old ladies among the maple tags at our feet. Andaddy has removed his two hats to talk with Willie — *Mr. Shields* to me; the wind whips his thin white hair to fronds, and tears of pleasure and laughter make their way down his cheeks like creeks in our mountain hollows.

Willie, who has on his maroon-silk-lined black wool cloak, has bowed low to me as if I were a queen, and as usual he's launched into a recitation: "As sweet and musical as bright Apollo's lute, strung with his hair; / And when Love speaks, the voice of all the gods makes heaven drowsy with the harmony . . . ."

Although I know what the words, by themselves, mean, for the most part, only every now and then can I see beneath their surface to glimpse their meaning. Poetry is harder to fathom than deep water, yet certainly my heart yearns to hear Love speak.

Willie works hard for his dinner, gesturing and bowing. The chapel bell tolling the noon hour blends with his melodious praise.

As Willie gets wrought up in the fabric of what he is reciting, which I have apparently inspired, something about "From women's eyes this doctrine I derive, / They sparkle still, the right Promethean fire," he raises his hands like a preacher, palms up, in the windy spring day, maple tags coptering down around him. All of a sudden, a swooping pigeon drops a splat right into his waiting hand.

Willie does not notice, goes on gesturing. I sneak a glance at Andaddy, who is still laughing merrily, enjoying the performance. Did he see? He digs out his crumpled handkerchief and wipes his eyes. A couple of W&L

students saunter by, nodding at our threesome. I of course cannot help breaking into giggles.

As when a musical group comes to the climax of the composition they are playing, I know and can predict its coming; likewise as Willie's speech rises toward its climax, I can hear the crescendo: "They are the books, the arts, the academes, that show, contain, and nourish all the world!" I *think* it's my eyes he's talking about.

Suddenly, Willie stops, drops his hands dramatically, and before I can do anything to avoid it, grabs my hand and smashes it firmly in between his two. Clutches of the handsomest cadets pass us by, saluting us and Robert E. Lee, who is buried in the chapel. Willie is congratulating me on being so beautiful, or at least on my blue eyes, and he goes on, pumping my hand over and over, his face a genial romp of wrinkles, squishing the pigeon shit in, perfectly unaware. I teeter between disgust and wild giggling, which apparently strikes him as a perfectly appropriate response to his performance. He pumps some more.

The scene freezes there, just on the brink of everything that the world is going to be. The passing boys glance at me, and I am paralyzed until I can get home to the bathroom and wash my hand clean of all those macerated worms and whatever else the dumb pigeons eat. Andaddy is still laughing, wiping his eyes and blowing his nose on that appalling handkerchief, the two hats once more back on his head. Gallantly, he invites Willie to accompany us home for Sunday dinner, and Willie, bowing low, accepts, as gracious as Sir Walter Raleigh, managing to convey surprise, joy, gratitude, all at the same time. He turns, his cloak billowing, to follow us.

I lean uphill into the March wind, into adulthood, my hair whipping in my eyes. I see what will be: Daddy will politely welcome Willie, Mama will be polite but unenthusiastic, Johnnie will be oblivious to it all, the twins will wiggle and show off, and Willie will wax eloquent on every knick-knack and end table in sight, and eat too much, and later there will be a scene between my parents.

I want to escape from the taint, the crowding and bickering and jostling. I feel more than ready to leave behind this nest my father has jury-rigged so grudgingly to protect us from the cold, to choose any one of those beautiful young men for my own, anyone who will teach me to fly.

But instead, my hand dangles immobile at the end of my wrist, a paralyzed wing, and I don't want to touch anything as we trudge on up the hill. The birds still soar around us, maybe some of the very ones my grandfather used to feed each morning but doesn't anymore, not since he's moved in with us. What will they eat now? For an instant I think sadly of them all, all those confused and abandoned animals that depended on him for food each morning. Do they still come, to stare up at the now-closed window, with memories of that daily cornucopia?

"Oh, my goodness, Little Sweetheart," Andaddy manages to mumble behind his handkerchief, "That was so funny!"

Mealtime, always Daddy's favorite part of the day.

Foodstuff

❈ 18 ❈

*M*ama and Johnnie and I, during the war, after we move uptown, are often invited to lunch, which Andaddy and Nainai call dinner. In fact, it's an open invitation, for every day, any day: all Mama needs to do is tell Nannie early in the day if we will come have dinner with them. Every day I hope, and sometimes I just go myself. Their lunches are all the things I love: creamy casseroles with bread crumbs and cheese, fried oysters, sweet stewed tomatoes, Virginia hams, corn fritters, lamb chops, cheesy vegetables, sweet hot desserts with melting ice cream on top.

Today it's to have some fresh fish someone has brought them. Food often arrives that way: a cut-glass dish of creamy golden custard, covered with a tea towel and delivered by a frail old woman whose husband Andaddy once helped out, a plate of cookies covered with waxed paper from a down-the-street neighbor. Near Christmas, a quart of yellow eggnog appears from some friend, the Mason jar covered first with a square of waxed paper before the zinc lid is screwed on. A chocolate cake appears on the sideboard, from Mrs. Colonel Somebody at VMI.

Today Andaddy has already sawed the small fried sunfish on his plate into squares with his knife and fork, as if it were a pancake, and ignoring the tiny bones, chews the morsels up, until one bests him, sticks in his teeth, pricking his tongue defiantly instead of giving way as he must suppose all of them will do.

Andaddy twists his face around, and takes his teeth out, to search for the offending bone. They are interesting, and gross, those disembodied ivories, unnaturally pink shiny porcelain gums, a bit of fish skin stuck to one tooth, a chewed celery leaf fragment protruding from another. Johnnie wants the teeth, reaches out making anh anh sounds, but Mama holds him back, studying her neat plate, one white half of the fish gently severed from the spine and laid back to receive her light touch of salt and pepper.

Andaddy picks the dentures up, studies them closely, turns them over on his plate, and probes around with a knifeblade, until he finds the protruding bone and removes it. Then he maneuvers the big teeth back into place, with monstrous grimaces and jaw gnashing.

I become aware of appalled silence from my mother, while Nainai, blind, eats slowly, unconcerned. Mother hastens to finish her fish, says she doesn't want any dessert, and grabs up Johnnie, who is uncomplaining, drooling, chewing now on a wooden spool out of Mama's pocketbook. She has suddenly remembered she has to go home to check on something.

FOOD MEANT A LOT TO ALL THE LETCHERS. They talked about food, and smacked their lips over what they enjoyed. Nainai's idea of a perfect meal seemed to be the same as mine: rat cheese sandwiches fried in lots of butter, black devils-food cocoa made without milk but with lots of sugar, the feast served in and on the very best china in the house, just us, at the kitchen table. Three times as much vanilla in the cocoa as you'd ordinarily put (that was Harriet's legacy) and about twice the sugar it needed. Nainai listened seriously to my view that Sultana Cocoa was the best, and thereafter that's the brand we always used.

She let me have anything I wanted, including coffee and tea, Charlotte Rousse with rum and whiskey in it, sherried grapefruit sent under the broiler to melt and caramelize the brown sugar on top, ice cream with the heady brandied peaches. William Jennings Bryan, campaigning for president, had been the only person ever to reject Nainai's sherried grapefruit, refusing to touch it when he came to their home for dinner in 1898, rabid teetotaler that he was. Andaddy ate everything zestfully. In food as in the rest of his life, he found pleasure and interest.

Again, my mother differed. Her family had just been a bit more delicate about food; you could admire it, and you could like it, but you weren't supposed to comment *while the food was still in your mouth*, and you weren't supposed to make noises while you ate.

IT WAS DADDY'S THEORY that eating whatever showed up on your plate proved character. He was proud of having eaten octopus, beaver, monkeys' brains, rattlesnake, and live baby eels. But I noticed he would emphatically and scornfully not touch tapioca, or okra, or anything called a casserole. "All that mixed-up mess you don't know what's in it." he'd say.

"Why," he fumed, after some dinner party, "would anyone in his right mind want to eat something with ham and raisins and rice and celery and peanuts all mixed up in it?"

Daddy's way was the right way, the natural way, the Only way. His bowels blew no ill wind. Like the Old Testament Yahweh, he was a jealous God full of wrath. If one of us had the bad grace to get sick, it was always because we never met his standards in taking care of ourselves. But if *he* got sick, it was because someone had poisoned him with rancid meat or some unnatural food, such as a casserole.

Daddy approved only of foods he liked. He could justify eating quarts of ice cream a day, and butter by the pound, while roundly condemning coffee (which he scorned) and oleomargarine (unnatural and therefore unacceptable). Hershey bars were fine (he liked them), but the Lifesavers I loved were poisonous. One time in the service he'd known a fat man who began every meal with the statement, "I'm a light eater, but I'm a glutton for — (whatever was on the table). Though Daddy laughed about that, I heard him say it a million times, helping himself to more roast lamb, more potatoes, thirds of chicken and dumplings. He was never happier than when he was eating.

Coca-Cola he detested and disdained; it would put you in an early grave. We knew a woman who (he said) drank a Coke and smoked a cigarette every morning upon arising; when she got sick and died young, it was absolutely clear to Daddy why, and occasion for lectures and cautions. One time he staged for us children a demonstration: he put a bit of hamburger into a bottle of Coke and left it overnight. The next morning, like a stage magician, he shook the bottle and forced us to look upon the gory remains of a perfectly good piece of hamburger: a gray dissolved mush now floated ominously in the clouded bottle bottom.

See what it will do to your stomach, he said darkly. It must have worked: to this day, *none* of us drinks Coke. His lessons did have a convincing quality.

The most outraged I ever saw him was once when a drugstore clerk mistook his order for a *chocolate soda*, and brought him instead a *Coca-Cola*. He told that story every time anyone ever mentioned Coke.

There might have been another reason, too, why he was against Coke; when he was a kid, he claimed, some salesman came around offering shares of Coca-Cola stock for a dollar a share. Daddy tasted the stuff, concluded that no one would drink such awful swill, and that it would never take off, so he turned his nose up at the stock. The idea of that loss as Coke's popularity rocketed and the stock made its owners rich was more than distasteful to him. He loved getting something for nothing (like free mushrooms in the woods), and he hated to lose a penny.

IN THE FALL OF 1947, WE COOKED A LOT. Daddy invented a sweet, dark, brick-heavy product he named Buffy Bread. We'd set up the old hand mill and grind wheat for half a day, leaving a fine flour film on everything in the kitchen.

While he turned the grinder handle, he made up stories about the history of that delectable loaf, telling how Cleopatra seduced Mark Antony not with her winsome charms but with Buffy Bread. And the real reason Henry the Eighth married and then disposed of so many wives was that he was simply trying to find a woman who could bake a proper loaf of Buffy Bread!

We'd stir in to 2 scalded cups of milk (for each loaf, though we never ever made fewer than four loaves at a time) 1 teaspoon salt, 1/2 cup honey and 1/4 cup molasses, and 1 dissolved yeast square. Then we stirred in fresh whole wheat flour, 4 to 5 cups, until our hands were numb and cramping with the sticky mountain of dough. Daddy thought it was more economical to make big batches of anything. He bragged that eating Buffy Bread was what kept us from ever getting sick that whole four months. And daddy might have said it was because we didn't weaken ourselves by over-bathing.

During the siege of Jerusalem the gallant Saladin (he'd say), hurled loaves of Buffy Bread from the battlements while the English were attacking. One struck King Richard on his helmet. The lion-hearted monarch, mistaking it for one of the coping stones of the battlement, shouted, "Odd Bodkins, Brave Englishmen! The place is falling to pieces. Charge again and it will be ours!" The English responded, swarmed the walls, and thus captured Jerusalem.

To me he would misquote Shakespeare on Buffy Bread: "Pâté de fois gras, bah! Wouldst I could have one sturdy loaf of Buffy Bread!" and, "Romeo, Romeo, has thou brought me Buffy Bread?" and, "Is this a dagger which I see before me, plunged to the hilt enloafed in Buffy Bread?"

I added my two cents' worth: Daniel Boone's leather nightgowns, I said, were all fashioned with small pockets for his nightly bedtime snack of several slices of Buffy Bread. And I opined that the real reason the sheriff of Nottingham hated Robin Hood was that Robin Hood stole his Buffy Bread, and distributed it to the merry men and the peasants.

Despite his scorn for casseroles, Daddy was extremely fond of his own messes. For example, for breakfast he would build a tower of oatmeal, nuts, brown sugar, honey, chopped figs, molasses, some dates, cream, maybe a ginger snap or two crumbled up — and then he'd ruin it by crumbling an egg shell over the top (for calcium), and eat it, crunching away while I cringed.

That fall, I invented culinary creations for him, for us, like my famous Tomato Ritzes: a piece of whole wheat toast layered up with crisp bacon, a slice of tomato, a slab of cheddar cheese, and Hellman's mayonnaise, then topped with a raw egg covered with a slice of Swiss cheese and baked until everything was bubbly. It was built of all the things Daddy loved best in a sandwich. If the egg wasn't cooked enough, next time I'd fry it first. Or I might fry the tomato first. Once I had perfected the dish, I invited friends to Saturday lunch, and entertained them with the successful Tomato Ritzes — or Strawberry Dreams, made of little pastry shells baked and cooled, filled with strawberry preserves and topped with whipped cream. Nannie cleaned up after us no matter how awful the mess.

Daddy was impressed, too, by huge *quantities* of food, and he never forgot some fifteen-course feast in Peking (he could remember what every course was), or a wedding reception he'd attended once where he estimated that the shrimp piled on ice would have filled two bathtubs. *Big shrimp, too, four or five inches long.* Telling it, he'd smack his lips, and you could see how visceral the memory was. He ate part of a Siberian crab once that he said must have weighed forty pounds. He said it was wonderful.

So when he cooked, he didn't do it on a small scale, then or later.

In the new house, he made gallons of an undrinkable alcoholic potion called ginger beer, and huge numbers of jars of chutney, and quarts and quarts of watermelon-rind pickle concocted over a week's time, scenting the kitchen, paralyzing the stove for any ordinary meals. Meanwhile, we had to eat up the watermelon, and none of us (except him) cared for its insipid cucumbrous flesh.

We, on the other hand, were totally reasonable: we had nothing against baked beans until we had to eat them for weeks on end. That project started with the rinsing of ten pounds of dried navy beans, followed by a soak in the sink for twenty-four hours. They were then simmered for hours. This was followed by the rendering of several pounds of salt pork cut up into little cubes, fried together with mountains of chopped onions. In the kitchen we stepped in and out of sprinkles of dropped onions, and puddles and smears of molasses, brown sugar, dried mustard, and catsup, which were added before the final day-long cooking in all our biggest pots over low heat.

During the final day, everyone in the house was adjured to check, to taste, to add water if things began to look dry. We'd end up with huge vats of beans, all the extra containers in the house full of baked beans, which we'd eat and eat and eat. Daddy went to junk stores and bought old crocks for a quarter apiece, and complained about the price. Just when we were sure the last bean was gone, he'd come up with another jar or crock of them from somewhere, under the table, in the cellar, out on the back porch, behind the stairs, the fat on the top sealing them from corruption (that was his belief), and it was beans for breakfast, beans for dinner, good ol' beans for tea.

Daddy's enthusiasm was marvelous; he thought during that period that he might start a business canning his Buzz's Famous Baked Beans. He designed labels, and talked to a canning company in West Virginia, but nothing came of it.

MAMA HAD PLAIN AND MODEST TASTES, and shrimp creole on rice once a year or so was about the limit of her temerity. She couldn't see the need for any of those pickled, sharp-tasting things. Daddy, on the other hand, thought everything he made was absolutely great, including roast beaver.

Bereft of all his former power and glory, his kibitzing in Mama's kitchen and interfering with the kids were probably the only ways he could feel powerful again. He interfered in everything, driving Mama crazy with his endless suggestions about decorating, eating, cooking, economizing, arranging furniture, storing food, raising children. He planned the kitchen in the new house the way *he* wanted it. He had begun using the kitchen while Mama was still down in Norfolk — and she had a time claiming it for her own.

As he did everything else, Daddy went at cooking with a horrifying abandon, and left in Mama's kitchen the same kinds of messes he'd left in Nannie's, so that it looked like tornadoes had touched down in his wake. He opened drawers and then spilled things into them, often closing them half back up with dropped eggs, molasses, God knew what, in them. If he scattered onions or dripped honey all over, he didn't bother to wipe them up.

He took things out but didn't put them back. I think he thought since he was doing us all a favor by creating these wonderful things, we should be delighted to clean up after him. It was the least we could do.

He decided one spring to make Boneless Shad, according to some method he'd clipped out of the *Richmond Times-Dispatch*.

It didn't deter him that the rest of us didn't care for shad. Daddy explained that away by saying we just didn't like coming across bones and having to deal with them. *This* fish we were going to like. In fact, except for flounder or the mild river fish we caught in Goshen Pass, we didn't like fish — and the oilier and stronger it was, the more we disliked it, and the more he loved it. He adored herring, and salted English breakfast fish. He loved mackerel. And of course the sardines. He mixed canned herring roe with scrambled eggs and ate it like it was going out of style.

The sink (which was the only thing big enough to hold the leviathan shad) had to be filled with water and vinegar, and the shad soaked for several days, during which time the bones were supposed to dissolve. They didn't, but we had to eat the fish anyway, bones and all, and all the dishwashing had to be moved to the downstairs *bathtub* while the sink was in use.

After two or three glum meals during which Daddy, in great spirits, extolled the virtues of shad, and ate of it heartily while the rest of us stared at our plates, almost the entire fish remained. At that point, he looked around at the sad faces and decided to make something he called Shad Chowder, which was ground-up shad.

The chowder only reduced the oily fishy meat to vinegary mush, with the bones all still quite intact, along with the strong fishy taste, so we picked at the chowder, too. Somehow Mama gradually got rid of it so we could have something else. I never got her to admit throwing anything out, but I think she did. It's no wonder we were secret candy addicts, all of us.

Daddy brought down at least one deer every fall, and we weren't allowed to buy store meat until it was gone. "Deer stew," Mama would sneer. "Venison stroganoff." She claimed to dislike venison in any form and called it "denizen." Even with my keen smell and taste, I couldn't tell it from beef.

We would just about get through the freezer full of frozen deer; Mama, breathing a sigh of relief, would head for the A&P meat counter and some good old hamburger, only to return home to Daddy, pleased as punch with himself, his red cap gleaming above his glowing red cheeks, skinning a huge buck in the back yard, blood and steaming innards all over the place, and the cycle would start again.

I asked for steak for my birthday once, having never tasted it, and Mama burst into tears to think one of her children could be so deprived. She had grown up on steak.

DADDY SHOPPED THE SAME WAY HE COOKED, made trips to the PX in Quantico to cram the car to the tops of the windows with whole cartons of the things he loved: mushroom soup and apple butter, peanut butter and Hellman's mayonnaise, Campbell's tomato juice. As a retired Marine, he got everything at discount.

Mama would fume to us as he pulled out of the driveway with another retired Marine Corps friend in the station wagon: "He thinks he's saving money, but just think of all that gas!" She would ask the air, "Where does he think we're going to put all that stuff?"

One wintry day just recently when I chanced to meet, walking in the cemetery, the friend who used to accompany Daddy on the food runs to Quantico, he began to reminisce about Daddy. He told me that Daddy used to say on their junkets, "Betty's just remarkable. She's a wonderful wife," just as though he understood that she was putting up with a lot.

We strolled on toward the statue of Stonewall Jackson, then veered off to the left where Mama and Daddy and Andaddy and Nainai rest. Dave went on to tell me that one time when they came in carrying boxes and boxes of stuff, he'd asked my mother, "Doesn't it bother you that Buzz takes over the kitchen with his awful recipes and things?"

And that Mama had replied, "Oh, heavens, no. That's nothing. If it makes him happy, it's fine with me."

And old Dave shambled off through the winter-faded rows of grass between the headstones, still murmuring about what a wonderful marriage they'd had, my mother and father. Standing before their graves, I felt I'd received a gift. I hoped that Mama really felt that way, at least some of the time.

Mama had come into her own In the years without him, and frankly resented his intrusion back into her comfortable female world, where her domestic talents shone with a quiet light. Her idea of heaven was quilting, sewing, canning, with her women friends, while the children played nearby. Mama preferred wholesome plain food, and never got used to greasy southern cooking. Daddy's return put before her eyes again her dashed dreams of a harmonious marriage.

I didn't know that back then, but Daddy must have known it, too, and, unable to admit it or perhaps even understand it, certainly not the sort to explore sensitivity training, he barged around being bossy, trying awkwardly to reestablish whatever balance of power the war and his absence had upset.

Mama tended to react with passive resistance, not daring to confront his anger. I think she *thought* he'd never hit her, but I think she was never sure he wouldn't. All she could do was fume when he invaded and occupied her kitchen for days on end.

She changed the subject, but kept the resentment. She never forgave him for visiting those old friends in California before he bothered to come home from the war. That she claimed as the cause of her anger. It wasn't, of course, or if it was, it was only the merest part.

Winifred presiding at my wedding reception, 1963.

Riding Lessons

❮❮19❯❯

In her wonderful living room full of gold leaf and rococo plaster, crystal and marble, Winifred, herself loopy as a hoot owl, snorts, "Anybody'd vote for Buzz Letcher, they'd have to be crazier than owl shit. How in hell did you turn out so sweet?" How I love her!

DADDY AND GEE HAD HORSES WHEN THEY WERE YOUNG, KEPT THEM IN THE stall part in the woodshed, and rode all over Rockbridge County. Daddy cultivated his riding later at Fort Sill and again at Peking. Even Mama rode as a young girl.

I don't like horses, but *everyone* else loves them and rides them. So of course I try to learn to love horses. I really am scared to death of them. They roll their eyes around at me in a crazy, alarmed way; they are smelly and have big bottoms that drop obscene scat that everyone else seems delighted to shovel endlessly out of their stalls. One big flat foot could crush mine to jelly. But I do try.

After all, if I am not part of the scene, the others will talk about me, and leave me out when they plan slumber parties and cookouts on the trail, so I put up with it, for two long years.

One day as I make my long way home, thirsty and dusty, my legs jelly-like from holding on with my knees, my arms exhausted from shoveling horse manure, there is a woman in the side garden of the biggest house, holding hedge clippers and sweating like a hog. She looks up. "Hey!" she says, "you look lower than a sunken ship. Lower than a worm with fallen arches." She stands up, wipes her face with a handkerchief, and grins. "You look like you could use a drink. Come on in here and get out of the sun!"

I follow her, back from the flowerbed through cool formal boxwood corridors to a shady porch, where we exchange names. "You're Buzz Letcher's child? Hmmm. You look like your grandmother. She was a beautiful young woman.

"So how come he didn't drive you out to Liberty Hall? He didn't have anything else to do."

Daddy drive me somewhere? It's not an idea I've ever even entertained. If you want to go somewhere in my family, you get your little red wagon in gear and go. On your own. Other parents chauffeur, but not mine.

"That must be tough."

This is interesting. I admit that it is kind of tough. I think about that while she turns her broad back to fix iced tea. She adds a slosh of whiskey to hers.

"He came out here lit up once when he was a cadet, and I kicked his ass out. But I loved your grandmother. Now she was a lady. Do you know, when her son, that's Gee — everyone loved Gee! I was *in love* with Gee — anyway, when he died, she took flowers to his grave every day for ten years. Every day. That's why she was blind, you know. She cried so much it damaged the nerves in her eyes permanently." She shakes her head sadly.

"You know Gee was her favorite?

"You hate horses? Gawd, I do too! *Hate* the goddamn big things.

"You know your daddy used to be the biggest rounder in this town? He'd get drunker than a boiled owl. And then when he quit, he turned into Holier Than God A-mighty Himself.

"Lookahere at this damn bee, trying to get at my titties. Get away, Bee, that there's a dried arrangement!" She slaps at her chest and laughs. I feel laughter bubble up in me in a whole new way.

I drink the iced tea, trying to hold myself back from gulping it down. She notices, brings more ice and more tea, more lemon, more sugar.

"I work down at Ruth Young's shop, part-time. How come you never come in there?"

My tea chimes when I lift the glass.

"What you mean, you don't have any money? Yo' daddy is the richest sonofabitch in this town. Stingiest too. Listen, you come on in on Monday and let me show you this new sweater we got. It's softer than cashmere, and you can wash it in the washing machine. It's called Orlon. If you like it, you can just charge it to Buzz Letcher. That'd squeeze the old geezer right in the balls."

Her name, I am trying to remember it, is Winifred.

I realize I've said almost nothing, but she hasn't noticed.

"You know why I hate your daddy? He kicked a Negro man off some land his father owned. Harmless old Negro man. Buzz said if he let him stay there over seven years, he'd have squatters' rights to the land, and so that damn Buzz kicked him off, and tore down his lean-to. That pore Negro froze to death out on the highway the next winter. Yo' Daddy didn't need that goddamn piece of land. Lord, I *hate* your daddy."

She's pouring more whiskey in her iced tea.

She slugs it down. "Whew, I ought to quit Ruth Young's. You know that American flag they got in the window for Fourth of July? Well, it's the tackiest damn thing you ever saw. Usin' the flag for a drape? Goddamn! I just might quit, go to work somewhere else. I was at that shop six months before I realized those goddamn flowers on the wall were plastic. Plastic! Watered 'em every day for six goddamn months! I swear!"

In the weeks that follow, I stop by and partake of this secret ritual: iced tea and shocking grown-up talk. I tell Winifred what I think about a lot of things, including riding and my father. By about the third glass of tea, she pours the whiskey straight into her iced tea glass where lemon and mint still float, adds sugar, stirs it around, starts on another outrageous story.

"You know Eulalia Fultz? You don't? Just as well. Lemme tell you. Biddie Grandin died last week, and her sister Helen Penning was in the store yesterday when here comes that fat Eulalia Fultz. She couldn't be quiet, that woulda killed her; started in about how *wonduhful* the funeral was. Then she said it, right out, I damn near fell on the floor: 'Helen, your sister Biddie was the prettiest corpse I have ever seen! She looked so *natural!'* I could have vomited! I doano why I work in that godawful store."

I am laughing, and she is laughing. "I am going to piss my pants if I don't go to the bathroom," she says.

I love this woman who talks this way, but it's getting way late.

"Now, listen, dawlin, I want you to come back. Would you look at this hole in my damn girdle." She smacks her ample side. "If I don't get a new cor-set, everybody's gonna think I got a *tumor*. It'd be all over this town in ten minutes. 'Oh, did you heah? Winifred's *dyin!* She's got a *tumuh!'"*

Mostly I love that Winifred doesn't like my father, for I have never found anyone else in the world who would admit it, and it is a validation and a relief to learn that somewhere, someone thinks he's not perfect.

Through the next few years, Winifred will tell me a lot of stuff nobody else will about the birds and bees. In a lecture about contraception, she will tell me a tale of losing her diaphragm once — "and when I found the damn thing, it had a chicken feather in it. *A chicken feathuh!"*

At supper I mention that on the way home, I met a woman named Winifred. That's all it takes.

"She's a hopeless drunk," Daddy says. "You stay away from her." As he carves himself more roast pork, he goes on. "When her husband went off to World War I, she carried on with other men."

He goes on to relate that they had awful problems with her at the church when he was Warden: when Winifred volunteered for extracurricular jobs at church, Jack Partridge, who was on the vestry, always voted to give them to her. He'd probably fooled around with her, Daddy said.

But she messed up everything she touched. Drunk at choir practice. Drunk in church. Drunk at her own mother's funeral. "I went out there once myself when I was a cadet. Winifred was frigging everybody."

"Dovey!" Mama protests mildly.

"Well she was," Daddy says, unrepentant.

WINIFRED'S VERSION, WHEN I PRY JUST A TAD, IS THAT THE CADETS ARE UNDER such pressure at VMI that she's always tried to provide a sanctuary for them.

As for the church, it has wasted her great talents, and all the new young people have taken over the church, and all they'll let her do is help with the after-church refreshments.

"Nuts!" she grumps to me. "That goddam pimply adolescent moron preacher — have you seen his Adam's apple? — put me in charge of the *nuts*! What the hell kind of job is that? You ask me, the whole *church* is full of nuts, starting with *him*!"

Another slosh of Virginia Gentlemen in her iced tea.

Me and one of the Willies.

Porch Swing

20

*A*lthough Andaddy continued to work his crossword puzzles, I had lost the zest for our word games. I was too busy becoming a high school student to walk through the woods to his friend Sam Walker's to visit on a Sunday afternoon. His homilies had no more power, for I soon learned nothing horrible would happen if a boy kissed me. I no longer cared about why lightning struck this tree and not that one; I had been struck by other kinds of lightning.

Mama tried to hide her revulsion for Andaddy, for what she saw as his unclean ways, but without much success. The other children never did get very attached to him, and of course age had set him in his ways and slowed him down a lot.

WILLIE IS MANY BOYS I WENT OUT WITH through high school, rolled into one. The aluminum siding has been ripped off the front porch now, as it made an entirely useless room. It's just a front porch again. We are there most every night recently, Willie and I, and every time either of us moves, the old painted swing we're sitting on protests, squeaking. Completely ineffectual all the 3-in-1 oil I've squirted down in its rusty greenish crevasses. Some people call them gliders. I'd call them shriekers.

The sound means Johnnie and Betsy and Pete, egged on by Daddy, if he's feeling devilish, can all sit in the darkened living room behind the screened window of an early summer evening and comment on what we are doing. Andaddy's room is off the other end of the porch, and his dim light casts a yellow square on the porch floor. His radio is on, an impassioned speech about something, a crackle of static from time to time.

Mama won't stoop to spying, but the rest of them might. When Smokey, now old and eccentric, jumps up with his greeting *myowl* to try to snuggle in my lap, the swing mimics his voice. Each time Willie's arm snakes an inch closer to my shoulders on the flowered canvas back of the swing, the swing cries out. Hush! I want to say. Every time I shift my thigh an inch closer to his, the swing tattles.

Already the family has been regaled at supper with tatters of our overheard conversations, which go like this: "You gonna be there Tuesday?" Daddy mimics Willie, whom I met at church camp, exaggerating his country accent. And he warns me darkly about something called the Clap.

Then Pete, goaded to join in, his voice high in imitation of mine, says, "I reckon so, I mean, I guess, well, maybe, probably I can."

And Daddy, laughing and laughing, forks another lamb chop onto his plate. "You gonna be there Tuesday?" Pete squeaks, imitating Daddy's imitation of Willie. "You gonna be there?" He wipes his eyes. Mama glares at them, gives me a sympathetic glance. Andaddy adjusts his teeth.

There's no place else Willie and I can sit. The living room, hot as a sweatbox, is out of the question. We could sit out in the grass, but there are the nightcrawlers snaking out of their holes and maybe up my shorts. Chiggers too.

In the dark, I can smell better than see: peppermint gum in Willie's mouth, starched shirt and Coppertone on his brown skin, browner than his hair, which is nearly white, or seems so in sunlight. He can skate backwards as well as I can skate forward, talking to me all the while, or singing the words to the songs coming over the PA.

I try to get Willie to skate next to me, like the other couples who stay in the oval and skate at the same rate as all the others and never run into anyone, for it makes me nervous to be skating full-tilt forward at somebody who is receding all the while, on whom I'd fall full weight if I slipped up. But he likes to weave in and out, or skate clockwise against the current. He grins and waves at everyone. He's King of the Rink, and I love that everyone knows him and watches him. And I love the heady smell of the honeysuckle that climbs rampant outside the screens of the rink, below the bright and watchful stars.

There, I can forget Daddy's disdain, his apparent disgust for every activity I love these days, including church camp and roller skating.

WHEN I MOVE, I MAKE LITTLE COOL AREAS IN BACK OF MY KNEES, OR UNDER my bosoms, where the sweat can evaporate. *Croink, squueenk,* wails the swing.

"Think you'll be there tomorrow?" Willie asks.

"Um, maybe," I say.

"Well, I'll be there every night — waitin'," he says. Willie is captain of the football team. In summer, he attacks skating with the same ferocity: he goes when the rink opens, to practice, he's so dedicated.

Waiting — for me? I don't ask, but the answer is yes.

Inside, behind that black screen, I am sure I can hear, barely, giggling. "Willie," I say, "I'll walk you across the campus, okay?"

He takes it as a hint. "I better go, reckon," he says. "I'll see you out' the rink."

"You gonna be there tomorrow?"

"There every night," he says. He glances behind us. I've told him to be careful, that sometimes my brother spies. But then he pulls me to him, and smashes a minty kiss right on my mouth, and runs his big hands down my back, along my bare arms, and I feel like my insides are all dropping out. The swing squeals like a pig. "Come on," he whispers, "walk me home."

And even that I can't do alone, for Smokey follows along behind us, complaining bitterly as we get farther away from the house. At the edge of the campus Smokey stops, but across the shallow bowl of front campus, we can hear his mournful wail as he cries after me to come back.

That's usually what's going on, these early summer nights until I leave for camp, with some minor variations, like sometimes I'll move Willie's hand off my knee, or he'll put a hand on my breast and it's so warm I can't stand it, and I'll move closer, and the damn swing rats on every move we make.

Some nights we walk each other home two or three times, crossing and recrossing the cool smooth empty bowl in front of the deserted colonnade at W&L.

One NIGHT AFTER SUPPER, EARLY IN THE EVENING, Daddy's gone somewhere fishing, and Bing Crosby in the kitchen is singing "Where the blue of the night meets the gold of the day . . . Someone waits for me." I'm thinking that Willie's probably already at the rink. The twins are playing ball over on the near end of the Parade Ground with the old gang, like I always did up to this summer. Johnnie has gone off with his straggly band of gangly preadolescents, all of them big-footed and clumsy this year. I've finished the dishes and had a bath and put Yardley's English Lavender on the back of my neck and the insides of my elbows, and I'm planning to ask Mama if it's okay if I ride my bike down to the rink to meet Willie. When I hear the swing telling on someone.

So I slow up, and stand still a minute in the door to the living room. Out beyond the porch roof the sky is turning to deep blue above what's left of the sunset, purple-pink, and there's one big fat low star, so I wish on it, wish I weighed five pounds less, wish I had naturally curly hair, wish I had olive skin and black eyes.

The porch swing squeals again. I step around the corner. Mama is in it and there is a boy, too. At first I say to myself, Willie? But no, his head is too big, and his hair is not straight and blond, but dark and curly; he doesn't look a thing like Willie. While I stand there, Mama laughs low and slaps at something. I see him raise a hand up, and she slaps at that.

I am frozen in the dark; I can't move a muscle. It's that friend of Daddy's, Jeffrey Fairchild, from Richmond. A traveling salesman. What's he doing here? Should I go out and rescue Mama? Again, the awful peeling metal swing squeaks and cries, and Mama turns blindly in for a glance behind her, to the right of where I'm standing. I know from experience you can't see a thing from out there.

Then I remember, she was humming and putting Jergen's on her hands after supper. Usually she only does that at bedtime, and that nutty-sweet smell of lotion is my night-time odor. She also put lipstick on after supper, which is not the norm, a swooping M across the top lips, pressing her lips together in a taut line, then smearing it with her permanently stained little finger pad like she always does, so it'll look natural.

A rare breeze wafts in the smell of cut grass, mixed with the ghost of some strong shaving lotion. I don't know what to do. Suddenly he leans over her, and she lets out a little cry, and while the swing screams, their heads become one, and I can't look anymore.

The kitchen is hotter than the living room, as hot as an oven, as hot as hell. The light is still on, the yellow walls shiny with glare. Walking in the door, I begin to perspire. I go on through and out the back door, where it is night already, the sky black and smooth, and put my feet down in the crisp cool grass. Sitting down on the steps, I pick a stem of mint growing by the back door, and chew it until my mouth stings, and cool my mouth by sucking in air. Mama loves mint, puts it in tea, and makes jelly out of it for the roast lamb.

Out of the night Smokey appears silently, comes close enough that I can feel his fur against my ankle. His tail is a question mark lifted in the light. Once more I hear the swing complain, all the way through the house. Anddaddy will be dozing now, his radio still on.

Is his hand high up on her leg? Are his fingers snaking up inside her shorts?

"I'll be there," Willie crossed his heart. But tonight he will have to wait.

Down the hill from the front porch, in the fenced-in big front yard running down to the creek, Chop and Curry bound after each other, startled by something or pretending to be. The darker the night gets, the more ghostly their blurry white forms. In the night their bleats sometimes sound like owls' cries. They are brother and sister, distant pets, and when summer is over we will eat them.

I see Willie in my imagination, skating backwards through the night, chewing gum, grinning, in his clean starched shirt. The storm is coming closer, sheet lightning flashing over the town, the wind rising. The porch swing screams, and already I can smell rain.

My church youth group in high school.
I'm kneeling in the middle.

What Glad Tidings

⥽*21*⥺

*D*addy (at the supper table): Did you wash your hands? They don't look
clean. There's a flu epidemic; it's all over town.

Me (in my soothing hospital voice): I know. We have four cases at the hospital.
(That "we" is calculated. My world versus his.)

Daddy: Well, if you come down with it, I hope the hospital will take care of you.
Go wash your hands. And don't fool with those mashed potatoes. Here, give me your
plate. I'll put some on it. I don't know if this job is a good idea or not. I'll see if there's
anything at the bank. . . .

Me: Oh, no, I love my job. (Big, innocent smile as I eat heartily, calming the fear
in my heart: what if I do get flu?)

WHEN I WAS A SOPHOMORE IN HIGH SCHOOL, I GOT A REAL JOB, A WEEKEND
and holiday job at our new hospital, as ward secretary and receptionist. It
was a step up from baby-sitting, I had a desk and dressed up for work, and
the dollar an hour I made was a rarity for high school students. I knew all
the doctors and nurses, and felt I was in something of a catbird seat.

Further, having grown up with Daddy's terror of hospitals, I was pleased that I could overcome my own learned antipathy. I was surprised at the power of my sympathy to elicit gratitude, even love, from the patients.

I worked sometimes through the night, sixteen hours at a stretch, two days running, so I made good money, though my final hours of a shift were sometimes silver-edged with sleep, a place where I could drift from life into dreams and back again.

The hospital was small and shining white, all on one floor; my desk was near the men's ward, and on weekends discipline relaxed, things slowed, the doctors came and went informally, and I could go sit in the pale winter sun on the edge of one of the beds and talk to the college boys recovering from appendicitis, broken legs, sports injuries. I was an angel of mercy, Florence Nightingale, astonished at the swelling of my own heart's energy.

At home I baked the sick and homesick young men brownies and cookies in my search for salvation and insurance, for I felt ready that year to start dating college boys, even if it were going to be over Daddy's dead body.

And I knew Daddy, who had a lifelong dread and distrust of the entire medical profession, would not dare set foot on these shiny white floors.

One of the boys that fall, a Southern Conference pole-vaulter, said to me, "Honey, if you were any older, you'd be dangerous." How I cherished that delicious hint!

As for the job, all I had to do was record temperatures, pulse rates, and so on, on the patients' charts, in each case drawing a line from the previous record to the new one, making spiky rickrack graphs that were important-looking and satisfying. If flowers arrived, I delivered them. I dressed carefully for work, usually a plaid skirt and a white blouse with a Peter Pan collar or a cardigan Orlon sweater worn with the buttons up the back in the fashion of the year. I answered the phone in a calm cheerful voice, and took messages carefully on pink pads.

I had a collective crush on all the college boys. They smelled mysteriously rank and animal-like, nothing like the Noxzema-scented girls I hung around with, better than the scentless boys I went to school with every day. I loved going into the college boys' ward of the hospital, where even the empty sheets were as good as ghosts at telling me where the boys had slept. The men in our family didn't wear deodorant or cosmetics or rings because Daddy felt that all of these were effeminate. I guess Andaddy did, too.

One of the college boys, Ralph G ———, had a smell that excited me almost to sickness. It was, at least partially, tobacco, the sweet stink of sophistication and sexuality and all the forbidden areas of adulthood. Ralph was in for pneumonia, and stayed two weeks. He snuck off to the bathroom to smoke, which he was of course forbidden to do.

I envied the noisy and jostling camaraderie of the college boys and did my best to enter in to it. The girls I knew bitched and gossiped, and never did anything more daring than calling some teacher from a slumber party at three in the morning, disguising their voices and saying stupid things. I liked that, but it was all so tame. I wanted sex and danger. Most of the boys in the college ward had injuries, or appendectomies, and they weren't contagious, so I could talk to them and breathe normally.

Those boys talked of driving to Hollins, fifty miles away, in thirty-five minutes. No matter how fast you drove through Buchanan, everyone knew to slow down at Dead Man's Curve near Natural Bridge. Every year cars crashed and people got killed there. They talked about dangerous mountain treks. They rode bikes all the way to Craigsville, or hiked up House Mountain, snuck into Natural Bridge the back way after dark to try to climb its inner faces. They slid down the dark throats of caves in the earth. They ignored any hints on my part that I might like to go along on some of their outings. Sometimes I even asked outright, knowing it as debasement but never totally losing hope even when they managed to escape me yet again.

Accepting at the same time that I couldn't go with them — that being a part of their group was no more in the nature of things than, say, being a Hollywood movie star was — I took what I could get and was grateful that they occasionally acknowledged me on the street after they got out, and sometimes they even discussed in my presence something important that had happened, or some situation involving a girl, trusting me not to tell.

I alone knew about the time several of them had let a pig into the college library on a Friday night, and I knew about the time Ed Reeves, a Sigma Chi, and Tyler Rakestraw from Sweetbrier were parking with a pump organ and a stolen department-store dummy in the back of Ed's father's station wagon. I knew about the time Jay Collins, who was president of the student body, got drunk right before a student council meeting, and how he went on and conducted the meeting anyway, drinking a whole bottle of Listerine beforehand to keep anyone from smelling the bourbon on his breath.

Ralph was different. He was a *lone wolf*, in Mama's lexicon, though I told her nothing about him. I sensed, even with those boys who seemed to talk about almost nothing, and to gossip not at all, that Ralph was on the outside. Ralph, when I was around, would be even more mute than he was around the boys, broodily studying his nails or maybe twisting the radio buttons irritably trying to find clear channels.

My heart swelled with sorrow for him, and I sometimes dreamed about him, and I wanted to touch him, and to save him, to be close enough to get all of his scent that I wanted, and when I thought about touching him, sometimes my stomach turned queasy. When I thought of kissing, I tried all the boys from church, and from school, all the boys from the hospital, in my thoughts, but for a time it was Ralph who was there finally.

Ralph did not kid me like the others did; in fact, he stared at me with such anger in his muddy eyes that it frightened me. What could he be mad about? I always smiled at him. Once I tried to ask another patient, Charles Something, what was wrong with him, but as usual my hunger for sensational information was not to be satisfied. Men seemed like that, just not very interested in gossip. The boy Charles mumbled something vague like "Oh, Ralph's okay, he's just got a few problems."

"Like what?" I prodded.

But Charles, recovering from a late tonsillectomy, just shrugged, as if it did not matter, and asked me to go find him some ice cream. The boys always had the power to deflect too much prying on my part.

Ralph took to calling me Blondie, and the day he left the hospital he kissed me on the top of my head, and my stomach did its roller coaster dive.

Some weeks later, when I worked up to asking casually of a football player named Glenn Bowes, in with torn tendons in his left leg, if Ralph dated anyone, he said, "Nobody I know of." I saw Ralph out in town a couple of times after that, but he only nodded at me.

I made good money that fall, and things at home were relatively calm. Daddy, paranoid about germs, lectured me about things like venereal diseases. He asked me a dozen times a day about washing my hands, which none of us had ever done well enough, thoroughly enough, to suit him. He scrubbed his own as painstakingly as any surgeon. But he was impressed with my job, I could somehow tell that. Maybe it made me seem a little more useful than he'd thought I was. And making money always impressed him.

On Christmas Eve, I was working late, and had to come back the next day too, as the hospital had only a skeleton staff on holidays. I was bundled up against the cold at ten minutes to eleven, planning to walk the few blocks home in the stinging cold night, and finish wrapping the presents my pay had bought for Mama and Daddy, Andaddy, Johnnie, Peter, and Betsy. Christmas carols played over the intercom, and the hall out to the main door was white and shining, peaceful and clean. As I approached the empty lobby I caught the sharp smell of the evergreens decorating it.

I looked forward to the walk home in the clear darkness, drawing in the icy air until my lungs would feel full of needles. Looking up at the heavens, I would try to think which bright pinpoint could have been the star of Bethlehem.

I was pretty certain I was getting the charm bracelet I had so longed for, the red cashmere sweater, and *The Egyptian*, a book by Mika Waltari that I wanted. My feet were tired from delivering Christmas flowers and presents all day to the patients, but my paycheck would be substantial, and I was pleased with myself, when Ralph walked in the front door of the hospital.

His leather jacket collar was turned up around his neck, and I watched him watch me the way he always did, that look of fixed anger on his face. I hadn't seen him in weeks. He stopped a few feet off. I smiled and said *Hi* and asked if I could help him.

He didn't say anything, just held up his hands in an odd position, his fists out in front of his forehead so that the undersides of his wrists showed a yard from my face. At first I thought he was going to attack me. Then I saw that beneath his cuffs was some odd color or substance I didn't understand.

Before I could speak, he said, "I tried to kill myself, but the slashes won't bleed. They froze." And he began to cry, those brown eyes brimming over with water onto his flat cheeks. "Come with me," he said. Then he turned away and swiped at his face with both hands. When he turned around again, the hard look was back in his eyes. The big clock on the lobby wall indicated one minute after eleven.

I had no earthly idea what to do. I wanted to get him back outside in the safe darkness so no one else could see. And so his cuts would not thaw and bleed. He had said, "Come with me," making me feel excited and terrified. Where? Was this really going to be my first date with a college boy? And with Ralph, the most compelling, the most dangerous, one of them all? And would he die with his head in my lap, like Sinbad and Robin Hood in the movies I loved?

Once outside, the odors of blood and leather and Camels dissipated some, and I could think. I asked him if he had a car.

He didn't answer me. In the darkness I could hear paper crackle between his fingers. In a second, a light flared, illuminating his hands, casting odd shadows upwards onto his bent face, and he lit the cigarette, took a deep puff of it, and blew out a cloud of smoke.

My own breath made smaller puffs. "Oh, Christ!" he said, under his breath. I didn't know what else to do but wait. "Want one?" he asked, glancing at me.

I shook my head, and he put his hand under my elbow. At his touch, the floor of my pelvis seemed to contract and twist in on itself.

He steered me down the street, then onto the crunching gravel of a parking lot. Down the row of cars we walked in silence. "Here," he said, stopping at a dark Studebaker, opening the door for me. I couldn't remember that anyone had ever done that before, and I passed very near him as I got in.

The smell inside the car was his smell magnified a thousand times, wonderful and terrifying. In the car, he stared ahead, smoking. When he just sat there, I couldn't stand it. "I haven't had any supper," I said. "Could we go get some French fries or something?"

"Sure," he said, but still he did not start the car, or even turn on the lights.

Then I remembered his wrists. "You really should be in the hospital," I said.

"No," he said. Then, "I've tried it before. It won't work."

"Tried killing yourself?" In that moment, he seemed immensely tragic. The thought of dying, of not being, ever again, made me feel sick inside, and seemed for an instant to blanket the whole earth with hopelessness. I couldn't imagine *not being*. The sun would never come up again, it would never be Christmas, we would all die. *Die.*

As he nodded, he rolled down the window and flipped the cigarette out into the night, where it arced up and over, then out of sight, like a meteor.

Suddenly, a loud version of "Joy to the World" chimed out in the church tower over in the next block. I must have jumped, because he gave me a wry smile that might not have been a smile at all, in that dim light. "Blondie," he said, "let's celebrate Christmas." When he said it, he relaxed his weight, settling back against the seat, and reached his right arm the length of the seat back, a gesture that made that same thing happen again in my stomach. That black sense of depth and doom passed over, though the memory of it still made me feel nauseated.

"Well, okay," I said, feeling very unsure about whether it was okay. If I didn't, he might kill himself. I knew Mama and Daddy were next door at the annual neighborhood Christmas Eve party, with country ham and biscuits, the turkey with rolls, all the men crowded in the den, its air dense with cigar smoke, the women in aprons bustling from kitchen to dining room and back again, moving plates, putting out more rolls, pouring spicy mulled cider into the glass punch bowl, the Letcher Avenue kids in the basement with cookies and stacked crates of Coke. It was the same every year. Johnnie and the twins would be there, too.

I estimated that I had an hour or so before they would notice I wasn't there and Daddy would start to work up a mad, and as I sat there in the smoke of Ralph's presence, I told myself that this might just be the Christmas present I had wanted all along. I prayed Daddy wouldn't get mad — but I'd be home before he was. I could already envision myself casually telling my friends all about it, how Ralph had chosen me to spend Christmas Eve with! — that he was nursing some tragic past —

So then I said, "You at least ought to put a Band-Aid on that. We could go by my house —"

"Nah," he said. "Look. I got a real strong clotting factor. They've quit bleeding." He stuck his left wrist out of his sleeve over toward me, and for a second I thought he was reaching for me, as his other arm was still on the back of the seat. I couldn't see very well in the dark, but I nodded, feeling relieved. I didn't know what else to say, but I thought I could still detect the rusty odor of blood even though his wrists, now that my eyes were adjusted to the dark, in fact looked more scratched than sliced.

For just an instant, his hand grazed my shoulder, and despite my wanting whatever was beginning to continue, I froze, and did the first thing that came to mind, which was to turn brightly to him and say, "Well, so, what do you want to do?" I hated that I sounded so — alert, so nervous.

His face was in deep shadow, but I could detect, maybe by the feel of the air, the anger that was so much a part of him. "How old are you anyway?" he asked, then answered himself. "Fifteen. Did you know Juliet was fifteen?"

"Juliet Who?"

A low, unpleasant laugh. "Shakespeare's Juliet. I don't know her last name. She killed herself. She killed herself when she was fifteen. Just your age."

"Capulet was her name, I think," I said. Fitz Flournoy had read me —

"Uh-huh," he said, irritated.

I knew the police shone lights into parked cars, and sometimes arrested the teenagers who sat in them. "We'd better go, don't you think?"

It seemed to me he sighed. Then, with sharp and jerky movements which I knew meant he was angry, he started the car, and I wanted to cry out, "Where are we going?" but at the same time, I wanted to appear suave and cool, wondering for an instant if smoking a cigarette would help. I said nothing.

He startled me by asking, "French fries? Isn't there anything else you want?" Why did I feel such a shiver at the question?

Of course I did, I was hungry, but saying so seemed somehow greedy, so I only said, "Well, anything you want."

"Oh, sure," he said, in that maddening sardonic way I did not understand.

I realized where we were heading a good while before we got there. Ralph was going to take me to *that* place, the one Mama and her friends called a "den of iniquity" that I had heard about all my life. It was out in the country, an illegal roadhouse. Up the stairs above it there was supposed to be a prostitute named Maggie, who gave S&H green stamps and had the body of a twenty-five-year-old and the face of a forty-five-year-old, or so the college boys told it in the men's ward at the hospital.

They had carried people out of there dead from drinking too much whiskey — which was illegal to serve anyway. Two men had killed each other in a knife fight there once. There was even supposed to be the ghost of a huge slave who had run away from his master sometime before the Civil War and gotten caught up with and shot to death in this bar! He had no shoes, only rags wrapped around his huge feet, and on certain nights you could hear the shuffling of his ragged footsteps coming down into the bar. "We're going *here?*" I asked.

"Sure." He got out quickly. When he slammed the door, the cold surged in so that I had a reason to shiver. What if someone saw me? What if —?

He opened my door to help me out and added, "Best French fries anywhere."

It was not much lighter inside than outside. Tawdry red and green crepe paper and artificial holly loops swung gently in the smoky breeze from the overhead fan. Four men sat at the bar, drinking beer and studying their own reflections through the array of bottles in front of the mirror and the blue haze that hung in the air. Ralph steered me past their curious glances to the line of booths in the back shadowed and dark, and I felt, or imagined, the heat from the palm of his hand on the small of my back. "Oh Come All Ye Faithful" played softly, and the air did smell like French fries. I was so hungry my mouth began to water. Almost at once the waitress showed up. Ralph nodded at her, while I wondered from her manner if she knew him.

"What do you want besides French fries?" he asked.

I swallowed. "What are you having?"

"Rye and ginger," he said.

"A drink?" He nodded. I racked my brain for the name of a drink.

"I'll have the same," I said finally. Daddy had made bathtub gin at VMI during Prohibition, and Mama sometimes mixed some pineapple juice and ginger ale with rum when she got a group of ladies together. In China they used to drink martinis.

"Make the French fries double," Ralph said. As she went away, he reached across the table and put his hand on mine. It was still cold. I could not move or look at him.

"Haven't you ever thought of killing yourself?" he said.

I kept staring at the table. "No," I whispered. He took his hand away again and lit a cigarette. I'd imagined myself dead and in a coffin, and Daddy *so sorry* that he was weeping above me. But how I'd gotten dead I'd never actually imagined.

At first I was chagrined, for the drinks, when they came, looked like plain old glasses of ginger ale. But by the time the French fries came I was relaxed and almost enjoying the cave of the booth where no one could see us. As my eyes adjusted, I could see VMI cadets in their undershirts in other booths. There were initials carved all over the wood, and I tried to figure out whose they could be. I couldn't make out anyone I knew.

Ralph said he had a gun that had belonged to his father in the war, that he had gone out to the woods in the afternoon intending to shoot himself. He had thought about it, wandering in the cold for many hours, thought how they would find his body on Christmas. "Killing yourself is the hardest thing there is," he said sagely, narrowing his eyes.

A woman who had not been there before wandered past the booth and slowed, as if she thought one of us might be someone she knew. Hesitating, she finally lurched off toward the back, where, I thought, the ladies' room must be. I had seen her somewhere before. Was it Maggie? I looked over at Ralph, and started to ask, then decided it was too unsophisticated a question. Silently, we ate the French fries, which were crisp and delicious, dunking them into little puddles of catsup on our plates.

Ralph told me about the car he had until he wrecked it: an old Franklin, the only car ever made, he said, with an air-cooled engine. The sound of the phrase rode like an easy carousel pony in my head, *an old Franklin: the only car ever made with an air-cooled engine.* His knee touched mine under the table, and I moved my leg away, pretending that I was changing my position. He stared at me for an instant, then looked down and took a long drink from his glass. "Don't you want to have good memories when you're old?" he asked.

"Well, sure," I said. But it couldn't have been the right answer, because he only gave me a hard, disgusted look. I tried to smile.

He said when he was nine a truck hit him and left him without any memory of his life before then. When he was twelve his mother took him back to Boston where they had lived when he was little, and they went to see their old house so he would have an image to associate with his growing up. But it didn't mean anything to him, it was just a house, and a man came out of it and asked what they wanted. Ralph's mother had explained and asked to take him, Ralph, into the house to see the inside, but the man had refused, so they had to go back without seeing anything. It didn't mean anything anyway, he repeated.

"Where is your mother now?" I asked.

He shrugged. "Who knows? She left years ago."

A mother who just went off — and never came back! It seemed too awful to think about. Mama had left, but she'd always come back.

The woman who had been by before wandered back by, slower this time, and paused, looking down at me. She had on too much makeup, and was vaguely, unpleasantly, familiar. "Honey," she said unsteadily, "let me tell you something. Stay pure. Stay the way you are." Embarrassed, I didn't have any idea how to reply, and looked at Ralph to do something. He seemed to be listening to her sideways.

Then it came to me; she had come one day into the hospital, nervously glancing around. Since she would not meet my eye when I asked if I could help her, I had grown suspicious and followed her around until she glanced angrily at me and left, drifting on back out toward the lobby. In the hospital I had power, but here I could not meet her eyes.

Suddenly Ralph lifted his chin up in a sharp gesture, and that seemed to dislodge her. "Okay, okay, I can take a hint," she said, offended, and then backed off, her teeth bared in a menacing grin. A coat rack stopped her, and she barely caught it before it fell. Did Ralph know her? Walking unsteadily, she went on back toward the front.

"Was that — Maggie?" I asked, unable to keep still.

"What do you know about her?" he asked, sounding surprised.

I shrugged. "I've heard stories."

He made a face then, and both of us laughed softly, conspirators finally for an instant in a doomed, pathetic world; and, miracle of miracles, there was nothing weird or unwholesome in that laugh. I thought I had never seen him just *laugh* before, and it made me feel better, so when he reached his hand across the table that time, I let mine stay under it. By then I had conjured up several other drink names, so I was ready when he said, "You want another one?"

"A martini," I said quickly.

He laughed sharply. "You can't get stuff like that here. I mean, you want another one of those?"

I was so mortified that when he next offered me a cigarette, I took it and let him light it, and smoked it — not as gracefully as I might have, but not disastrously either. "Hold the smoke for a minute," he advised. "Then inhale." After a moment he said, "You look sexy with a cigarette. Older."

After our second drinks, our third drinks came.

I decided to ask him why he wanted to kill himself, because that seemed a foreign thing to me. By now, he was holding my hand under the table.

He narrowed his eyes at the question, seemed to ponder for a moment, then said, "I don't know. I hate holidays. I hate Christmas."

"You hate Christmas?" It seemed I had to mock him, I had no choice. "Golly! If you hate Christmas, then you must not like anything." And I heard in my ears how stupid my words sounded, how prudish.

"I like sex," he said, staring at me, his hand holding mine very tight. I thought of the blood, so near.

My lips felt dry and I ran my tongue over them and tasted salt. "That's what I want for Christmas," he said. "Here, feel this."

But I jumped to my feet, grabbing my hand back from under the table, exclaiming, "Christmas, to me, is the single best day of the year!"

"Take it easy," he said.

"What time is it?" I cried, too loud.

"Take it easy," he said again. "It's just eleven-fifty."

"Eleven-fifty!" I shouted. "Ralph! I have to go right now! My father will be — I forgot —"

"Take it easy," he kept repeating. "Just take it easy! You're not going to turn into a pumpkin."

He dropped me in the cold in front of our house, making no move this time to get out and open the car door for me. His brake lights glowed at the far end of the street like wicked red eyes, and the odor of exhaust fume hung in the midnight air.

Inside, the house smelled of spruce and tangerines and the *L'heure Bleue* that Mama wore to parties. When I began, in the front hall, to try to clear my head to remember what I needed to so I could explain, Daddy in his undershirt and boxers interrupted. "Don't rub your eyes like that. You could have gonorrhea."

When I put my hands up to cover my face, they smelled of cigarettes and rancid fat. Now I took them down. The alcohol coursed through my brain. "Wait a minute," I said. "Just what the hell do you think I've been doing?"

He wasn't used to that; he stopped, turned back. "I *know* what you've been doing, and don't you ever speak to me in that tone of voice."

"You don't know, either, and you're dirty-minded!" I fully expected him to knock me down, but he didn't. Without the drinks, I'd never have had the nerve to say it.

Mama stood as bound to the spot as if she had turned to a pillar of salt. "Dovey —" she began, timidly, but it gave me courage.

"You have no reason to distrust me," I said, right up in his face.

For a second he glared at me. Then he turned away, and started upstairs in his bare feet. "I'm going to tell the hospital she's safe," he said over my head. "Go take a bath and go to bed." He was talking to me. He had to get the last word. Mama was crying, trying not to let me see.

As I climbed the stairs, the church bells downtown began to ring. It was Christmas Day. Jesus was born. Keep yourself pure, she had said. Did Mary —? No, Mary was a virgin. I knew what that meant. You couldn't have a baby without — I felt weary thinking about all of it.

At the top of the steps Johnnie stood, waiting, his face solemn, a lanky serious twelve-year-old. "Are you okay?" he asked. I nodded, but I felt dizzy and couldn't quit crying.

"It's okay," he said, hugging me. "It's okay. I understand."

It wasn't, and he didn't, but I let him hold me until I could stop crying, clinging to his familiar boy-smell. All births were bloody, even Jesus's. Things being what they were, I wondered how anyone ever got born.

Camp Kiwanis, 1950: I'm in the front row,
fifth from right, and Jeanne is on my left.

Return of Anne Ivy

Daddy, at supper: Go wash your hands! You just don't know what you might pick up at that place.

Mama: So how did it go today, honey?

Me: We had a baby tonight. Some poor high school girl.

Daddy: Anybody you know?

Me: It must be awful to have a baby.

Mama: Thank goodness I was out cold every time. But they said I screamed and screamed.

Daddy: Pass the butter.

Me: How come you screamed if you were out cold?

Mama: Twilight Sleep. A drug called Twilight Sleep.

Daddy (to me): Well, you better not be getting pregnant. If you ever get pregnant, don't think you can come bringing some little bastard back here. (to Mama) Dovey, what you got for dessert?

IN MARCH, WHEN I WAS ABOUT SIXTEEN, a Saturday came that I looked up from my desk at the hospital to see a girl standing there who looked, for just a second, to be a stranger. But when she opened her mouth to speak, I knew at once who it was. Sharlene Rawley (I'll call her) was appalling; gone was the old wicked sexy swagger; pregnancy had bloated her once-shapely form, and made her sluggish, sullen, and sloe-eyed, and she had never gotten her front tooth fixed. I could barely remember her as the ripe bosomy girl who'd fainted in the arms of someone — oh, Buster — the brazen creature who'd shimmied up and over the fence separating Mrs. Garing's yard from the school yard to retrieve our balls, her underpants flashing a lying, pure white. Now her tawny curly hair was messy, and her eyes haunted.

I backed up from the first shock: Sharlene stood at my desk with her mother and a ratty cardboard suitcase, and no sign of Roscoe, the high school boy I knew from the grapevine had made her pregnant. I knew that she had failed to show up for school this January as her pregnancy became undeniably real. I did emergency check-ins when the desk was closed, and the OB ward, from Saturday noon until Sunday night. But I had never expected this. A long-forgotten moment came rushing at me like a 3-D movie, so popular that year:

> When Anne Ivy's smiles turn to frowning,
> And the practical jokes are few,
> When Addie stops all her good cooking,
> Then the family I'll come back to you, to you!

I HAD SUNG THAT SONG IN THE TENTH SUMMER of my life, my voice swelling along with Jeanne's, Susan's, and the others, strong with the surprising joy of being a part of the marvelous group. I absorbed all the camp songs like a dry sponge, hung on to every detail of the camp's lore, keenly envious of the history I had missed by not being at Camp Kiwanis until then. Submerged in that group, I was relieved of the tyranny of my self, my terrible individualism. I was, in a sense, reborn, and each summer after that for several years I fled to camp in freedom and relief from Daddy.

Anne Ivy. It had seemed to me back then that it would have been the ultimate joy to have a song written and sung by eighty people about you! This one started, "Last Tuesday they wrote me a letter, / And asked me to come back to them, to them —" and went on to declare that *only* when the mountains tumbled into the creek, *only* when the stars fell from the sky, only when *Anne Ivy's smiles turn to frowning* — would we come home. The mysterious Anne Ivy and Addie loomed larger than life, like all those guys we sang about, like John Henry, like the Noble Duke of York, like Ivan Skavinski Skavar. I leaned over against my buddy and friend from home, Jeanne, and I'd never loved her more than when our synchronous voices soared and danced in a rhythm as perfect as raindrops. And Sharlene was a part of that memory. She'd been at camp the year of the flood.

Sharlene's mother hurried off quickly, leaving her daughter forlorn and slope-shouldered, her stomach unbelievably huge. The nurses on duty were both new, and young, and Sharlene was led to a room and put to bed. She screamed and shrieked and groaned enough to make them call Dr. Brush, though it was, both nurses muttered to me, way too early. They didn't know *what* they were going to do with her. I had not been around when a baby got born, for up to now labor had occurred on the separate OB hall where I did not work, and during the week.

I could not stay away from Sharlene's room, drawn and repelled equally by her plight. If this were typical, I told myself, *surely* no one would ever have a baby. Perhaps this pain was payment for her sins of the flesh? I could hear her yelling and swearing, and Mrs. Agnor telling her to pipe down.

Back at my desk, I thought about those camp days five endless years before. Addie, as small as I was but old, black, and shriveled, ruled the small kitchen staff that made cocoa for us every morning to drink with our scrambled eggs and toast. Addie and her assistants each day turned out homemade biscuits, corn on the cob, hamburgers and beef stew, lima beans cooked in sugar and butter, and the hands-down favorite dessert, hot chocolate pudding with vanilla ice cream melting into it. Sundays we awoke to the smell of frying chicken that we'd eat at noon. Although Addie never smiled that I saw, I imagined that she smiled when we sang her song only a room away, in the camp dining hall with its wonderful unfinished-wood scent.

The smiling and lovely Anne Ivy in the song existed only in my mind. She had been at the camp in past years, but the summer I was there, she was only a part of history. It did not matter to me who she was or what she'd done at camp, for my vision of her was clear and strong, and I knew only that she was popular, and must have been wonderful to have merited a song in her honor, recording her name forever!

I was much taken with all the counselors who were so much older and more sophisticated than I, and envied Joy and Pat and Felicia the rebuilt chicken coop in which they got to sleep, with the clever sign over the door saying, "COOP." I envied the curlers on their heads, their filled-out bathing suits, the lipstick on their mouths, the pimples on their shoulders or chins. Every detail was something I longed for.

But the queen of them all, in my mind, was the absent Anne Ivy. The name was redolent with glamour, suggesting college with its promises and ivy-matted brick buildings. I saw her so clearly I'd have recognized her on sight, a tall cool blonde named for queens, with blood-red smiling lips, a waterfall of smooth bright hair perhaps down over one eye, like Veronica Lake. Anne Ivy was beauty contests, Hollywood movies, everything that the future meant to a skinny ten-year-old with uneven braids, whose chiefest claim to fame was more mosquito bites than anyone else in camp.

In my bunk on the back porch of Main with Jeanne and all the other youngest girls and a nail-biting jaycee who got on my nerves with her repetitive baby-talk, I dreamed Anne Ivy to life, and I dreamed my own life a swift train ride away from childhood, from home, from Daddy, from the depressing grit and whine of everyday.

Down the hall, Sharlene continued to groan and shout. I remembered how I was hungry that summer to know everything there was to know, longed to be a part of the in-group, Sharlene's group. Sharlene was on scholarship because she couldn't afford the twelve-dollars-a-week cost. You could see her developing bosoms through her thin t-shirts. She'd started a secret club during rest hour, in the bunk against the wall, down at the end of the sleeping porch. Sharlene had come late to camp, and, the spaces for the older girls all being filled, she had to sleep with us Hummingbirds, which was fine by us because she had been to camp before and knew things none of the rest of us did. Her conversation constantly alluded to kissing, dates, and secret things, rituals and activities so delicious they made her lose consciousness. In one story, a boy named Buster picked her up, carried her upstairs somewhere, and laid her down on a bed!

"What happened next?" I asked.

Sharlene only looked at me pityingly and said, with great scorn, "Oh, Christ, don't you know *anything?*"

Jeanne and I, talking of it later, thought that must have been when she fainted. Her club met during rest hour, the lower bunk turned into a tent by the draping of two red blankets around the ends and in front. I had inquired discreetly about joining, but Sharlene smiled mysteriously and said I wouldn't understand, I was too young. I understood that under the draped blankets were whispered jokes, giggles, muffled talk, and suppressed laughter like steam in a pot wanting to burst out.

A girl called Beanpole told me that when a friend of hers named Peanut started to join, they said she had to take off all her clothes, so Peanut didn't. "That's all *I* know," Beanpole finished.

At my desk in the hospital ward, I felt restless, prickly. The ward was for once empty; all the old sick people were asleep in their rooms.

I went and stood in Sharlene's door. Under the starched sheet her huge stomach rolled and heaved as waves of pain took her. I thought a Coke, which everyone but me thought was great, might be in order for her, and so I took out my own nickel and went to buy her one at the canteen just inside the hospital door. They were planning to put in a snack bar soon. "When Anne Ivy's smiles turn to frowning, / And the practical jo-oaks are few . . ." was still replaying itself in my head, as I stepped carefully on the polished black granite floor.

WORD WAS THAT ANNE IVY WAS COMING OUT TO CAMP ON SATURDAY, which was designated Visiting Day, a day on which anything might happen: some parents might bring corn, or enough watermelons for the whole camp. One girl's parents brought thirty carved wooden whistles for the Hummingbirds, but they had to be confiscated because just when you thought all was quiet for the night, someone could not resist the temptation to blow a shrill "TWEEEEEE!" waking up the entire porch. One father, presumably employed by Wrigley's, brought a pack of gum for every girl in camp. Eighty packs of gum, easily the most amazing display of generosity I'd ever seen!

I had a dream of Anne Ivy coming up to me that Saturday and smiling, and of our becoming best friends. I saw the excitement among those who had known her, and I, already so envious of the history I was not a part of, began to feel nervous about meeting her. What would I say?

But as fate would have it, I missed the Return of Anne Ivy. I had to leave camp suddenly, because Mama's baby brother Jack decided to get married on the spur of the moment, his bride's dress having to be remodeled for some reason that I couldn't understand. The wedding was going to be in Richmond, and there would be a tent on the lawn, and a band, shrimp, and mints at the reception, and Mama had hurriedly made me a new dress to wear.

I was surprised at how relieved I felt, though I outwardly complained bitterly about having to leave camp early. I knew that in reality Anne Ivy would probably spend all her time with her old friends, and have no time for someone she didn't know. Still, I entertained the regret of someone who has missed only barely a significant event of history.

And so I left Camp Kiwanis on Saturday morning, vowing to return next year, forever, every summer for the rest of my life, hearing only faintly my mother's worried static about whether the dress was going to be too small, I'd grown so, and getting my hair washed and dried in time for the wedding, barely hearing Daddy's instructions about sitting down and turning around frontwards. As camp receded in the cloud of dust our car raised, I pressed my hot face to the window and waved until the last beloved face faded. Despite that Daddy was mad about everything the whole weekend long, I had a wonderful time staying in the hotel and playing hide-and-seek with my cousins through the formal boxwood gardens at the reception.

Six weeks later, two weeks after camp had closed, on the peninsula of land where Camp Kiwanis was located, a flash flood washed away the entire camp one night, probably in a few minutes. Two vagrants were supposed to have been staying (illegally) in the Coop when it vanished. No bodies were found, but then nothing else ever was either, and the hoboes may have been made up, their story no truer than the campfire tale of the slave who wandered the peninsula on stormy nights in search of his lost arm, cut off by a cruel master.

School had been back in session for several weeks before we went back out to camp to look at the devastation, on a brisk glorious October weekend. Uncle Jack and my new aunt, had, astonishingly, had a baby that morning, and from the backseat my friend Jeanne and I could hear my parents talking in low voices of money and drinking and outrage and living with her parents and who was going to pay? Already Uncle Jack had, since the wedding, twice asked Mama for money. I knew about that, and knew that twice they'd ended up sending some, but that Daddy thought Jack was just *ordinary*, a word he reserved for the very worst people, and said both times he wouldn't give them any more.

The fences along the road from town were still clogged in spots with junk from the flood, trees and muddy mats of roots, boards, car pieces, whole porches, small lost things like jars and pans. In low places the mud had not washed out of the roadbed.

Daddy spat out the window. "Lou's just common, and her people are common," he declared.

At one place a hundred vultures rose like black umbrellas as we approached, and a terrible stench told us before we saw it that in the tangled fencerow, feet up, was a cow's tattered corpse. Jeanne and I broke into song at once:

> Old cow died by the side of the road,
> And the jaybirds whistled and the buzzards crowed,
> And the old king buzzard he flew so high,
> That he wished to the Lord another cow would die!

THE MAIN BUILDING THE KIWANIS CLUB had built us with cakewalk and barbecue money was gone, nothing but a severe edge of the cinderblock foundation poking up at a queasy angle from under several feet of sand and debris. Only mild indents showed in the sandy soil where cabins had stood. Addie's iron woodstove with its eight burning eyes, enormously heavy, had vanished as easily as the light wooden chairs.

Jeanne and I ran around the peninsula, pointing out things to each other: the outhouse pits totally filled in, the outhouses vanished; trees uprooted, the canoes gone. Jeanne called me to the riverside to point out that not only had the raft that was our adit to the swimming hole washed away, but also vanished was the dam of rocks we repaired every day to deepen the shallow river for swimming. The shoreline was so altered that it was impossible to say precisely where our beach had been. Twenty feet up in one of the few remaining treetops I spotted one twisted mattress.

In the sand were many baby toads, as though that flooding, which scoured away our forms, had released the spot to another form. After we'd looked around, Daddy was restless to go; on the way home, I cried in the backseat as I had not while reading the description of the flood in the newspaper, for the loss of a wonderful dream, and felt my life would not ever be the same again. Anne Ivy, whom I'd never met, was a major part of the loss.

At school that fall, in the telling, we put ourselves closer to the flood, barely making it to dry ground before the rolling waters gulped the camp. We felt important who had been part of the now-bearable ruin, and at recess as we played ball we chewed over the facts, the stories, the incredible disappearances, until what we'd seen and what we'd heard and what we'd imagined all became one.

Someone observed that eighty people had been there, which meant eighty mattresses, eighty chairs, eighty bed frames, and at least eighty cups, plates, forks — all lost!

Just over the school fence, beyond the bare dirt playing field where every day at recess we took up the ballgame we called Five Hundred, had lived the woman who was my boss now, head nurse at the hospital, Mrs. Garing, Typhoid Garing, as I secretly called her to my family. I loved regaling Mama especially with tales of Life at the Hospital, and Mama was the perfect audience, fascinated, mildly shocked at my boldness, laughing at the right times.

Typhoid Garing's presence was the only thing marring my total happiness with my job. Fortunately, she wasn't there often on my time, as she relegated weekends and off-times (my very hours) to the youngest, newest nurses, but her reputation was intimidating. She was imposingly large in her stiff whites and square cap, and her crackling presence made me sit up straighter, and lower my head over my charts, in the hopes that she would not recognize me from grammar school, nor recall the times we had invaded her yard.

We felt in fifth grade we were justified in making fun of her, for Mrs. Garing stole our balls, had stolen the balls of Ruffner Grammar School kids for ages and ages. Time had no limits then; old meant as old as time, as old as the Civil War. I could still see Sharlene, her green skirt hiked daringly high to get over the fence, Mrs. Garing's winter garden beyond stiff and faded as a painting, the greenish lily pond frozen over, the muted petrified weeds thick around the gray paving stones.

Nervous, unable to sit still and finding nothing to do as the charts were all neatly completed, I moved again to the door of Sharlene's room, thinking we might reminisce about the old days. She was silent. I worried that she had perhaps died, but on careful examination I could see her breath rising, falling. On her forehead beads of perspiration picked up the calm green twilight from outside, and her mouth gaped open.

Sharlene, smelling of onion sweat and kerosene, got a front tooth knocked out when Annette Somebody flung the bat and lit out for first. After that, tossing the bat was a penalty of fifty points.

Our softballs were folk artifacts: unable to bear the purity of their smooth responsive surfaces, we wrote all over them: our names, hearts with our boyfriends' and our initials done like addition problems, all in ballpoint, quick hearty or flirty sayings like the ones on the little heart candies you bought to hand out to your friends for Valentine's Day. BE MINE! HI PAL. TE AMO. KL+PH. The same thing I'd done in Norfolk with sailors' hats.

The school owned the one bat, which was by chance a good one. It had the most satisfying sensation of any bat I've ever held when it made contact with the ball. It was wrapped halfway up with filthy once-white adhesive tape for a better grip, and had an oval brand burned into it just above the wrapping.

Once in a while, a ball would glance off the bat queerly, veering over to the right, skimming the sturdy wooden fence, and disappear into Typhoid Garing's garden. Mrs. Garing, large and menacing, would if she were home stalk out, pick up our ball, and take it inside with her, ignoring us as though we weren't there, her back door slamming angrily twice, first the heavy winter door, then the lighter screen. When she failed to appear, we'd hang around the fence awhile, looking at each other, but that usually didn't get us enough nerve to go over.

It had been Sharlene, who also braved truant officers and teachers uncowed, who was the one bold enough to retrieve our balls. Her strong beautiful legs could climb anything; in an instant she'd hike her skirt high, flash over the fence, get the ball, throw it back hard, raise her dark skirt over her winter-white legs again, and be back among us before Mrs. Garing could appear.

It was known that Mrs. Garing had called the police many times; if one of us was caught in her yard we would definitely go to jail. One time in the far past a father had gone to her house after school to try to retrieve his daughter's softball; he had entered, *and never been heard of again*. When I thought about it, I didn't think that would happen to Daddy. But Daddy would never have retrieved a ball in my behalf, seeing as he did all losses (on my part) as lessons.

I don't know if we invented the game we played day after day, and year after year, in the Ruffner school yard, or if someone before us did. We argued the rules, contradicted, lied, inflated our scores, claimed victories, from recess to recess. While the boys in their separate yard out back played baseball, we imitated their game, with girls manning bases, even infields and outfields if there were enough of us, three strikes to a batter, four balls. We scored by numbers. A caught fly was 100 for the opposite team, a home run 100 for ours. Batting order, complicated and ritualistic, had to do with grades on recent tests. Hitting the ball into Mrs. Garing's yard lost the entire game for whatever team was unfortunate enough to do that. Further, it often meant losing the ball, vexing its owner, and suspending any game until another ball could be dug out of some bookbag or scrounged up at home by another one of us.

When a team accrued 500 points, it was the winner, and we started a new game.

What did Mrs. Garing do with all the balls? We didn't know, but the problem was standard fare for years at slumber parties, where fact and folklore got forever entangled. More than once we wondered aloud among ourselves if Mrs. Garing could "do" anything to us by holding captive our stolen names, initials, handwritings, handiwork.

In my months at the hospital, Mrs. Garing had paid scant attention to me, been nothing but pleasant. But I could sometimes hear her laughing about something with the nurses. She might loom over my desk and say cheerfully, "Got to find my rusty bent needle, give that old sourpuss in 14 his shot." Or, "Record a 3-H enema for Mrs. Fortson. That's High, Hot, and Helluva lot." And then she'd whoop loudly.

Once when Mrs. Sisley, a shy white-haired woman, came as she did every day to visit her dying husband, Mrs. Garing watched her scurry by the nurse's station, then leaned close over me and said when she was out of earshot, "She's only thirty-four. Her hair turned white overnight when he got cancer."

Mrs. Garing's unquestioned authority made me fear her occasional sudden appearances on the hall on a sleepy Saturday when there wasn't much going on, when I might be caught lounging at the end of a college boy's bed with my loafers off, talking. Once she caught me fast asleep at the desk, my head on someone's chart, and said to me sharply, "Been out with the boys, have you?"

The boys? What did she think about me? The only thing that scared me was that she might tell Daddy something awful about me.

Another time she caught me writing a letter to someone, on pink paper with roses, after I'd finished the charts. All she said was, "Better put a little salt in that shaker." It didn't exactly sound unkind but it made me so nervous that I immediately put the stationery away, and got out the charts again, even though they were all perfectly up to date.

It crossed my mind to ask her about all those balls, though of course I never did, never would. I didn't want her to connect me with our sins against her property. I imagined her peering down her cellar stairs at them, our letters fading, sliding into oblivion, mounded in the moldy darkness of her cryptic museum. What part of us was still in those balls, captive forever of her selfishness?

I COULDN'T GET COMFORTABLE at my desk, and moved nervously again to the door of Room 17. The afternoon had stretched thin, and gone on forever. Beyond Sharlene's window a sharp bloody red-purple stained the sky, and a sudden flurry of leaves rattled and scraped across the glass. Sharlene's baby did not come and did not come, and she woke groaning and straining, her stomach bulging like a mountain.

Dr. Brush had come and gone twice, his stethoscope swinging on his pinstripe shirtfront. I went to see if Sharlene wanted anything, and she was quiet, just staring at the ceiling.

"Sharlene," I said, "remember the times you went over the fence after our ball, at recess? Well, you're lucky, because Mrs. Garing, you remember her? is the head nurse here, but she's off for the weekend. Remember how she used to steal our balls?" I wiped at the sweat on her face with a washcloth wrung out in cool water.

"They went in her flower beds and broke the flowers. She loved those flowers," Sharlene panted.

I was surprised. I'd never thought of it that way. "You want some more ice?" I asked. I went to the basin to rinse the ineffectual cloth. I stood by her bed spooning in tiny bits of crushed ice, but it didn't seem to help her lips, which were pale and cracked. For a few minutes she dozed off, snoring lightly, and I got up to return to the desk.

But childbirth apparently made your mind wander, for as I left the room, Sharlene awoke, let out a scream, and I passed Mrs. Agnor running in. "I can't stand this!" Sharlene yelled. She called my name. "Get Anne Ivy, can't you?" and her voice ground off into a groan behind me. I turned back. Anne Ivy?

"It won't be too long now, honey," the nurse was saying, reaching her gloved hand up under the sheet. "Keep up the good work. Now pant."

What had made Sharlene remember Anne Ivy? I'd been thinking of her, of camp, but I was sure I hadn't said ...

As I stood in the hall, I heard her yell, "Damn that Roscoe! He ain't even — He won't even come to the hospital. He should be here! Damn him! Damn!"

I wanted to run, could not leave. I stood in the doorway, wanting it to be over, thinking no baby was worth this. But Mrs. Agnor shook a thermometer expertly against her wrist, and said to Sharlene, "Anne Ivy can't do *you* any good."

Sharlene groaned by way of answering, and I was horrified to see the mountainous bulge of stomach under the sheet peak to a point like an Alp as her bellowing groan also peaked in a scream. "Oh God, please let it stop! Oh God!"

Now I was really confused. What secrets were under that sheet? In my mind floated the red blanket that had covered Sharlene's earlier secrets. What was I missing? How could Mrs. Agnor know about Anne Ivy? Mrs. Agnor peered down at her watch. "You should have thought of this nine months ago."

"Oh, damn! Why isn't Anne Ivy here? Anne Ivy —"

I was baffled. Nurse Agnor didn't seem perturbed at all, just ignored the yelling, holding Sharlene's flailing wrist and squinting her eyes at her watch. "I think it's time to go to delivery," she said.

Sharlene caught sight of me, rolled her eyes, and said, through clenched teeth, "She never kept the balls, you little — she gave the balls back. She gave them to Miss Nettie, and Miss Nettie gave them back at the end of the year."

Her whole stomach seemed to heave, like a ship riding a wave. Miss Nettie, the principal of the school and our seventh-grade teacher, rang the brass bell for recess and for the day's beginning and ending.

"She gave them back? But —"

Once again Sharlene's face darkened with strain, and she began to pant like someone who'd been running forever. "Listen," Sharlene begged the nurse, "please, can't you call her?"

"I told you," said Mrs. Agnor, "she's not on duty until Monday. I'm not bothering her on her day off." She turned to me. "You," she said, "help me get her on this roller."

"Who are you talking about?" I asked the nurse.

"Ivy Garing," Mrs. Agnor said. "Who did you think? Here, grab this sheet and pull."

"But Anne Ivy —" I said. "She wasn't —" And I saw her clearly, her smiling lips, slim body, platinum hair, all against the red brick and ivy of some lovely campus, Fred Waring singing "Halls of Ivy" in the background.

"Not *Anne*, it's *Aunt* Ivy," Sharlene gasped, just as her weight shifted heavily onto the stretcher.

"Get the other end," said Nurse Agnor. "Let's go."

"Aunt Ivy Garing?" I said dumbly. At that moment warm water gushed from under Sharlene's sheet and drenched my loafers. "Oh, my God!" I said, stepping back.

"Oh, for heaven sakes!" Mrs. Agnor said. "You've been here all these months and this is the first time you've seen someone's water break?"

"She was the greatest nurse that camp ever had," Sharlene said. "And don't you forget it! My God, it's coming. It's coming! I can feel it. Oh, *hell!*"

Wet shoes caused illness directly. Daddy was right, I shouldn't have taken this job. But I had to do it. I brushed Sharlene's damp hair back from her forehead as we wheeled her out of the door and ran down the white hall pushing the stretcher between us, my loafers squelching. "It's all right," I said, but Sharlene, who was pushing her voice in a scream out of her lungs, didn't hear or care.

As we rolled faster and faster down that shining hall, Sharlene turned her eyes up at me, imploring, and in that gesture I saw again the long sleeping porch at camp, the endless row of bunk beds, the last one at the end sideways against the wall, red blankets around it hiding the secret club where the girls giggled and where I did not belong.

At the entrance to the OB wing, we stopped a moment while Mrs. Agnor went ahead to fold back the double doors. Stupid and uncomprehending, I stared down at Sharlene's ravaged face. It was as if we were back on the porch at rest hour, with all that mattered going on apart from me. I wanted to lean down in her face, and demand, "What is it? What is it?"

But I knew her; she would only have replied, "Oh, Christ, don't you know *anything?*"

The lights overhead receded as we pushed into the bright room where Dr. Brush waited masked like a robber, all in white even to the odd alien rubber gloves on his upturned hands.

The Dance: me with A. Collins Pettigrew to right of center, 1954.

My Own Mind

❊❰23❱❊

A. (for Arthur) Collins Pettigrew, I'll call him, has asked me to the dance! Formerly he has dated a girl I know who is small, thin, flat-chested, sparkly where I am ill at ease. She is a cheerleader, and has little feet, chic clothes, and dark lipstick. She is also bad: once pinned to a fraternity boy at Washington and Lee, and ringed to a cadet at VMI — at the same time! But Collins, handsome president of his fraternity, BMOC, has, against all odds, seen the light and called me! Justice is for once served. Welcome to Paradise, Population 2.

But at the dance, feeling glamorous in a fog-gray silk dress Mama has made me just for the occasion, silver high-heeled slippers, and white gloves, I am quickly deflated. From the outset, already too late, I sense that Collins has brought me here only to make his old girlfriend jealous. He is not with me in any sense. He responds lethargically to my conversational efforts, and his eyes search the gym with its dimmed lights, for her. I follow his gaze, seeing through his eyes now as tawdry the blue and green streamers I spent all day draping from rafters and basketball hoops, the candles on each table tied with blue and green ribbons, the picturesque painting of an arbor, and trees, a boy and girl holding hands, that I'd done a big hunk of.

As soon as he can manage it, Collins is dancing with his old love, while I sit on the side simmering and miserable, feeling betrayal at every hand. People are paired off, and only one or two goony leftovers skulk in the corners, and finally come to the rescue and dance with me.

HE'D BEEN THINKING, DADDY TOLD ME, that summer before my last year in high school. And here is what he'd decided: I should really skip college, and join the Marine Corps because I liked to travel and I liked people, and my name would be noted there, and I'd have preferential treatment because of him. College would be a waste of money.

Or, if I chose instead to stay home, he could get me a position as a bank teller in the bank he was now on the Board of Directors of.

"A bank teller? Me?" I can feel the mercury rising in my thermometer.

"Well, if you don't want to travel, it's secure work until somebody marries you."

It took me years to figure out what was so appealing to him about that bizarre idea: I'd be in a cage from the waist down, protected from predators. Furthermore, the people you'd meet in that position are generally going to be Men of Means, for who comes into a bank unless they have checks and stock dividends to deposit? Only worthless day-laborers get paid in cash and keep their money in socks.

As good an auction block as existed then, I guess. How he must have yearned to be rid of the squirming intrusive all-too-present me, to shift the responsibility to some other poor man!

"I'M GOING TO HOLLINS," I said firmly.

We'd already had a lot of discussion. After it was decided that I *would* go to college (for Daddy was really against it, couldn't even grasp the concept; girls just didn't go on in school, or if they did there was certainly no return on the investment — I'd just marry someone and not finish, and waste all that money), once we'd gotten over that hurdle, Daddy decided I should go to Randolph-Macon, because some ancient distant relative was registrar, and could "keep an eye on me."

He hauled me, reluctant, to Lynchburg, where we toured the tree-dotted campus in the company of the old lady, obscenely ancient, tottering about in nurse shoes, detailing the rules and regulations, shifting her yellow false teeth, and swapping genealogy details with Daddy.

But I had begun to sort out that I was a democrat like my grandfather, and having observed the damage and foolishness of fraternities for too many years, found a reason for rejecting that college: I told him I found it silly to go to a school where there were *sororities*. I told him if I went there, and refused to join a sorority, I'd be an outcast. After all his objections to my going to fraternity parties, he couldn't very well contradict that argument.

Mama's vote was for Sweetbrier, with all those *nice* girls from old families. That was the kiss of death as far as I was concerned. Mama, always less persuasive than Daddy, didn't insist on a visit. She just knew they had a May Court, and she'd been there once, and it was a lovely campus. . . .

A current beau advised Wellesley, where *his* mother had gone.

Hollins was never mentioned, so it became *my* choice. I applied to all four schools, and all four accepted me.

Randolph-Macon was out.

All I knew of Sweetbrier was horse shows, definitely not for me, as I had never gotten over my opinion that horses were big dangerous animals that smelled bad, could bite, step on you, or brush you off, and took a lot of dumb demeaning work.

I wanted nothing to do with masculinized bookworm girls with bunned hair and rhinestone cat-eyed glasses and no lipstick and complexes about standing up straight (like my beau's mother), so I rejected Wellesley, along with that particular beau.

That left Hollins. Daddy was grumpy, and stomped around some, for he still clung to the idea of Miss Cousin Nurseshoes keeping an eye on me.

But he didn't give me too much in the way of an argument. He just plain figured college was a waste of time for girls, and they were all out-rageously expensive, so it really didn't matter where I went.

But I was going to be a teacher. (I had throughout my childhood and high school envisioned myself as the head of a pleasant and old-fashioned room, the walls dingy and unimaginative yellow above, green below. The old wooden desks are there, the hundreds of romances forever recorded on their carved surfaces: Lois loves Harry, Helen and Boo, CD and KW, Cindy and Mike locked forever in a wooden heart. The windows are large, with shades that must be raised or lowered with a complicated sys-tem of pulleys and handles, and they still have the inslanting glass panes at the bottom to discourage birds or squirrels entering and children exit-ing. The door still has a glass transom, which opens at a slant to let in air and the smell from the lockers in the hall, where millions of lunches have yielded up their vague aromas, to linger like ghosts in the air: egg salad, peanut butter, sour milk, potato chips, and over it all, bananas gently rot-ting through a million school mornings. A glass shelf encloses books in duplicated sets; the cloakroom shelf still holds muffs, hats, and gloves on the shelf, coats beneath on double hooks. In fact, I will spend the next three summers teaching in rooms like this one, rooms where I've gone to school — and the next lucky thirty-five years teaching college English, mostly in lovely high-ceilinged rooms like those.)

My freshman fall at Hollins, eager to assure Daddy that I had chosen rightly, I wrote my parents what I was taking: English, history, calculus, Latin, humanities. I was proud of that schedule: no fat.

But in a hasty letter back, Daddy wrote, "Take something useful, like Typing. Drop that Humanities, whatever it is. You're human enough already."

I was going home that weekend, and I was all set, articulate and right-eous. The course was *required*. As Daddy generally focused only on his requirements, not those of others, I had assembled several arguments; my ace in the hole was that I knew vaguely that Andaddy had set aside money for my education, and Daddy could not keep me from getting it.

He was combative: "I won't pay for this stuff," he said.

But I was ready. "I *have* to take humanities," I told him. "It's *required.*" That was only my first argument.

To my surprise, I didn't have to go any further. "Oh," he said, only mildly surprised. "All right then." And that was the end of that.

He didn't know much about liberal arts colleges for women, and he stood cowed before the mystery. I used that claim later many times, and it worked exactly the same way every time; he'd tell me to take shorthand or typing, and I'd stare him down and lie (after the first time) that Creative Writing or Twentieth-Century Southern Drama was required. End of discussion, with no more punishment to bear than the scorn in his shrug, for a college for frippets that would *require* such frippery.

I heard a lot in letters about his military education: mechanical engineering, surveying, military history. I heard dire reminders of the only *other* English major in the family, the meteoric John Letcher Harrison, Ph.D. in English — who went to New York in a Stutz-Bearcat and returned home in a cardboard carton.

But I didn't pay much attention to anything he said after that: the strings were loosening; I was almost free.

I had learned early, and from him, that outrageous was okay; if one were charming, one might get away with anything on earth. I was my grandfather's child, loving lots of people and thriving in the intellectual challenge and social excitement of college.

I went to Hollins, and Daddy paid the bills. I took the famous beaver coat along, and wore it to dances, spraying it with perfume first, and hoping to get asked about it so I could regale some new beau with the story of its creation.

On weekends when I came home, I still sang in the choir at church, as I had done since my discovery of Boys. Sassier by then, and defensive about my chosen loyalty to the church he'd left, I would demand to know how he knew that the preacher and the vestry and choir were wife-swapping back then when he was the warden, but he'd only say, "I just do." Later, like every other college student of my generation, I told my parents I had concluded that I was an Existentialist.

Andaddy died of heart failure, or perhaps it was a broken heart, just after I went off to college. He was by then bereft of everything that had meaning, inhabiting an environment sad, sterile, and hostile, and I reckon that he had no choice but to leave. I was too busy adjusting to college to go home for his funeral.

Later Johnnie told me that Daddy, "to make a man of him," made him go into the room and stand, and watch, as Andaddy gasped and writhed in his final death throes, heaved himself to a sitting position, foamed at the mouth, and died.

Lexington, Va.
Jan 9th, 1956.

Dear Kaish:

I was glad to get your letter. I have to go to Richmond Wednesday but I will get back Friday night and will be glad to see you. Sorry that you missed the quail, but maybe you'll have one Saturday. No news here, cold but I expect you are also. Hope you get more humans or whatever is required to pass that course. Better stop reading comic books and take up something serious, like the Rover Boys.

Love always, Daddy.

"Quail" refers to a boy I dated named Bob White.

Love

I hear Mama from another room tell Prissy over iced coffee in the living
room how furious it made her that Daddy, arriving on the West Coast
after nearly four years away at the war, stayed out there for a while visiting old
friends before coming home.

"Oh, Betty! How could he?" Prissy sympathizes.

To Prissy Flournoy and others Mama tells the story of the wet branches ruin-
ing her hairdo in Peking. "I've never felt the same about him since!" she declares.

MIDWAY THROUGH COLLEGE, I fell under the spell of a lawyer from Florida
exactly twice my age, already established, settled, handsome, and mature.
He was ready to marry, I thought I was ready to leave college, and I knew
I was ready to leave home. I'd decided on a career in radio.

I was showing him around Rockbridge County when he asked me,
"Could you trade all this for an orange grove?"

I said I thought I could. The announcement appeared in the *New York
Times* (because my great-grandfather had been governor of Virginia in the
Civil War).

It was not until ten days before the wedding that I put together the terrible mosaic: he figured I would be a dandy ornament for his life. He called me "Kitten" and wanted me to formally adopt that nickname because it rhymed with his last name. I also listened to him say early on the day at the end of which I finally returned his impressively large diamond, "No wife of mine's going to work," when I had been all along planning to launch my career in radio the second we got settled.

"Date with Kate" was going to be the name of my show. I'd met the station owner at our engagement party in Florida, and we were in the talking stage. My fiancé apparently hadn't thought I was serious.

Finally, he had decided to give me braces for a wedding gift. No, he certainly wasn't, I said. My teeth might not be perfect, but they were okay with me. No dentist had ever suggested I needed braces. "But I'm going to pay for them," he told me, angry and hurt at my indignation.

When I saw how far he'd missed the point several times, that was it. I couldn't explain how tacky I thought it was for a first and last name to rhyme, or how insulting it was to be told (by a man supposedly madly in love with me) that I needed braces. So I didn't explain. I didn't care whether he understood or not.

I wrapped up the ring in a sweater his mother had knit for me and sent them back; I called Mama and told her everything was off. I went home a week later to wrap and send back over a hundred presents, each with a brief explanatory note — and was confronted by a *tsunami* of Daddy's anger and disapproval. *You've always been a failure! You'll never amount to anything! You are a damn fool to give up a good man like Bert Britten! I'm going to "disown" you!*

Exhausted, humiliated by all that had occurred, I burst into tears as he stood over me. That time, it was Mama who said sharply, "Oh, hush up. You are not."

Daddy looked startled, slammed out the screen door, leaving it to bang angrily, and went away for a few hours. When he came back, perspiration was rolling off his face and bald head, and his face was beet-hued. I held my breath, waiting for what would come, but he never said another word about it. He'd swallowed the camel.

I thought nobody would ever forget, and I felt naked and stupid and careless. Then Edith, a friend of Mama's, came for coffee one morning, and to help us package up the crystal, linens, ashtrays and lamps, Revere bowls and food warmers, and confessed over the broken landscape of brown paper and tape on the dining room table that she'd broken an engagement years before, and that her mother had fainted and taken to her bed, and refused to get up for two months. I was astonished and comforted and gratified, having never thought of Edith as anybody but the mother of Bill and Joe.

During our wrapathon, Mama had tactfully suggested I call the camp where I'd worked as a counselor for two previous summers and see if they might not need me for the summer. They did; I returned that summer and for two more years, and I stayed in college and vacationed at home for a little longer.

COLLINS PETTIGREW AND THE GIRL he had been in love with were GET-TING married. She hadn't finished college; he had. It was a summer wedding, and at the party the night before, Collins got terribly drunk and kissed me on the mouth and when I pulled away said, whispering wetly in my ear, "You were the one I wanted. You were the golden girl. I was scared to touch you. You were the *General's daughter.*"

Then he wove loosely across the room, his walk and talk slurred from booze, greeting and kissing the other guests. I watched him go, feeling proud, and angry, mistrustful of his slack mouth, and most of all, relieved. The next day the wedding came off as planned.

ONCE, A DECADE AFTER THE SUMMER I KNEW HIM, when Fitz Flournoy was near retirement, I invited him to speak at Hollins where I was a senior, graduating in less than a month, an editor of the campus literary magazine and president of the literary society, headed for graduate study at Johns Hopkins.

I remember him in a dark suit with a shining red satin vest moving slowly toward me across the green and shadowed spring quadrangle at sunset with the same ponderous grace that had always characterized our meetings. The wisteria was in bloom, amethyst cascading down the columns of the sedate academic buildings, and he cast a long shadow behind him that I watched, with the sun at my back and my shadow stretched out in front, until he moved from his brightness, bronze, crow-black, blood-red, into the dark shape of my shadow on the grass, and kept on until he stood in front of me.

But I can barely remember that visit. I'd had my wisdom teeth removed that day, and distracted by my discomfort and the dulling pain medicine, I took him to dinner in the school cafeteria, awoke to find myself chewing on a hard fried oyster with the new stitches in my mouth, switched to ice cream instead with the taste of blood in it.

I later walked with him along the colonnade of profuse blossom and into our elegant green drawing room, and on the hour stood and introduced him to the rustling roomful of young women as an old friend and a great scholar. But I don't recall at all what his talk was about, I believe I fell asleep during it, and I think I hardly spoke with him. I do remember that later that evening my friend Trudy commented that he was better than Allen Tate in her opinion. He had spoken on *The Tempest*. Trudy's dress that spring night was pale flowered chintz, and she wore a stiff crinoline underneath to make it stand out.

I remember that part, and the achingly beautiful spring evening, but not a word Fitz Flournoy said. I would like to have told him, though I hope he knew, what a difference his fathership made to me, the difference between shadow and light.

If he was a drunk, I never knew it. He was sober at our meetings, sober that evening at Hollins. I was the one who needed drugs to get through his visit.

I have since understood that, though I was trying to make it up to him by inviting him to speak to my club, and by showing him what a record I had made for myself, I did not have the courage to face him, as he had me, much earlier, sober and without armor.

Mama, 1971.

Butterfly

≈≪25≫≈

The July morning in 1979 that my mother died, Daddy and I sat on the
steps of the house he had built and Mama had hated, and he said to me,
his hands hanging helpless and empty, "Mama was a wonderful wife. We had a
wonderful marriage. The only thing we ever disagreed about was having a dog."

I was flabbergasted, actually struck dumb. I know truth is not the same for
any of us, but that remark was unbelievable, especially following as it did the
months of his refusals to give Mama what she wanted to eat, his anger so close to
the surface that once, when someone had set a gift bushel of tomatoes inside the
kitchen screen door and he found them in his way, he furiously kicked the entire
bushel through the screen, spilling tomatoes everywhere on the back stoop and
leaving a cartoon-like hole in the bottom half of the screen door.

My brothers and sister remember different things than I do, and often they
remember the same things differently than I do. We can't even agree on so apparently simple an issue as why our parents' marriage seemed such a prison for them
both, though we all do agree that their marriage was disastrous. But even that is
only our collective judgment; Mama definitely felt trapped, but obviously Daddy
didn't, not if he could say what he did the morning of her death.

BUTTERFLY: AN APT IMAGE FOR MY MOTHER, for she was delicate in her sensibilities and taste, extremely feminine, loved bright colors and gay clothing, and was short-lived.

She collected bolts and bolts of Chinese silks during the years in Peking; our attic still harbors big trunks full of it — often there are thirty or forty yards of one color. I knew the story: they were called "tribute silk" and had been brought from all over China as tribute to the Mandarin emperors for many centuries. But after 1911, when the last Manchu emperor died, and the city needed funds, the endless warehouses crammed full of the silks collected over centuries were opened up, their contents auctioned off to the small merchants of Peking who in turn sold them for many times what they paid. Some were nearly a thousand years old. They were still, to Americans in the thirties, ridiculously cheap. The exchange rate was such that one American dollar spent in Peking translated into about twenty American dollars' worth of merchandise.

Thus there was always a ready source of silk (of nearly any color I could wish for) whenever I (and later Betsy) needed a dance dress or a new blouse or skirt for a party. Only after Mama died, and Daddy remarried, and Betsy and I went through the trunks, did we discover and rediscover bolt after bolt, roll after roll. It didn't make sense; my mother never would have made, for instance, mauve curtains, yet there were forty yards of a wonderful silk in that color.

I think I know why now, after years of thinking about it; I don't think she intended to sew them all into dresses or curtains or quilts, though her sewing was famous, and all our prom dresses were of turquoise or pale blue or water-green or electric-blue embroidered Chinese silk. My wedding dress was of creamy white silk, with little sprigs in subtle relief. A generation later, we were still dipping into the silk to make Betsy's daughter's wedding dress.

I am sure that Mama bought them because she could not bear to leave behind in China the amazing colors, which were not available in America until many years later. They were colors that you could drown in, colors that you couldn't hold in your head: rusty roses, teals, persimmon and cantaloupe, dusty greens, pale indigos, deep spruce greens, mellow golds, and every conceivable shade of blue, which was Mama's favorite color. There were burnished metallic sunset corals, soft cloths of warm gold that shone, and where they draped or folded, magically changed colors.

A few of the pieces were intricately embroidered, possibly by hand, with birds or vines or flowers, and there were even some pieces with scenes of cityscapes, of children flying kites, of warriors on horseback. The colors were like heavenly hues people report from near-death visits to Paradise: unearthly colors — a hue somewhere out of the spectrum but in the realm of blue, green, and gray, or a color we'd name orange for lack of a better description, but that was no more "orange" than is the pearly blush at the center of a ripe peach.

In some, threads of real gold gleamed from glowy sea-turquoise or royal purple. We knew about that, too, how the Chinese wove in solid gold thread, for it was the only metallic thread that would never lose its luster.

Mama showed no more preference than butterflies do in her purchases; she just had to own them, and they cost almost nothing.

Mama became an artist late in her life. She moved from tentative watercolors of wildflowers to bold collages and landscapes, brilliant abstracts and subtle seascapes. She put her utilitarian sewing skills to artistic ends, and perfected wall hangings, sewn pictures, silk collages. She made stuffed and decorated Christmas tree ornaments. She won awards and got her work into major shows apparently effortlessly.

When her mother, Laolo, died, Mama showed remarkable acumen, buying with her modest inheritance a few choice stocks she personally liked: Kroger and Revlon among them. ("Kroger? A&P is a better stock!" Daddy protested. But she wouldn't be advised. "They're nicer out at Kroger's," she replied serenely. It was her money; he couldn't do anything but fume.) But the main stock she bought was Fritos, which she thought was the single best food ever invented. She even decided that Fritos were healthy, as they were made of pure corn, corn oil, and salt. Up to then, she'd been an enemy of all junk food, which had proliferated since the war.

She did very well in the stock market, baffling Daddy, who chose stocks after studying their annual reports and keeping up with the market. The only emotional decisions he ever made were not to buy Coca-Cola or any tobacco products. But he had never heard of choosing stocks because you ate one of their products, or liked "Fire and Ice" lipstick.

That little bit of money-generating income did wonders for Mama's self-esteem, and made her sassy. She took some trips with her sister Polly, at her own expense, to the Caribbean, where they sat in the sun and drank rum things with fruit.

At her death, she left all her money immediately to the children; perhaps she knew Daddy would try to avoid doing that. Each of us had from her an inheritance which, well-managed, would bring in five or six thousand dollars of extra money every year.

My mother was extremely self-effacing about her art, and disparaged it relentlessly, even after she became successful, and, at least locally, somewhat famous. She made clothes for friends and for us, made herself evening wraps, a long regal purple-blue gown for the annual Marine Corps birthday party, a wine-red going-away dress for my honeymoon.

Still the silks held out, and at the end of her life crazy quilts appeared, pieced with scraps and remnants of the gorgeous silks, decorated with exquisite silk needlepoint. She made one large quilt for each child, small ones for each grandchild that came along, and a few more for friends. She was generous with her paintings, and today in Lexington the hospital, banks, and library display her work. At Christmas, I spot her ornaments on trees all over town.

All of us throughout our childhood were dressed sensibly for the most part in navy as our "basic" color. Practical, she said. Doesn't *show* dirt. I always had a navy winter coat or jacket, with my one brazen exception, the glorious fuschia fur-collared coat with rhinestone buttons I chose when she was hundreds of miles away, which I wore until the shoulders split apart with my growing. I always had a navy skirt and a navy sweater, whatever else I owned. To this day. The silks were our *icing*.

"There goes your Mama," our daughter says, as a silver-spangled fritillary bounces by. She's a believer. For I have had, since Mama died of bronchiectasis brought on by breathing in spray fixatives that she used in her painting, an odd fancy, a conceit, that Mama comes back to check on us — in the form of butterflies, many different colorful kinds, my dear mother bopping around in midair changing from one glorious outfit to another.

Mama had the strangest talent: she could, at any given instant, stoop down in any grass and come up with a four-leaf clover. I don't mean once, or twice, or several times. I mean I never saw her fail to, and I must have asked her or watched my sister ask her, or seen our friends ask her, a thousand times. She pooh-poohed it herself, saying four-leaf clovers were much commoner than people realized. But I never saw anyone else who could do that. Bust clouds, yes; dowse, and feel that coathanger yanked downwards as if by a magnet, sure. Remember the words to thousands of poems or songs, easy. But that stooping down, and coming up with a four-leaf clover every time, that was *grace*.

In her art, especially after it had escalated to smashing large-canvas collages and brilliant watercolors of whole imaginary cities reflected in water, the gorgeous quilts, Mama used spray fixatives to hold her pastels and watercolors and collages on the paper or canvas. Nobody knew they were dangerous. Nobody knew what was going on when she came down with a tenacious lung congestion as I was getting ready for the birth of my first child in 1971.

There followed six and a half years of benign-sounding pronouncements: *Nobody dies of bronchitis. It may be an auto-immune disease, and maybe cortisone will help. We think it's tuberculosis. Penicillin will take care of this in no time. Ah, it's just a persistent sinus infection.* Each opinion was followed by biopsies, heart catheterizations, steroids that made her moon-faced and swollen, horrible sinus treatments. The list grew of all the things it *wasn't*: syphilis, emphysema, her heart murmur, lung cancer, psittacocis, lupus.

Primary pulmonary hypertension is what they finally said. She could learn to live with it; it was just chronic bronchitis, and wouldn't kill her.

She got worse. Osteoporosis combined with her constant coughing eventually cracked every rib, and several vertebrae. Weakened, she was put into an oxygen tent. She could not get out of bed without help.

Before she died, Mama and I talked about death. I have said we were nominal Episcopalians. Yet neither of us believed that a human is more than a biological accident in a random universe.

That summer, her coughing racked us all, hacked the air, snaked her chest, cracked our ears. Daddy, believing that milk caused phlegm, would not give her the one thing she craved, chocolate milkshakes. He extended that veto to the only other thing she loved: coffee, with generous dollops of both cream and sugar, hot in the morning, iced later on. She grew thinner and frailer. Prednisone made everything taste funny, and her appetite disappeared completely.

Fastidious as she was, she absolutely detested the hawking and spitting her illness necessitated, and was in constant pain from the coughing which caused the hairline fractures in her osteoporotic ribs. She wanted to die, and asked my help.

I approached two doctors, two lawyers, two pharmacists, and finally two chemists — eight people in all, seeking a kind death for her. One of the doctors told me, "Medicine used to be an art, and a few years ago I might have been able to help. Now that it's a science, I'm accountable for every grain of any drug I prescribe. I can't help you any longer, but I feel for you both."

The other seven advised that I was crazy, that I'd end up in prison if I helped my mother die. Yet all of them admitted they knew how she could kill herself effectively and with a minimum of suffering. They just wouldn't tell me.

She'd ask fretfully, "What was it spies kept in rings in all those old thrillers? It was something you could take if you were going to be compromised, and it killed you instantly. That's what I need." I actually leafed through spy novels, looking.

At any rate, I sat, and we talked, long hot hours, for her slow dying was in the summer, bunches of the wildflowers she loved, chicory and butterfly weed and Queen Anne's lace, in a jar renewed every day on the desk at the foot of her bed, until my father took yet another notion, and said, *Take them away, they make her cough. What if she's allergic?*

Then they took her off the cortisone. For a while her appetite came back. She wanted milkshakes, but my father prescribed instead beef broth, and made it himself by boiling raw hamburger in water, and straining off the gray hot greasy liquid — no salt, as she had a heart murmur — and somehow, the doctor's directions were not sought, and my mother, a prisoner, was forced to drink that gagging brew.

When she was too ill to paint, she took up needlework, and asked Daddy to find her a small chest with drawers to keep her supplies in by her bed. Daddy found her a little nineteenth-century walnut marble-topped cabinet that was perfectly beautiful. But the drawers stuck, and the front wouldn't stay closed, and it was the last bitter draught to her that he had not even cared enough to remember that she *hated antiques.*

Daddy *was* angry, though he protested of course that his ministrations were all for her good. He was angry at her for dying, angry at us children for wearing her out, angry at her sister Polly for always having smoked. Angry at *her*, for having smoked when they were young, out in China. Angry at anyone he could find to blame.

Guiltily, when I knew he was going to be out for several hours, I'd sneak in the ingredients and make her a chocolate milkshake, and clean up any traces carefully, hiding the ice cream cartons and syrup cans in the trunk of my car, fearful for my safety if he discovered what a scofflaw I was, and fearful, too, that he might be right, and that I might hasten her end. Though I believed in her right to do it, I didn't want to kill her.

The dice of death rolled in her chest, and it sounded as if pebbles of bone cluttered the space where her heart rankled.

Mama had a richer life than I had known, but only in her dying months did she tell me much about it. I'd long known of her crush on Stewart Granger, and the autographed studio photo of him she'd sent off for once that she kept in her underwear drawer (scented with an unused cake of Yardley's Lavender soap), but that was all I knew of her love life.

In the long hot days between coughing fits she recalled men she'd loved: there was Roger, who'd loved penguins, and was, I learned, to my surprise, responsible for all the penguin clocks, vases, drawings, and statues, we'd had around all my life, and that I'd assumed were her own quirky collection. Roger had wanted to marry her, but she had not loved him enough to spend the rest of her life with him.

The one she'd really loved, a beautiful and gentle boy in the Navy named Pete, had come to see her in despair one day to say that he'd been walking down the street, and had fallen in love on the spot — with a handsome sailor — and did not know what to do. This was around 1930. Horrified, she had turned him away forever, having never heard of homosexuality, as possibly he had not either.

There is a later interesting twist to this story. Pete did marry, long after Mama and Daddy wed. He was killed standing on a shipbow staring at the Hawaiian dawn with binoculars the morning of December 7, 1941, equal in death at least with so many other American sailors. I'd never even wondered where Mama came up with Peter's name.

Mama's Pete left a widow and a son. The reason I know this is that, through Fate's vagaries, that widow served on the board of the college where I taught for twenty-five years during the first few years of my tenure there. We became friends, though of course we never discussed anything personal. All I knew in those days was that her husband had once courted my mother.

And Mama had almost had an affair once, incredibly with the dead-handsome captain of a cruise ship she and Daddy were on. The flirtation lasted beyond the cruise, and died away after a few letters back and forth. There was no chance they could ever meet again, and she regretted that.

"How about that Richmond friend of Daddy's?" I asked, made bold by her confession. "You know, that Jeff Fairfield, or whatever his name was."

"Oh, him!" she said, and closed her eyes, and smiled. "He was a mess. Came to see me a couple of times when he knew Daddy was away." She sighed. "It was flattering, that was all."

And I see her, eyes closed, wryly amused, despite her misery, at the memory. As Ralph had said, we all need good memories for when we're old.

Mama promised me before she died that, if she and I were mistaken, if it turned out that there *was* an afterlife, that she'd find a way to let me know. Our glances met when someone came to visit who told her they were *praying* for her; later she'd say, "You and I are the only ones who know what to pray for."

"What's it like?" I would whisper. I'd squeeze her hand, already cool.

MAMA HAD A LIFELONG CURIOSITY about psychic things, and had visited a Madame McLaren in Washington when she was young, with her sister Polly and Polly's husband Lamar and some friends. One recently married friend who went with them named Laura took off her wedding ring to try to fool Mrs. McLaren.

Madame McLaren said to the bride, "I have nothing to tell you. My secretary will give you your money back." Mother was next, and during her reading, Madame McLaren gave her a sealed envelope to give her friend in two weeks, but not before. Mama agreed. A week later, Laura committed suicide.

Sometime after that, Mama came upon the forgotten paper in her purse, and opened it, since Laura was dead. It read, *You have no future.*

Madame told Polly's husband, *Beware a bay mare,* and several years later, Lamar was thrown eighteen feet and severely injured while riding a bay mare. The psychic told Polly to beware deep water, so she always has, and still does today, at eighty-four.

Madame McLaren also told Polly that she would lose twins in a foreign country. Polly never did, but my mother did just that. Before she conceived me, she miscarried twins in Peking. She and Polly thought later that Madame had gotten them confused.

So Mama was at least open-minded about things you couldn't explain. That's why I asked her to promise that if there were something beyond, she'd find a way to let me know.

"Want a cup of coffee?" I'd ask, when Daddy was away, for coffee had all her life been her single most favorite thing. But when she merely shook her head wearily, I knew she'd die.

And so she did die, quietly, with the dignity she'd have wanted, near the end of that July, only sixty-eight. She'd had a terror of being buried, connected perhaps to her loathing for worms and dog excrement, and had asked to be cremated. I was prepared to fight for her wishes, but Daddy, though opposed to cremation, assented without argument.

I took up running, feet pounding the pavements up Main Street, through the cemetery. I ran at night, angry and forlorn, after the air had cooled. I would cry and sweat and run.

I remembered Mama's promise, and tried to notice tiny things, in the hopes of receiving a message. I would suddenly notice the way the sun fell on a bowl of lemons I'd set on a table. A picture would for no reason fall off the wall. I'd see my keys lying on a chair in some odd configuration. And I'd wonder in those moments if she was perhaps sending a message, but one I couldn't read. But I didn't really think so. There seemed no reason to believe anything but what I'd always believed, that Mama was dead and gone.

I had a vivid dream early one night shortly after her death; *someone calls me from downstairs, saying to hurry, that Mama is in the kitchen. I am very excited, anxious to see her again after so many months, and get out of bed, into my bathrobe, and halfway downstairs, calling to her out loud, before my husband comes to meet me at the bottom of the stairs, puzzlement on his face. Then I wake up enough to realize it was only a dream.*

SEVERAL WEEKS AFTER HER DEATH, I was in the woods alone in August hunting chanterelles, when I was joined by a big navy blue butterfly called a Diana. I had learned most of their names with her. The Diana tracked me, stayed with me for more than an hour, blipping about overhead, resting on a branch: the message was, it seemed clear to me, though I can't say why, the word *happy*, over and over again. The Diana wrote its message on the air, then floated weightlessly to the next stob, or branch, to alight, then flew off again to repeat, *happy happy happy.*

At home, my husband and I had a drink on the terrace, and I told him about my afternoon's companion. As I told the story, another Diana came bounding across the terrace. "Like that," I pointed, "only bigger."

"The females are bigger," my husband said.

I kept running, restless and driven, often ending up in the cemetery. "Where are you?" I'd complain.

She wasn't there, though it was peaceful and beautiful there in the graveyard where Stonewall Jackson also lies, keeping company with Governor Letcher surrounded by most of his children, nineteenth-century local poet Margaret Junkin Preston, and of course Andaddy and Nainai. Mama's ashes are with the Letchers, though her own parents and her younger brother Jack, who died young and wretched, rest only fifty feet away, across a gentle walk, easily within calling distance should they be inclined to converse.

At some point, it began to occur to me that maybe the butterflies were really her message.

At home that winter, there was chicken burning in the oven, children with colds. All that fall and winter, Daddy would come, stay, not leave. He wanted to talk, of his will, of his constipation, of his anger at the price of everything. He would hack into his handkerchief. The baby, who hardly ever cried, would cry. Daddy would not take supper, but he'd stay and kibitz while we ate in silence.

"Don't eat so fast; it'll make you sick." "Yogurt? Who would eat yogurt?" he'd say, making an icky face. My jaw ached from gritting my teeth together, from holding my tongue.

"How much you pay those New York Jews to print your books?" he asked me once. *New York Jews? Print* my books?

I exploded, listened to myself yelling that, *God dammit, I'd made fourteen thousand dollars on my writing last year, and that in my line of work, I GOT PAID!*

Clueless (you could tell by the puzzlement on his face), he replied, "Is that so? I paid McClure right much to have my books printed." And he never understood why I'd gone ballistic.

He would not go away. Our son, eight, would slink off upstairs to his room, me promising to be right up. The baby would cry. Clearly she felt our tension in every nerve of her tiny body.

Whenever I'd hear a faraway dog bark in the white winter air, the sound was an ironic mimic of Mama's coughing.

Standing halfway up our darkened stairs holding the baby, light below me, light above me, I feel wracked. Above me, our little boy struggles alone with homework or stares at the pages of Playboy *(I once asked him why he liked looking at all those naked girls, as they all looked alike. He gave me his big blue-eyed gaze, and replied, "Not to me they don't.")*

Below me my husband struggles alone with our unwelcome visitor. I wonder in the dark how much tension we can continue to take before we crack. I can't help either one of them, and I can't help myself. In the hall, I find the big dictionary we keep there, and look up "wracked" to see if that is what I mean, and find that it is related to "wreak" and "wreck" and "rack." The word comforts me, and I go on.

IN TIME IT GOT SO BAD WE'D HIDE IN AN UPSTAIRS ROOM, LOCK THE FRONT and back doors, pretend not to be there, until he finally went away. We actually considered moving to another town, and looked at real estate around Charlottesville. I'd run more. I'd run all over town, all through the cemetery, twigs snapping in the cold, brick the only color in the winter landscape of gray-green.

Three times (unable to confront him in person) I wrote Daddy letters asking him to stay away until I invited him. He'd do it for maybe three days, then back he'd come, so lonesome he couldn't stand it. His loneliness broke my heart, causing me real, nearly physical, pain. But I couldn't stand having him around either.

On my runs, I'd stand in the spot where we'd buried the fake marble plastic book I suspected was a Bible — containing Mama's ashes — and talk to her, but I felt like a phony and I was sure she wasn't anywhere around. And I guess I didn't want her to be: she detested winter.

Time passed. One day when I was running, my heart pounding, my sneakers gathering the soft mud, snowdrops appeared in the cemetery. Then crocus. Before long there were enough daffodils in my yard to fill a jar and take them to place on her grave.

Where are you? I demanded, the smell like Pledge rising from my packed jar. What is it like? Can you see spring is coming?

Suddenly, something cruised in sight, darting, weightless, like the dots and lines on that machine by her hospital bed, then hovered blue, her favorite color, over the yellow flowers. A spring azure!

By then I'd gotten used to the idea of the butterflies. "Mama," I said aloud, "how corny can you get?"

Yet when I started again, the tiny blue creature paced me, swimming ahead, larking in the redbud blooms. "What's it like?" I asked aloud.

Happy, happy, happy, the butterfly spelled, dipping blue in the high moist air. My eyes followed it up and up, until sunshine intervened.

It seemed to happen often enough that soon both my children would remark on the attentions of some tiger swallowtail that came to call while we were picnicking or swimming, or sitting out in the garden.

Even friends after awhile would say, "Oh, there's your mother, Katie," and sometimes we'd have to explain the Red Admiral or Blue Hairstreak to strangers. One summer day, a pair of coupled dragonflies made their erratic way over the river where we were lounging friendly in innertubes, drinking beer. "There's your mother," a friend remarked, "and she's got a boyfriend!"

There is one recent, bemusing episode: I record it here, for whatever it may be, transcendence of time, space, and matter — or coincidence:

I still have the habit of walking by her grave occasionally — not to see her; she's not there — but I find it a comfort. Just the other day as I did so, I happened to glance down at what I thought must be one of my lipsticks lying right on the ground in front of her marker. My brand, expensive. Puzzled, I then figured I'd maybe dropped it out of a coat pocket last time I was there. I picked it up, opened it, and it was definitely not mine, but it was — I swear this — *a particular shade I'd been thinking of buying* to go with a new burgundy sweater, a darker shade than I've ever worn, which is why I'd hesitated to spend eight dollars for something I might only wear once or twice. This lipstick was used, but otherwise fine.

I stuck it in my pocket, thinking of hepatitis, maybe worse, but when I got home, I decided a little soap and water, and some boiling water to clean out the top — well, anyway, I cleaned it, and now I've used it, several times. It doesn't belong to any of the women in our family, and I can't think who in the world would drop an expensive lipstick a foot from my mother's headstone. It just seems so odd.

Morel, 1989.

Morels

❦ 26 ❧

I used to think the only thing that could kill Daddy would be lightning or a house falling down on him. But a cabin he'd built did that once: lightning split a tree, which fell on the flimsy structure, which collapsed on him as he was sheltering out the storm. He crawled out from under the heavy timbers and raining roof-panels and came home to regale us with his adventure.

"He leads a charmed life," Mama remarked afterwards, somewhere between admiration and irritation.

EVERY SPRING I GO IN SEARCH OF MORELS AND INNER PEACE. It was Daddy, for all the things he didn't teach me, or taught me wrong, who taught me to find morels, as well as other edible wild plants — just as Mama taught me to identify the showy orchis and the red-spotted purple, the zebra swallowtail and the cardinal flower.

Daddy was interested in what you could eat, Mama in what was beautiful. She was afraid of deep woods, fearful of ticks and mosquitoes and wild anythings, but would collect wildflowers along the roads or edges of the mountain woods we'd haunt, take them home in mayonnaise jars of water that we'd carried out for that purpose. Once home, she'd draw them and paint them in, in pale watercolors, and all her children would learn the names: Bouncing Bet and loosestrife and joe-pye weed.

Daddy, on the other hand, remembering some remote stand of paw-paws, would barge out across fallen trees and through poison ivy thickets as high as his head, daring any copperhead to come within a mile, going so fast I couldn't keep up, taunting me when I fell behind or got ensnared by some berry thicket.

Suddenly he'd stop, point his walking stick, and say, "Over there, Chick. That was a house site. See the periwinkle and mustard? Someone lived there. There'll be a spring nearby." And he'd stomp around some more, ignoring whatever got in his way, tangled grapevine, last year's honeysuckle, or spruce thicket barriers, and soon we'd find it sure enough, full of leaves and mud maybe, but there, just as he'd said. He was truly amazing.

And sometimes he'd dig out the spring with his hands, and we'd wait a few minutes watching until moisture would seep in clear, filtered by time and our famous limestone, and we'd cup our hands together to drink of the cold sweet water. Then we'd crash on until we came to the pawpaws, black and mottled on the ground, and fill up his hat, or a paper bag, or the old enamel potty, triumphant that we'd once again gotten something for nothing.

THE SERVICEBERRY'S WHITE LACE HAS GONE, and the leaves on the hardwood trees are faint green and the size of mouse ears. Wild strawberry blooms strew the roadsides and the old trackbeds. This is when you hunt for morels.

Daddy first took me when I was ten or eleven, and we'd moved back to Lexington. With four children and no job, he was trying hard to keep his head above water, too proud to ask his father for help. He had then and later more time on his hands than he wanted.

He took me to the hill of trillium and mayapple and tall hardwood, oak and tulip poplar, where he'd hunted as a boy, and was tickled at me when I found two the first time out. "Damn, I didn't see that one. Takes good eyes," he said. For you need special eyesight, a knack, to see morels.

Those are the kinds of times I like remembering. But at least as many times in my life with Daddy were haunting, miserable, scarring.

Today he is, in a phrase, out of it. Yet I know what these intense spring trips could mean to him, even now. For all our differences, we are two of a kind, he and I, both in our time loving these Virginia mountains, with an all-day passion for the morels that few understand or care to keep up with; and when I'm ninety and senile, I hope there'll be someone, even if I can't remember who it is, who'll still take the time to take me out looking when April comes.

Daddy's second wife, Sallie, ever alert, cautions me not to let him get tired, not to let him out of my sight, worries him about his hat, fusses about the possibility that his feet will get wet, hands him his walking stick.

Daddy stands there looking somehow *stuffed*, as if he's been taxidermied, baffled at the instructions and attention, but not anxious — sort of content to be at the center of a small bustle, his personality seeming to be off down the driveway, across the field, or perhaps floating free, tugging to be loose from earth.

Once we are in the woods, I point out pink and purple trillium, jacks-in-the-pulpit. (Suddenly I remember my mother's wildflower paintings. Later I think she destroyed that early notebook, in which she first drew, then watercolored, a summer's supply of wildflowers, berries, butterflies, for I have been unable to find it. It was about 1950. I used to sit, turn the pages of the book until I found my favorite ones, the lushly pale-green luna moth, the gorgeous puce trillium, the old-gold honeysuckle. I loved them, though Mama would always turn self-deprecating if she found me looking at her sketchbook: "Oh, those are terrible. They aren't right . . . I'm going to do better." Then she might say, "But look over here at the butterfly bush I did today. I kind of like the color, don't you?" I'd give anything to have even one of them now, but they have all vanished.)

"Daddy?" I say. "Look here. A jack-in-the-pulpit."

He frowns. "Hunh," he says noncommittally.

"Do you remember how Mama used to paint flowers?"

"No," he says slowly.

"Trillium," I point out. No reaction. "They always come out with the white morels," I say, determined to be cheerful and conversational.

"They do?" he says, and the words hang there, mere reflexes. And we are silent as he stumbles along, leaning hard on my arm.

"Do you remember that eel you caught, and made me hold it while you cut its head off?" I ask him, for there are glimmers of understanding when we bring up the far past: Peking, VMI, his brother Gee.

For a second he looks puzzled, then says, "Yeah."

"Scared me to death," I say.

He only grins, his blue eyes bleared.

"Remember how your soldier invented the Slinky?" He chuckles as if he does, but doesn't answer.

If I were to tell him I'd just been elected the first woman president of the United States, overturning the law that says you have to be born here, he'd only say, "Is that so?" He still wouldn't tell me he's proud of me.

In fact, the last thing he "remembered" about me was wrong, and negative. He said it to everyone, for months. "They got her teaching down there at Hollins, when she couldn't even get through the first year. Now you figure that out."

"How many times you been married?" he asks me.

"Just once," I say. "Over thirty years."

"Aw, naw," he goes on. "You been married more times than that." I know he's gotten me mixed up with one of my siblings, but he won't be corrected.

Jeanne and I have talked through the years about parents' different realities. Her mother, at the end of her life, invented huge successes for her daughters, claiming that one was editor of the *Philadelphia Enquirer* where she worked, then that the other was the head librarian at the university where she held a perfectly responsible job, though not that of head librarian. This kind of inflation (if not exactly invention) I understand, and am anxious to portray my own children in the best possible light, even perhaps in a better light than the rest of the world might.

I think what upsets me so is that my father's reality for me seems unnaturally negative and diminishing. I graduated pretty high in my class at Hollins. By now I've published many books, some of them with foreign editions, many also appearing later in paperback. I've won awards for my writing, been honored as one of Virginia's fifty-nine most important writers of the twentieth century. Me paying "New York Jews" to publish me? Can he really believe that?

Maybe I should just say, *Hey, Daddy, they gave me the Nobel Peace Prize. Daddy, I just got invited to sing on the Grand Ole Opry. Daddy, they want me for Playmate of the Month!*

"Daddy, look," I say. "Three morels, in a line. You get them."

Buzz, Cap'n, and Teddy, who replaced Scout, 1917.

Barefoot

❦ 27 ❦

During the War Mama chatted in letters to Daddy about my progress and disgraces, and Johnnie's development, and relayed the local gossip. In a 1944 letter to Daddy, Mama wrote, "The other night I went to the movie, 'Winged Victory' with Scott and Anne and enjoyed it very much. Scott loves to kid me about your bare feet, and I always pretend to get huffy, which tickles him no end, and he is forever teasing me with such questions as, 'Does Buzz take his bedroom slippers when he goes to dances, or does he dance barefooted?' So I have got a comeback now for every person who talks about your bare feet to me — I am going to say that you are the only person who has ever been allowed to remain in the Marine Corps despite your refusal to wear shoes, and in your case they waived shoes as part of the uniform because you are such a valuable soldier. On your part as a special concession you wear shoes with mess jacket for the sake of the reputation of the Corps to formal functions, but never at any other time! How's that?"

MY FATHER'S CHILDHOOD WAS HARD, even by the standards of the turn of the century, but even more important, he *perceived* it as unpleasant. Nainai and Andaddy's first child, John Paul Letcher, had died in 1901 when he was only one and a half, just at that magical time when babies are learning everything, toddling like chubby drunken sailors, labeling the world anew with words. Just at that special moment when you can really begin to see a baby's character, and sense what sort of adult he will become, baby John, fat and funny and delicious, got meningitis and died, suddenly, suddenly, absolutely swamping Nainai, Mrs. Letcher, who was at the time recovering from the difficult birth of Gee, her second son.

That first time, she wore black for a year, but at least she had another baby to tend. Slowly she crawled back up from the blow of that death, and let herself fall in love with Gee, who was, by all accounts, an especially endearing and charming child.

When Gee was three, and her heart sang with his winsomeness ("Tuesday's child is really full of grace," she once wrote about him to her husband, absent on law business), she had a third son, my father, Seymour, whom they called Buzz.

From the beginning little Buzz was angry, energetic, temperamental and difficult. Miss Katie wrote a lot of letters to her husband, who traveled a lot in his legal duties. The letters reveal a woman plagued with frustrations, already unable to see well, by choice a homebody. Her home was her life, and the letters are a record of dailiness. She hired and fired maids, quarreled about the cost of food, complained about the temperamental heating system in their big old house, wrote fondly of Gee, not as fondly of her third child.

A typical letter, when the baby was just under two, says, "I don't know what to do with Buzz. He is so *fresh*. Colonel Nichols came by today, and Scout barked and grabbed his trouser leg. The Colonel tossed a stone at him, and Buzz came rushing out, hollering, 'Bad Man frow rock Scout! Bad Man! Go home!' He would not be hushed."

All boy, Buzz tugged at his mother's skirt to "Less go see dead 'nake," and dreaded attending some birthday party for which he would have to wash and dress up in uncomfortable clothes and unforgiving shoes. Even the promise of ice cream, with which he had a lifelong love affair, was sometimes not alluring enough to make a party worthwhile. He wanted to be in the woods hunting, or fishing. Sometimes Nainai made him go to the birthday parties anyway.

Buzz was required every other day (Gee had to do it on alternate days) to arise early in the chilly house, go down alone into the coal-black basement, and stoke up the furnace for the day. Three times one week, four times the next, all winter long, he had to choke down the terror of descending those narrow steep steps to the underworld. It was a cellar so dark you could believe anything lurked in the corners. Daddy early formulated the peculiar notion that there were *wolves* in the cellar. The basement — which I probably went into fewer than a dozen times total — had a truly malevolent air, as if angry spirits — why not wolves divested of their homeground? — lurked there.

Even Nannie, if I were home, would try to inveigle me to "help" her if *she* had to go down there, with the promise that I could lick the pudding dish, or make strawberry jam tarts in her kitchen.

In the next generation, neither I nor Johnnie could ever bear to go down there alone.

After starting the furnace, Daddy had to walk down to the train station to pick up the newspapers he would deliver until the sun came up. Sometimes he had no time for breakfast. (Buzz and Gee had to eat cold breakfast alone, as their father wanted Miss Katie to breakfast with him later, when it suited *him* to get up.)

Then Daddy had to go to school, which he loathed. Nainai once told me that he came home after the first day of first grade and announced to his mother that he didn't think he'd go back, that school was boring. Generally speaking, he never changed his mind from that day on, which was typical of him. He was not interested in forgiveness. If once you fell out of his good graces, you were not likely ever to get back in. School was only one of many, many things like that. Others included Sunday school, church, doctors, and, excepting his mother, girls.

Gee, on the other hand, like his father and his grandfather the governor before him, regarded life differently altogether. Gee made friends easily, loved school, and was talented on the ukelele, an instrument just then coming into fashion. He excelled as a singer and dancer, and was much in demand socially. Teachers were crazy about Gee. He was popular with other kids. Girls fell for him. Gee was handsome, and won awards at school. And his mother, Miss Katie, doted on him.

My father, finding school and social pursuits puerile, had a hard time trying to understand how Gee's life seemed so easy, while he, Buzz, was in constant trouble. He couldn't learn the times tables; he wanted to be out fishing or swimming or camping or hunting, and he was forced to sit in school instead. He and Gee did naughty things together, but only *he* got caught. He and Gee smoked monkey-cigars, the pods of gum trees, but only he was discovered and whipped. Together the boys stole their Uncle Hootie's rum-soaked Cuban cigars and *only Buzz* got caught, and tanned in the woodshed.

By himself Buzz shot out some streetlights, and of course Andaddy found out, strapped him to one of the streetlights, and beat the stars out of him.

When he'd leave for school or play, Nainai would say to him, and make him repeat, "Don't fight nobody, don't call nobody Fool," for his school reports read, "I am sorry that Seymour's deportment is not better," and such backhanded remarks as "Seymour appears to be improving."

But Nainai taught him to be a good hater, and banded together with him against the fools of the world, and they decided on and listed and kept track of some of the world's worst fools. I feel that this early instruction infused into my father a lifelong cynicism about human nature. In fact, he seemed to trust nobody else but his parents and usually Mama, but certainly not his own children.

Apparently, unless history has filed to softness the sharp edges of truth, such cautions rolled off Gee's back. But maybe Gee never heard them, for Miss Katie may never have felt that defensiveness for Gee that she felt for Buzz. Or maybe Gee was by nature just more like Andaddy.

Of strong mind and frequently frustrated at what he tried to do, little

Buzz spent a great deal of time angry. Their dog Scout got rabies and bit *him*. Not Gee. It was Buzz who had to go to Richmond on the train with his mother and get the terrible shots, one a day, for something like twenty days. The compensatory trips to the zoo, the museum, movies, the Peter Paul Mounds Bars his mother let him have every day, did little to comfort him. Each morning on the streetcar to the hospital, he'd sniffle and cry. "I'll go," he'd say, "but I won't like it." It led to his lifelong dread of hospitals. And it led to our famous family saying, by anyone who had to go somewhere he or she didn't want to go: *I'll go but I won't like it.*

And then, when Buzz was thirteen, Gee, hero and competitor, came home from Augusta Military Academy with a cold that wouldn't go away. It turned into Spanish flu, then into pneumonia. There was nothing they could do.

Miss Katie's grief is legendary; people in Lexington today still remember that she cried for years. Her personality changed then, they said, to cold and cynical, reclusive and resentful.

My father adored his mother, and was such a dutiful son that he wrote her a long letter at least once a week from the time he left home in 1927 until he retired to Lexington twenty-one years later. His mother wrote him rarely, but Daddy kept all his life in his shaving kit one letter from his mother, which she wrote to him in the spring of 1931, while he was stationed aboard the battleship *Oklahoma*:

My lovely Buzz, The roses came Easter morning fresh and beautiful. How like you to send them. Later in the evening I took them up to the cemetery where the grass was soft and green. Somehow since you went out into a bigger world and found your heart's dream and have seen all the beauty of seas and sky and new mountains and forests I am so much happier thinking of Gee in his new world. Of course he was always just away, but he is nearer now. I ought always to have been happy to have him there, remembering how after an hour's delirium, his fever and restlessness faded from his face and he lay for a little quiet and very beautiful and turned his head from us and looked up with such wonder and love in his eyes seeing something or Someone wonderful and lovely beyond our knowing — and was gone, to be "this day in Paradise." Mother.

After the enormous change in Buzz's life of losing his brother there came another: for three more winters, he had to descend into the cellar and turn the furnace on *every* morning.

Nainai had, amid her grief, a practical problem: how could they protect their third, and last, boy, Seymour, called Buzz, then thirteen, the son who had lived his whole life in his charmed older brother's shadow? Nainai called on the doctor for a consultation, and the doctor came to the house and sat in the parlor and told her, looking sternly over his glasses, that it was wet feet that killed young people.

How could they cope with that? Buzz must never again have his feet encased in wet shoes. Bare feet would dry as soon as they got away from the wet.

My father never wore shoes again until well into college. In most of his VMI pictures, his feet are discreetly out of camera range.

He kept one other thing in his shaving kit, which he must have been proud of: his page torn carefully from the 1924 VMI annual, the *Bomb*:

Seymour Letcher. Nicknames: Buzz Hambone Mirandy. "His laugh as light as wine or chaff breaks clear at witty salleys." To the delight of the entire third class our Buzz in a moment of enthusiasm threw on sock and shoe and matriculated with '24. His early determination to make a name for himself was materially hastened at the outset by his exploits with the bayonet in fending off "hard" upperclassmen. In no wise daunted, however, he survived every ordeal devised by cadet cunning and emerged triumphant at Finals. The following year at the first appointment of officers he appeared with chevrons and commenced the steady climb in the military line which landed him high in the list of officers his graduating year. An inspection of his chevron curve will testify to the good opinion held by the authorities of his military prowess.

Deciding that the chemistry department offered the greatest opportunity for his genius, the second class year found him starting in the pursuit of knowledge of the elusive molecule under the guidance of "Old Rat."

The last ten months of his cherubic youth residence at VMI seems to be occupied for the most part by disputations with "Doc" and "Matt" Davis over the woes of the Quartermaster's Office.

In affairs of the heart, Hambone is something of a puzzle. However, the fair sex does seem to have some hold over his affection, and of late years interest in them and the "hops" has been steadily growing.

Characterized by a largeness of stature and heart, a wide infectious grin, a keen sense of humor, truthfulness and steadiness, loyalty in adversity and steadfastness always, Buzz leaves the Institute. With him go the best wishes of Old '24, and if success in life is proportional in the least measure to the good wishes in the hearts of his classmates for him, the future is assured. "Turn on the Vic!"

Daddy and kin, 1986.

Twilight

❦28❧

*I*t was during the years in Peking that a curious event happened to my father; a single psychic event in a long life untroubled by anything else beyond this plane of linear time and three-dimensional space. I know only the bare outlines of the story. Daddy had a dream, I think early one morning, that one of his soldiers was kicked to death by a horse down in the stables. As it was an extraordinarily clear dream, he mentioned it during the bridge foursome he was part of later in the day, so that two other people as well as my mother heard about it.

When the event occurred two days later exactly as it had in his dream, when the man was found exactly as my father had described him, word got out that my father had "foreseen" this death, which had some apparently ambiguous elements about it, the nature of which I have forgotten. This led to an investigation.

My father was cleared of any involvement, but as with other supernatural events, the questions raised are puzzling to this day, the implications enormous of our ever being, under any circumstances, able to read a future event before its occurrence. It has haunted me all my life that my earthbound father had this one episode, never another (at least not that he remembered), and that he was not especially curious about it. Whenever I'd pump him about it, and ask him what he thought had happened, he'd shrug, and say,

"*Coincidence, I guess.*"

But somehow, it's always given me a flash of belief, a scrap of hope, that there is some part of us that transcends time and space. So, for even my infirm faith in things unseen I must, to some degree, credit Daddy.

DADDY'S RELATIONSHIP WITH SALLIE caught us all broadside and off-guard. He'd been lured around to dinner and candlelight by several lonely widows in town. He'd been visited by the widow of one of his VMI brother-rats, who, he reported to me with mild indignation, tried to *neck* him, but he wouldn't let her because she smoked and her breath reeked of old cigarettes!

We all thought no one would ever marry him, as peculiar, as tight, as difficult, as he was. For awhile he dated a much-younger woman, a sculptress, but I knew it wouldn't last. She seemed superficial to me anyway, and she must have been interested in his money, which was by then considerable, but he was smarter than that.

Then one night at dinner at our house, Mama's sister, Aunt Polly, turned to my father and said, "Well, Buzz, are you going to marry this new woman?"

I perked up to listen, and remember well Daddy's double-entendre answer, which was, "Well, I certainly hope you don't think I'm just screwing around." Truth is, I was a little bit shocked. Screwing around? Where had he learned that kind of talk?

Soon he was engaged, and Sallie, who reminded me a lot of Mama, who dressed like Mama and even *smelled* like Mama, was taking me aside, telling me about how he proposed.

He asked her on about the fourth date if she liked to travel. She said she did. He then announced he was going to Russia in the fall.

"That's nice," she said.

"Well," he went on, "it is, because you'll be with me."

"I certainly will not," she replied. "I don't travel with men I'm not married to."

"Well, who said you weren't going to be married?" he asked her.

The autumn wedding was in a tiny church in eastern North Carolina where one of Sallie's nephews was minister. Three of us, Daddy's children, made it to the wedding, where I could not stop crying, for every reason in the world: relief that no longer would he plague our days and nights, sorrow for my mother and her sad and forgotten life, wonderment that this woman found our father so attractive, but most of all, pure amazement that he had found someone to love, someone who seemed to love him, maybe all for the first time.

Sallie had buried two other husbands, had had no children with either.

When they were leaving the reception to catch a flight for Russia, I whispered in Daddy's ear, *Now don't go getting Sallie pregnant too soon*, and he blushed lobster-red. Most of all, I prayed it would last.

Later, when I saw Sallie at work, I knew it would. She moved smoothly around his cantankerous behaviors, his negative reactions, handling him like a child. Her patience was endless, her devotion total. She'd have been a terrific mother.

These days he's docile as an old dog. He eats the wonderful old-fashioned southern food that Sallie loves to cook: a little fatback in the string beans, a bit of sugar and butter in the limas, fried chicken, Smithfield ham, roast beef, potatoes au gratin, sweet fruity desserts served hot with ice cream on top — foods my mother didn't cook, being health-conscious and not southern, and terrified of *fat* long before it was so fashionable to be thin.

What my daddy has found with Sallie is gravy, icing, seconds, postscript, love and kisses. He is still handsome, gracious and cordial now, though his health is failing and his memory is gone, and Sallie doesn't believe us when we tell her what he used to be like. She just thinks none of us understood him. As he gets more confused, less able to tell her of his needs, more dependent, he stays closer to her, often clinging to her hand.

Once, just a couple of years ago, when I had begun to believe that I am more than my physical body, and to explore other states of consciousness, I went in a meditation to visit that essential, eternal, *whole* part of my father; that part therefore that is not senile.

I imagined him standing before me in Sallie's tasteful traditional living room, and I said, *You can go now. You don't have to stay in this useless body.*

His response seemed immediate. *No, Sallie wants me here, even the way I am now.*

I told him I wanted to help him go in his imagination to prepare a place to go when he dies, so he will not wander in darkness. I had in mind the place Jesus spoke of when he said, *In my Father's house are many mansions.* Other religions mention it, too. The idea is, that if you go there now in your mind, before you die, and create what you want in the way of an imaginal place for yourself, it will be there, waiting in the area of imagination, for you to go to when you leave the body of flesh.

Daddy in my imaginary journey seemed passive, but willing. I explained as we went. I told him he needed only to imagine himself a place, and it would be there.

A farm would be nice, he said.

So we conjured it up, on a nice big piece of hilly land, an old house with a woodstove, an orchard, a stream with fish and a swimming hole. He asked if he could have a dog. I replied that you could have anything you wanted, and asked, What kind of dog? *Just a good old dog,* he said, so we called up a dancing brown medium-large one. Daddy went along, seeming skeptical but amused. When we were done, I suggested he leave a sign so he could find the place again easily when the time came.

A Marine Corps insignia, he replied instantly. So we placed a big one, high up on a tree just at the entrance to the farm lane.

On the way back, I asked him for a blessing (a suggestion of Aunt Polly's, who is a recent born-again Christian; her religious conversion is a subject on which we argue constantly and disagree pleasantly), and Daddy said yes, he'd give me one, but that was all. He didn't do or say anything, though I waited.

Are you proud of me? I asked him finally.

Well, he considered. *You're a hard worker.*

Anything else? I prodded.

You're a good wife and mother.

Still I prodded, *That's all?*

Well, he finally said, *you stick to things.*

I left him back in Sallie's living room, where he's chosen to stay a bit longer. Perhaps imagination is the gateway to eternal reality. It all felt very real, and definitely *in character*. I felt convinced I'd been in touch with the real soul of him, and I felt, for the first time, resolution.

DADDY HAS BEATEN TWO KINDS OF CANCER and he has had the good fortune to marry on the second go-round a woman who thinks he is the most charming of men, who told me on their wedding day that, of all her husbands, my daddy was the smartest, the handsomest, the kindest — and, she added, dropping her eyes and blushing sweetly, the most sexually attractive. I was a bit startled to think what they'd been up to, she seventy-seven, he eighty-three.

He's living on a farm like he always wanted to, in Sallie's elegant eighteenth-century house, surrounded by people who love him and take care of him. My sister Betsy and I, at one of Sallie's Easter or Fourth of July gatherings, elbow each other and whisper, "Can you believe this?"

No longer does he rage about the lesbian priesthood or the liberals. The good hater is at long last transmogrified into country gentleman, with emphasis on *gentle*. Maybe there *are* miracles of transubstantiation.

The world falling apart doesn't bother him anymore, though he still holds the paper and stares at the headlines every day, frozen in an unimaginable reverie sometimes, Sallie says, for as long as an hour. He is content, and he often laughs to himself, as if attending to a secret, interior conversation. He doesn't initiate anything anymore, not action, not conversation.

But if you catch his eye and grin, or wink, he'll come back for a moment as from a great distance and grin and wink back, for all the world as if the two of you shared an old cozy secret, as if he still remembered that you were his Chickie, as if no time had passed, and no bad feelings, between then and now. Oblivion may be a mercy.

And if you say, when you're leaving, those words that are so hard, yet so true, "I love you, Daddy" — now that he no longer has the wit, ironically, he's got the words to reply, as he does automatically to anyone saying it, including Sallie, the grandchildren, and the night nurse Arlene when she leaves — "I love you, too."

Daddy among old friends, c. 1980.

Ending

Daddy was so convinced of his own immortality that everyone around him believed it, too. He thought if you could lick your wounds, they'd get well faster. Dogs did that, he pointed out, and we should, too. Mama would shudder, but since then I've always licked wounds. They've always gotten well.

Daddy avoided doctors for nearly all his life. Once in Norfolk he got a splinter of metal embedded in his eyeball. Instead of going to the medic, he went out and borrowed a powerful magnet from a local high school science laboratory, held it up close to the eye, and attracted the offending thing out. Though his eyeball stayed bloody red for a long time, he got over it eventually. I was very impressed. He later bought a heavy, powerful magnet, to have around in case such a thing ever happened again.

JOHN S. LETCHER DIED FOLLOWING A STROKE and a probable heart attack, and a brief week's illness, at Sallie's and his home on August 9, 1994, at 91.

Although he is dead, in me he will always be alive, or at least kicking. He was never a slight, or retiring, or pale, man like the other fathers I knew. His reaction to people was like mine; he rose to the occasion, and could banter with nearly anyone. And he could charm them, too; I can see how if that's all you ever saw, that florid face all glowing with laughter and good health, that genial clever raconteur, you couldn't believe that other part of him that hated in fear and anger, that punished in rage and without restraint, that judged everyone and everything and found them all lacking. He never admitted to an error, and he could not apologize. He was so scared and mad and disillusioned that all he could do was strike out.

In the end, I had to pity him. For in his bones, he must have been sorry sometimes, looking at the whipped defiant faces of his kids and knowing at least for a moment that any one of us hated him. And he must have known Mama didn't love him. He had ultimately failed in the Marine Corps; though he blamed the service, he was smart enough to know at least sometimes that nothing is one-sided, and that in certain diplomatic ways he did not measure up, as he was never even considered for super-intendent of the United States Marine Corps, despite a war record hero-ic as any in history. If they'd wanted him to stay badly enough, they'd have found us somewhere else to live besides that rotten Quonset hut. Even a child could see that.

Most of us Americans have a movie view of heroism: but what happens after the curtain falls, when a hero comes back to earth to try to live normally following that terrifying, triumphant, transforming experience? Odysseus, restless hero home from his adventures, has inspired many writers to seek the answer to that question. Their depressing conclusions can be summed up by Housman's words in "To an Athlete Dying Young": "Smart lad, to slip betimes away / From fields where glory does not stay."

That is where I have to leave Daddy, for he transcended most men in bravery and in rage, and the peccadillos, the dopey human failings, of his wife, his children, of people in general, may have seemed unforgivable because of what he'd seen on Iwo Jima and Corregidor and Guam. No less than any savior, he offered his life to save us, and when it was not required, he couldn't figure out what to do with it.

So I forgive him for being a hero and for being a human being again later with a hero's heart and a hero's memory and a hero's sorrow in a family and world that forgot what he'd offered to keep us safe, and to let us live. I hope in the end he forgave me for being largely pitiless about his bravery and heedless of his gift, and for being headstrong and defiant.

He composed early the words he wanted on his tombstone:

Brigadier General John Seymour Letcher, USMC, commanded the artillery of the V Corps at Iwo Jima in World War II. He was the youngest officer in the history of the Marine Corps to have a General's command in battle. "Colonel Letcher's personal valor and professional competency were in large measure responsible for the success of our forces" — General Holland M. Smith, United States Marine Corps, commanding the landing force at Iwo Jima.

Note

ABOUT TWENTY EPISODES FROM THIS MEMOIR have been read in occasional five-minute "commentaries" throughout 1994 and 1995. They originated on WVTF, a Virginia national public radio station, and have been picked up by other NPR stations. "What Glad Tidings" appeared as "Christmas, Fourteen" in *Shenandoah*, Vol 38/2, 1988. "King Lear" appeared, in a slightly different form, as "Neighbor" in *Artemis*, Vol. XV, Spring 1992. Most of "Naming the Enemy" appeared in *Good Old Times*, Summer 1992, as "Slinky." "Women" was part of an article in *Americana* in April 1992 entitled "Berry-Picking: a Lost Art."